Embodying Asian/
American Sexualities

Embodying Asian/American Sexualities

Edited by Gina Masequesmay
and Sean Metzger

A division of
ROWMAN & LITTLEFIELD PUBLISHERS, INC.
Lanham • Boulder • New York • Toronto • Plymouth, UK

Published by Lexington Books
A division of Rowman & Littlefield Publishers, Inc.
A wholly owned subsidiary of The Rowman & Littlefield Publishing Group, Inc.
4501 Forbes Boulevard, Suite 200, Lanham, Maryland 20706
www.lexingtonbooks.com

Estover Road, Plymouth PL6 7PY, United Kingdom

British Library Cataloguing in Publication Information Available

The hardback edition of this book was previously cataloged by the Library of
Congress as follows:

Library of Congress Cataloging-in-Publication Data

Embodying Asian/American sexualities / edited by Gina Masequesmay and Sean
  Metzger.
    p. cm.
  Includes index.
  1. Asian Americans—Sexual behavior. 2. Asian Americans—Attitudes. 3. Asian
Americans—Race identity. I. Masequesmay, Gina. II. Metzger, Sean, 1973–
E184.A75E43 2009
306.76089'95073—dc22   2008038343

ISBN: 978-0-7391-2903-6 (cloth : alk. paper)
ISBN: 978-0-7391-2904-3 (paper : alk. paper)
ISBN: 978-0-7391-3351-4 (electronic)

∞™ The paper used in this publication meets the minimum requirements of
American National Standard for Information Sciences—Permanence of Paper
for Printed Library Materials, ANSI/NISO Z39.48-1992.

Printed in the United States of America

Contents

Acknowledgments

We would like to thank the contributors for their patience during the years it took to take this project from conception to publication. We specifically would like to note their courage in allowing us to publish shorter works meant to introduce a general readership to research, community work, and artistic practice that bear on understandings of Asian/American sexualities rather than the sorts of more specialized and elaborated arguments common to academic publishing. We owe a debt to Tim Fong for his support and encouragement, in general, and the introduction he provided to our initial editor Patrick Dillon, in particular. To Patrick and his successor Michael Sisskin, thank you for facilitating completion of this book.

Individuals at both California State University–Northridge and Duke University have also supported this volume in various ways. While limitations of space prevent us from listing each individual, we recognize the graciousness of our colleagues. In terms of logistics, the book would not have been finished without the assistance of Stacy Lavin. Funding was provided for various parts of this collection from Duke University's Arts and Sciences Committee on Faculty Research and its Asian/Pacific Studies Institute.

Finally, we thank the Ford Foundation, which financed final publication of the collection as well as the conference, "CrossTalk II: Embodiments of API Sexuality," that inspired it. The book is a response to the request from several participants at that event for an accessible anthology that might serve as a kind of introductory text.

Portions of this book have previously been published. Noël Alumit's *Rice Rooms: Scenes from a Bar* appears in its entirety in Quang Bao, ed., *Take Out: Queer Writing from Asian Pacific America* (New York: Asian American Writers' Workshop, 2000). Eugenie Chan's *Novell-aah!* is available through the online resources Asian American Drama and North American Women's Drama from Alexander Street Press.

Introduction

Embodying Asian/American Sexualities

Sean Metzger and Gina Masequesmay

In the April 2004 issue of *Details*, Whitney McNally offered a piece entitled "Gay or Asian?" as part of the "Anthropology" page of the magazine.[1] This regular feature, which previously showcased "Gay or British?" as well as "Gay or Jesus?" pages, refers to the study and classification of cultural behavior in an ostensibly humorous manner. Adhering to conventions that evoke both fashion and documentary photography, "Gay or Asian?" offers for the viewer's consumption the image of a young Asian male. A paragraph to the left of the model elaborates the "Gay or Asian?" title:

> One cruises for chicken; the other takes it General Tso-style. Whether you're into shrimp balls or shaved balls, entering the dragon requires imperial tastes. So choke up on your chopsticks, and make sure your labels are showing. Study hard, Grasshopper: a sharp eye will always take home the plumpest eel.

In the center of the page against a gray background, the Asian man stands at a forty-five-degree angle toward the camera. His head is turned so that he directly faces the photographer. On the right hand side of the photograph are a series of numbers with arrows pointing to various parts of the Asian body that correspond to the nine descriptions offered in the left-hand corner of the page. The descriptions follow a head-to-foot order starting with the "Dior sunglasses" atop the Asian man's "Ryan Seacrest Hair" and proceeding down to the model's "Evisu Jeans" and, finally, the "Metallic Sneakers" that adorn his feet.

At the lower left of the page, the list of nine descriptions informs the reader about the model's apparel, physical features, and accessories. Item 1 is the pair of Dior sunglasses that can substitute as a "headband and am-plifies inscrutable affect." The "Ryan Seacrest" hair of the model is inter-preted as the "Asian" wanting to look like "the crazy cool Ameri-caaaaaaaan!" Item 3 points to the model's "delicate features" that are "refreshed by a cup of hot tea or a hot night of teabagging."[2] While the Dolce & Gabbana suede jacket keeps the "last samurai warm and buttoned tight on the battle field," the white V-neck T-shirt "nicely showcases [his] sashimi-smooth chest." The $400 Evisu jeans provide "delicate tending" of his "bonsai ass." The model's "ladyboy fingers," described as "soft and long," are "perfect for both waxing on and waxing off,[3] plucking the koto, or gripping the Kendo stick." Lastly, he wears metallic sneakers because "when the Pink Lady takes the stage, nothing should be lost in translation."

The wide-ranging associations of "Gay or Asian?" drew much criticism from a variety of sources, including the media watchdog group called the Gay and Lesbian Alliance Against Defamation (GLAAD), as well as community-based organizations and Asian/American professional groups. Several letters express-ing indignation circulated on the Internet, and *Details* published a number of these responses in their June/July 2004 issue. The magazine's editor-in-chief also printed an apology that not only ascribed responsibility for the piece to him, but also stated that "[s]ometimes you set out to be funny and simply blow it."[4] This "letter from the editor" included a photograph of a protest as well as two full pages of "letters to the editor" on the topic. President and vice-president of the Asian American Journalists Association (AAJA), as one example, protested:

> We're not sure which is the more offensive aspect of "Gay or Asian?" . . . its re-duction of two minority groups to grab bags of demeaning stereotypes,[5] or its utter lack of humor. But we'll focus on the former. While we can't figure out ex-actly what the feature is trying to say—Asian men are gay? Asian men look gay? Asian men would be better off gay?—there's no disguising the fact that it com-bines leering sexual innuendo and a litany of the most tired clichés about both Asian and gay culture with no goal other than to ridicule both groups.[6]

Letters from other groups elaborate some of the negative stereotypes to which the AAJA may allude. For example, the Steering Committee of the Gay Asian and Pacific Islander Men of New York (GAPIMNY) took issue with the lumping together of Chinese and Japanese references as if all Asians were the same. GAPIMNY also contended that the mention of Ryan Seacrest as the "cool Americaaaaaaaan" positioned Asian-looking people as foreign or not American. A coalition of gender and sexuality activist groups attacked the assertion of "Asian men as passive and effeminate," suggested through *Details'* description of the man as a "queen" (item 7) and a "Pink Lady" (item 9), as well as mention of the Asian model's "ladyboy fingers" and his "bonsai ass" that needs tending.

The last letter included in the magazine serves as a sort of conclusion. An individual author wrote: "I feel insulted by the magazine, and I am neither Asian nor gay—or even male, for that matter. It is not about being politically correct or incorrect; it is about respect."[7] Although this final comment on the "Gay or Asian" piece offers a plea for respect, the context of the other letters that point to a "lack of Asian and Pacific Islander representation in the media" and the possibility of "hate crimes" occurring because of "misconceptions of the LGBT[8] and Asian community" suggests that the stakes are both greater and more specific.[9] The concern expressed about a mainstream magazine, which usually displays a majority of white men, using the intersection of "gay" and "Asian" for a few laughs reveals the power dynamics that have shaped Asian/American[10] representations in dominant media and suggests the continued need to explore discourses[11] of race and ethnicity as they inform, are constructed through, and intersect with those of gender and sexuality.

Although the particular example of *Details* reveals the efficacy of both individual and community actions in creating productive dialogues about difference, the issues raised in this exchange persist. In the August 17, 2004, issue of *The Advocate*, which bills itself as "the national gay and lesbian newsmagazine," a "Bear[12] or Straight?" feature appeared.[13] The piece stated that "whether or not you were offended by the *Details* piece, there's no denying that, in this age of metrosexuality,[14] the whole notion of gaydar[15] is getting more difficult to fine-tune."[16] The rhetoric presented, which echoes the AAJA letter's structure, implies that *Details* has correctly marked a historical moment in which the signifiers of sexuality are so in flux that they cannot be distinguished from racial ones. Never mind that the editor-in-chief of *Details* has called the "Asian or Gay?" piece "indefensible."[17]

To understand why so many people perceived the *Details* piece as demeaning, we must understand the social and historical contexts behind particular and persistent conjunctions of sexuality and race. As our first example has revealed, such pairings emerge forcefully around bodies—both real and represented. Three overlapping registers may help define and analyze the example in question. In popular discourse, body image refers to self-perception of one's body. Extrapolating beyond this definition through the discussion of the *Details* page, we use body image to express how representations of Asian/American bodies construct fantasies and also the material effects resulting from those ideas. We also consider what we will call the bodily frame, by which we mean various theoretical frameworks and methodologies used to explain Asian/American genders and sexualities. In both the *Details* piece itself and the published reactions to it, the bodily frames are ambiguous. No articulation of the criteria for evaluating the representation appears, although many of the critics seem invested in a historical methodology, given that the most-often stated objection is to stereotype. For purposes of this discussion, stereotypes are fixed images used to characterize a group that rely on repetition for effect. Finally, our example raises issues of communal bodies. That the individual body is meant to represent larger communities is obvious from the "Asian or Gay?" header. But a number of communal or coalitional bodies as evidenced in the letters to the editor have used the incident of this publication to take a stand against *Details* and, by extension, the dominant media that the magazine may represent. Communal bodies often function as sites of negotiation and contestation, and they continually evolve. Indeed the editors of *Details* demonstrate an investment in potentially new communal formations when they offer their own pages as a site for protest.

These three categories of concern—body images, bodily frames, and communal bodies—implicitly and/or explicitly recur, albeit to different degrees, in all of the chapters in this book. For example, Dan Bacalzo's succinct chapter serves as a sort of study guide for Margaret Cho, perhaps the most famous commentator on Asian/American sexualities. Emphasizing Cho's body image and her attempts to reframe it through the genre of autobiographical performance, which also serves as the lens of his analysis, Bacalzo attends to the audiences to which she appeals and the communal formations that both sustain and form in relation to her work. While some of the chapters do not fully align with and may even contradict some of the arguments in this introduction, we feel that such disagreements are not only productive but also essential to the field of Asian/American studies. This point will receive further elaboration a bit later when we introduce Amy Sueyoshi's chapter. First, we articulate a bodily frame useful in unpacking both the *Details* example and the constituent chapters in this book. This frame is suggested in some of the letters, but elaborated in what follows— that is, a historicized introduction to the general subject of Asian/American sexualities in terms of field and analytic concepts. We briefly explore notions of race in the United States as well as the utility of other related areas of inquiry, including Asian/American studies, women's studies, sexology, and queer theory.

In the United States, perhaps the most influential conjunction of sexuality and race is white and black, where "whiteness" and manhood have historically been linked to civility, intelligence, and control of one's sexuality, and blackness and manhood have most often been linked to savagery, low intelligence, and hypersexuality. This particular project of "racial formation" began with the conquest of Africa and the Americas by Europeans that separated certain Europeans from "Others," Christians from heathens.[18] Religious justifications and financial considerations fueled both challenges to and support for acts that we now see as a violent history of exploitation, appropriation, expropriation, and domination.

With the advent of the Enlightenment, religious and economic rationales for racial difference were supplemented by and sometimes yielded to scientific ones. Although inspired by the Enlightenment philosophy of the "natural rights" of "man" to declare its independence from the British Empire, the newly founded United States of America was a nation that depended on and thrived through slavery.[19] Thomas Jefferson thus had to delete a passage about the freedom of the slaves in the draft of the Declaration of Independence in order for it to be adopted by other revolutionists.[20] In other words, the formation of the U.S. nation-state was rooted in slave trades and colonial expansion into the frontier.[21] "Scientific" racial theories often served to validate these processes. Applying such work as Linnaeus's 1735 *Systema Naturae*, many scholars of the eighteenth and nineteenth centuries conceived of "race" as a biological concept, a matter of physiological differences among people, and invested their work in the identification and ranking of variations in humankind; such research once again established that black was the antithesis to white, the apex of human evolution.[22] Slave became synonymous with black as racial classification became a racialization system to justify slavery.[23] The criterion of who was black was based on the hyper-descent, or one-drop blood, rule, which assumed that "white" was pure and superior and that any racial mixing would contaminate it. That is, a person was no longer considered white if he/she had a drop of another race's blood in him/her. Citing studies on cranial capacity and other physical characteristics of human bodies as well as supposed cultural traits, both popular and scientific documents asserted, often with questionable evidence,[24] a racial hierarchy with white at the top and black at the bottom. In short, race, as an organizing principle of U.S. society, determined who has the right to what resources, both economic and non-economic, and associated specific images with specific groups of people to support a regime of supremacy that, despite its internal complexity, was coded as white both historically and today.

By the late 1800s in the United States, Social Darwinism and the eugenic movement as advocated by people like Sir Francis Galton (Charles Darwin's cousin) found fertile ground to spring amid the great wave of immigrations from Asia and eastern and southern Europe[25] as well as through projects of U.S. imperialism,[26] including involvement in the opium wars,[27] the U.S.-Mexican War,[28] the annexation of Hawaii,[29] and the Spanish American War.[30] Fearing the republic would be contaminated by darker beings of supposed inferiority and concerned over economic competition from Asian migrants, the U.S. government passed laws that curbed immigration, penalized miscegenation (e.g., the Chinese Exclusion Act of 1882, the Cable Act of 1922), and restricted citizenship.[31] When Asian racial categories emerged, they were often seen in relation to black and white,[32] rubrics that designated not only race alone, but also, as the laws implied, information about supposedly appropriate gender, class, and sexuality.

In different ways, several of the essays in this volume address this issue of relationships among categories of difference, or intersectionality.[33] Perhaps Cathy Irwin and Fiona Ngô most explicitly engage it. These chapters articulate the stakes of racial intersections and multiracial subjects at different moments of the twentieth century. Ngô focuses on spaces where bodies collide, specifically urban dance halls in the 1920s and their representation in fiction of the period.[34] Such public yet intimate spaces evoked both anxiety and the potential for new understandings of race and sexuality at a moment in history when gender norms and the demographics of the workplace were visibly shifting in cities like New York. In contrast to the concern over the sight of racialized bodies in physical contact and proximity, Cathy Irwin's spoken-word chapter marks in a more oblique manner the often illegible multiracial body. Her case study is, appropriately, Brandon Lee (the son of legendary martial artist Bruce Lee and Linda Emery), who died during the shooting of his last film *The Crow* (1994). Because his physical body was not available for the final days of shooting, he was replaced by doubles and CG effects. The film works to render the image of a whole Brandon Lee out of a series of quite disparate parts. Irwin mimics this practice of pastiche in the structure of the chapter; her own spoken-word text speaks for the absent Lee even as her words are themselves interrupted by other materials that have worked to describe topics potentially relevant to understanding Lee's career and life, from studies of Asian/American masculinity to media reports on "ambiguous" heritage. Animating both chapters are questions of desire for and of mixed-race subjects.

Although the sheer number of anti-miscegenation and exclusionary laws passed in the United States evinces a governmental view of Asian/American people as a "yellow peril"—unassimilable or otherwise un-American—it is important to note that this perspective was never the only one nor was it static. For example, although conditions in Japan after the 1868 Meiji Restoration facilitated emigration for farmers, educated elites also participated in overseas journeys to the United States. Amy Sueyoshi highlights one such figure: Yone Noguchi. The earliest chronological case study in the collection, Sueyoshi's piece intervenes in our discussion in significant ways. Perhaps most importantly, she shifts away from an emphasis on the body and bodily acts, such as the fellatio she mentions in her title, to expressions of sentiment as the site at which emotive connection can certainly and eroticism might possibly be located. Her work on male-male interracial friendship and potential romance reveals an early articulation of interracial desire that suggests a range of Asian/American male sexualities and forms of communal affiliation were operative, even during periods of intense anti-Asian sentiment (the 1907–1908 Gentleman's Agreement between Japan and the United States, for example, severely restricted Japanese immigration to U.S. soil).

To varying degrees, anti-Asian sentiment has been a recurring feature of U.S. political and social life since the 1870s. In its quest for raw materials and labor, the United States secured new markets with political and military force. Given that the Western frontier was declared closed in the last decade of the nineteenth century, Asia and the Pacific became new sites for the United States to realize its manifest destiny or engage in its imperialistic expansion. The increased contacts with Asia added nuances to the racial hierarchy even as the structure of white supremacy continued to crystallize. Historian Ronald Takaki called World War II a watershed or "a crucial dividing line" in Asian/American history.[35] People were forced to ally themselves with Asia or America. This situation increased the signification of claiming Americanness, but it also produced many contradictions.[36] Soldiers of color returning from World War II, including the Japanese/American infantry unit the 442nd, which had fought imperialism abroad, began to question their status at home. These soldiers demanded their rights and added fuel to spark the civil rights movements.

The civil rights movements of the 1950s and 1960s that included legal challenges, boycotts, civil disobedience sit-ins, protests, and marches had its first major landmark victory with the *Brown v. Board of Education* case in 1954 that led to desegregation. Other de jure acts of discrimination were contested by civil rights leaders; their work culminated in the Civil Rights Act of 1964 and the Voting Act of 1965. The liberalization of immigration laws were also pushed with the passing of the Immigration and Naturalization Law of 1965. These legislations drastically shifted U.S. demographics and political participation as immigration from Asia and Latin America increased. The thirty-year period between 1945 and 1975 generated quite contradictory images of Asian/American peoples in general, and sexualities in particular. From war brides to prostitutes, from foreign spies to refugees, and from "yellow peril" to "model minorities," Asian/American images and the actual social conditions that fueled them became increasingly complex.[37]

This volume addresses some of these complexities, for example, in relation to refugee and diasporic populations from Cambodia and Vietnam. A collective of women offer their corrective account of the non-profit organization Khmer Girls in Action (KGA), which was formed in part to address health and sexuality with girls and young Cambodian/American women. The analysis raises issues of individual and collective agency in relation to Asian/American activism and inquires into the consequences of theory being grossly abstracted from the bodies it purports to illuminate. Through the frames of literary and trauma studies, Cathy Schlund-Vials investigates related issues but focuses specifically on a Cambodian/American memoir by a woman of ethnic Chinese descent. What, she asks, are the stakes in this representation? How is Cambodian/American memoir reception and interpretation facilitated by its intersection with, for example, Jewish American literature? She turns her attention to sexuality by asking what are the conditions of possibility for sexuality and individual desire in the world of the Khmer Rouge in which one occupies the position of daughter of the state. How is sexuality reconfigured when the Khmer Rouge destroyed and replaced normative family structures with the state? Julie Thị Underhill's contribution provides a kind of coda to the volume as a whole in asking what remains of bodies after they disappear. Her autobiographical text links sexuality and violence and testifies to how individuals live and die in the face of traumatic events both in spaces of U.S. imperialism and in U.S. domestic spaces, where individual bodies have been scarred by those larger geopolitical events.

As in the case of Khmer Girls for Action, a collective body can be organized to frame and legitimate certain bodies of knowledge while marginalizing others. In Eunai Shrake's commentary, she inquires into how Confucian practices, a fundamentalist reading of the Bible, and fear of assimilation converge in a stance on anti-homosexuality by Korean/American Christian churches. Unlike the liberating effort of KGA, we witness here how Asian/American bodies, in an effort to sustain a notion of community in the face of assimilation, restrict and constrain other Asian/American bodies from expression. These liberating and confining currents flow simultaneously.

In the wake of these multiple iterations of belonging in and disidentification from the United States, the persistence of the model minority discourse is perhaps surprising. Nevertheless, it endures. Citing mainstream media and J. Philippe Rushton,[38] an evolutionary biologist who argued that different "races" have different physiologies and correspondingly different intellectual and sexual abilities, filmmaker Renee Tajima-Pena argued in her 1997 documentary that the model minority discourse characterizes Asian/American men with the description "big brain and small penis."[39] According to some writers, although many Asian/American men have had the opportunity to catch up economically with their white male counterparts as indicated in occupational and income achievements, Asian/American men still experience discrimination through the perception that they cannot fulfill the role of "real men" in U.S. society.[40] Asian/American men might fare well economically, but sexually they are seen as undesirable and, therefore, not really "masculine" men. In other words, while model minority discourse may account for economic successes among Asian/American men, it also reconstructs them as deviant in terms of their sexuality.[41] Meanwhile, African American men are still often seen as hypersexual and not intelligent, and European American men are considered "normal" on both counts of brain size and penis size.[42] In short, this theory renders only white men as "normal" and desirable and deviantizes men of color as mentally and/or physically inadequate.

Given this recurring image of Asian/American men as undesirable geniuses, it is understandable that the feminization of the Asian model in *Details* strikes a nerve among Asian/American psyches. "Why can't the page exist with only the image of an affluent, built Asian/American man who looks cool?" some Asian/American students have asked. They hypothesize that this "cool" image goes against the stereotype of nerdy, undesirable, unassimilable Asian men.[43] Whether the model is Asian, gay, or Asian and gay, he serves as an "inscrutable" amusement for the spectators. Asian/American studies as a field emerged in part to address these sorts of perceptions. The standard narrative of Asian/American studies traces its roots to the student protests movements in the 1960s and 1970s. Asian/American studies emerges as one leg of an ethnic studies quadruped, a hybrid creature that represented the concerns of Asian/American, African American, Native American and Latina/o populations in the United States. The institutionalization of Asian/American studies, initially within the halls of San Francisco State University and the University of California at Berkeley, promised to redress historical erasure, and to locate and validate the contributions of Asian/American communities within the contours of the American nation.

As the concept of the "American nation" has come under scrutiny, however, so too have the constituent parts of ethnic studies become increasingly fractured. In part, the growing pain of Asian/American studies indicates a shift away from the imagined unity of a body politic defined by U.S. "Americanness." The civil rights movement in the United States coincides with both the Cold War and the decolonization struggles of a number of "third world" peoples. The intersections of these movements have produced subjects that do not fit neatly into cultural nationalist frameworks of assimilation and resistance.[44] For example, May Joseph has used the example of performance artist Shishir Kurup, an Asian/African/American, in her larger discussion of how citizenship sometimes "extends beyond the coherence of national boundaries and is linked to informal networks of kinship, migrancy, and displacement."[45] Aihwa Ong's work follows a similar trajectory, elaborating how transnational Chinese networks produce "flexible citizenship" for people with a certain level of economic means.[46] Not surprisingly, although both Joseph and Ong now live and teach in the United States, they spent at least part of their childhoods in "third world," hybrid spaces that bear the marks of colonial struggle and postcolonial transition. Migrating from such spaces undoubtedly inflects their experiences of and writings about citizenship in the United States. And, while both of their bodies may now signify as Asian/American, the cultural nationalist paradigm of Asian/American racial formation created in the 1970s and 1980s does little

to explain the conditions of life they describe for themselves and their subjects.

Of the many chapters that interrogate the coupling of national belonging
and sexuality in this volume, perhaps playwright Eugenie Chan's *Novell-
Aah!* is the most imaginative and, in some ways, expansive. The Chinese
women she depicts speak in English, but the format of a Mexican tele-
novella shapes their interactions. The principal relationship might be characterized by its lesbian, mother-daughter, and/or incestuous dynamics. But
even as Chan's stage creates a world without men's bodies, masculinity still
informs much of the dramatic action. The piece raises intriguing questions
about bodies and the ways in which they do or do not correspond to social
norms. Such issues are picked up elsewhere in, for example, Anjali Arondekar's discussion of the Indian rubber dildo. But that item we will discuss
later.

Notwithstanding Chan's and others' potential challenge to the dominant
scripts of American nationhood, a master narrative of American citizenship
continues to circulate. Based on myths of founding fathers and self-made
men, this dominant fantasy of national construction and belonging has
worked to define "the American citizen," to borrow the eloquent phrase of
Lisa Lowe, "against the Asian immigrant, legally, economically, and culturally."[47] Despite the presence of the many people of color involved in the development of the U.S. nation-state—the "Manila Men" in the eighteenth
century and Chinese laborers in the nineteenth being representative examples here—the history of the American dream has been visualized in black
and white.

Both the "official" documentation of self-reliant white men as well as the
counternarratives of Asian/Americans such as Filipino and Chinese migrants indicate that conceptions of masculinity anchor the national narrative. Representations of the U.S. nation, therefore, are often coincident with
the assertion of manliness.[48] It is perhaps no surprise, therefore, that when
Asian/American studies attempted to carve out a space in the American historical trajectory, male voices would come to dominate the movement in
terms of its protestations if not its cultural production. In the early 1970s,
for example, the four editors of the first anthology of Asian/American writers, called *Aiiieeeee!*, wrote a manifesto that profoundly influenced the direction of early Asian/American studies. Concerned with "Filipino, Chinese,
and Japanese Americans, American born and raised,"[49] the collection's
goals included debunking stereotypes like that of "passive Chinese men,
worshiping white women and being afraid to touch them."[50] Such a statement implicates the editors' efforts in a project to reclaim an aggressive heterosexuality for Asian/American men, whom they feel have been emascu-
lated. Indeed the original *Aiiieeeee!* contained fourteen selections, only
three of which were by women. But again, Asian/American masculinity was

never articulated univocally. Russell Leong remembers that his gay-themed short story "Rough Notes for Mantos" appeared in *Aiiieeeee!* under the pseudonym Wallace Lin and that Lonny Kaneko's "the Shoyu Kid," now discussed in queer terms, appeared in *Amerasia Journal* in 1976 (the periodical began printing in 1973).[51] In *Embodying Asian/American Sexualities*, we also include a fictional tale centered on masculinity, but Noël Alumit's excerpt from his performance *The Rice Room: Scenes from a Bar* uses humor to engage the vexed issue of Asian/American masculinity. This piece also explicitly places the gay man center-stage, both literally (since Alumit performs the piece) and figuratively. Alumit's solo show might therefore be seen as a counter to the lack of *explicit* gay Asian/American male representation by Asian/American producers in the early years of the movement.

Similar to the direction in Asian/American studies that has been heavily heterosexual or anonymously homosexual, early studies on gender and sexuality were often heterosexist. After first-wave feminism (that is, the late nineteenth- and early twentieth-century women's suffrage movement), the studies of gender that came out of second-wave feminism from the 1960s forward focused not on a model of universal rights but on difference (e.g., "herstory" instead of "history") and centered the experiences of women in research amid the prevalence of men's stories represented as universal human stories. In reaction to male dominance, or patriarchy, these studies of gender opened new theoretical and methodological frameworks for research on topics like work, family, and selfhood. Discussions of reproductive rights, sexual pleasures, and gender roles challenged an old patriarchal paradigm of "sex" as a biological destiny and brought in a new paradigm of "gender" as a social construct and social process.[52] In other words, women and men could no longer be reducible to biology. The social world became a new site for investigation into how sexed individuals become men and women. This fundamental change in distinguishing anatomical difference from gender paved the way for later studies on sexuality as something socially constructed rather than physiological.

Centering on women in revolt against patriarchy, early work in women's studies allowed room for a separatist movement away from men. Lesbianism must be a new politics for feminists, argued Adrienne Rich.[53] Monique Wittig explained that the notion "lesbian" exists outside of heterosexuality and, therefore, challenges patriarchy.[54] In a patriarchal world, perceived differences between men and women end up serving as a justification for women's oppression. Wittig argues that "lesbian" can be a term independent of woman (which, in a heterosexist and patriarchal world, is always defined in relation to man), and so Wittig's lesbian interrupts and contests patriarchal authority. However, the integration of lesbianism as a feminist politics was hampered by the rampant homophobia, or intolerance of homosexuality, in the 1970s women's movement. The "lavender menace,"

Betty Freidan warned, would discredit and destroy the women's movement.[55] Coupled with homophobia is heterosexism, or the belief that heterosexuality is the only "normal" category of sexuality.

Sexology has both reinforced and contested the normalization of heterosexuality. On the one hand, research on sex has been used to validate existing cultural norms. Terms like "sexual inverts" and "sodomites" pathologized people and helped to justify their confinement in prisons or psychiatric wards. On the other hand, work by Richard von Kraft-Ebing, Magnus Hirschfield, Karl-Heinrich Ulrichs, Havelock Ellis, Sigmund Freud, and others chronicled variance in gender expressions, sexual practices, and erotic desires. Such documentation offered public discussion of previously taboo subjects. In 1948, a controversial and landmark study, *Sexual Behavior in the Human Male*, and again in 1953, *Sexual Behavior in the Human Female*, by Alfred Kinsey and associates challenged the assumption of "normal" heterosexuality by exposing a continuum of sexual behaviors and attractions using interviews conducted in the United States. These studies revealed a "natural" spectrum of diverse sexual and emotional expressions with homosexual behavior being one of many possibilities. Despite the finding that 10 percent of men have sex exclusively with men, the dominant perspective of the time clung tightly to the normality of heterosexuality and also ignored the other 46 percent of the male subjects who said they had "reacted" sexually to persons of both sexes in the course of their adult lives.[56] Similar findings on women (up to 6 percent of women were exclusively homosexual in experience/response) were also recast in the framework of "normal" heterosexuality.[57] Curious about the "deviants" or sympathetic to the "abnormal," sociological researchers in the 1950s through the mid-1960s continued to detail the lives of gays and lesbian people as well as other categories of perceived sexual deviants (e.g., hustlers). By the late 1960s, images of gays and lesbians began to change into ones more sympathetic when homophile and gay and lesbian research contributed to this scientific and political enterprise. Reflecting the gay and lesbian movement's challenge to discrimination in the 1970s, the American Psychiatric Association in 1973 removed homosexuality from its list of mental disorders after a close vote among members. In sociology, the focus shifted from "deviants" to "deviantizing processes." Instead of assuming gays and lesbians were abnormal and exploring what made them deviant, researchers shifted their attention to the social processes that deviantized people and processes that made them into "gay" or "lesbian" subjects. Thus, social processes of identification and labeling now fascinate social scientists. In summary, like the evolution of studies on race and gender that have moved from viewing them as natural occurring phenomena, current studies in sex and sexuality have denaturalized sex and sexuality and shifted the focus to the social.

The roundtable on the various uses and meanings of pornography revises and elaborates discourses of sexual practice and representations that were the mainstay of sexology. The scholars gathered for the discussion all work on pornography from different perspectives, based on archives in different locations. The conversation includes Richard Fung, whose essays and films were pioneering examinations of this topic. Anjali Arondekar works on colonialism and sexuality and the circulations of materials and desires that move between such locales as England and India. Rather than tracing the movements of bodies, however, Arondekar comments on objects like the Indian rubber dildo and how such items might help us understand how bodies become legible in the first place. From a film-studies approach, Sylvia Chong discusses the spectacle of pornography and what it might share with spectacular violence. Finally, Darrell Hamamoto, who joins the conversation at the end, offers a brief word on Asian/American production of pornography, an issue that has lately placed him in a media spotlight.

The issues raised in this roundtable revise much of the early scholarship on race, gender, and sexual desires/practices that we have traced in this introduction. Like almost all of the chapters in this book, shifting critical vocabularies for these issues have enabled such revisions. Of all of these shifts, perhaps some of the most influential have been generated under two overlapping rubrics: "transgender studies" and "queer theory." In the last couple decades, a significant body of work in transgender studies, in particular, has recentered the corporeal to expand our understanding of the complex intersection between the physical, the social, and the psychological.

A simplified but useful starting point for understanding the difference between heterosexuality, homosexuality, or bisexuality and the category of transgender is articulated in our interview with Pauline Park, chair of the New York Association for Gender and Rights Advocacy (NYAGRA). As Park explains, sexuality pertains to sexual orientation or desire, while transgender pertains to gender/sex identification. For some transgender people, their sex/gender assignment does not match their identification. For many, they seek physical alteration of their appearances (through clothing, binding, packing) and/or physiologies (through hormones, surgeries) to match the gender/sex that they perceive themselves to be. Contesting the physical body, transmen and transwomen traverse a complicated terrain that challenges the culturally taken-for-granted understanding of sex as biologically given. In a study of biology and medical practice in the United States, Anne Fausto-Sterling explains how physical bodies become male or female through the culturally biased assumptions that structure the medical profession. Anthropologists, whose research argues that some cultures have more than two sex/gender categories, have also observed such challenges to a male-female binary.

Queer theory designates a body of scholarship that, according to the most widely circulated narrative, first emerged in the United States during the late 1980s and early 1990s alongside and often in response to the AIDS crisis. While the halls of academia and the "streets" of protest are not mutually exclusive, university researchers began to produce knowledge on the normative as opposed to the "normal," while activist groups like Queer Nation and ACT-UP (AIDS Coalition To Unleash Power) were experimenting with new models of civil disobedience.[58] In examining the normative, scholars like Judith Butler, Teresa de Lauretis, and Eve Kosofsky Sedgwick asked questions pertaining to how norms emerge and become standards of correctness.[59] More specifically, they queried why and how we have come to regard certain sexual desires and practices as "normal." A reference point for many of these studies was the work of French philosopher Michel Foucault,[60] whose research into how norms function as regimes of power to normalize heterosexuality and differentially deviantize homosexuality and other alternative sexualities and genders has had a profound impact. Linking knowledge and power, Foucault and radical sex theorist Gayle Rubin[61] illustrated how the discourse on sex and sexuality is also about social control and resistance by conflicting groups. In recognition of this work, and as distinct from some work in gay and lesbian studies, queer activists and theorists attempted to reimagine and/or reconstruct the conditions that led to the adoption of oppressive norms in the first place. Rather than arguing for the inclusion of, for example, gay and lesbian people within existing social and political structures, queer theorists sought to expose and disrupt politics "as normal."[62]

As Ruthann Lee's contribution to this anthology demonstrates, while the queer theory–informed studies in the genealogy outlined above have contributed much to the field of sexuality, the studies of its intersection with race, class, and ethnicity have been somewhat limited, although articulations of what has recently been called queer of color critique promise much. This queer of color critique often looks to older texts by artists and scholars such as Gloria Anzaldua, Audre Lorde, and Cherie Moraga that attempted to create spaces for the articulation of multiple and simultaneous categories of difference, such as lesbian, feminist, and Chicana. In Lee's case, her own body in the classroom serves as the touchstone for her ruminations on the efficacy of queer theory for racialized subjects. Lee argues that the classroom is a primary site for the negotiation of politics and knowledge and a site where the individual body matters.

The conference "CrossTalk II: Embodiments of API Sexuality," held at California State University–Northridge in 2002, also attempted to account for these multiple and simultaneous indices of difference, with a specific but not exclusive focus on underprivileged "Asian Pacific Islander (API)" communities in Los Angeles.[63] The follow-up to a previous public forum, CrossTalk II addressed how intersecting discourses of race, ethnicity, class, spirituality, gender, and sexuality both inform and are constructed in relation to changing understandings of API bodies. Obviously, CrossTalk II had a predecessor. CrossTalk I (1997) was the first national conference on sensuality and sexuality in API communities. It began an interdisciplinary dialogue on subject matters that have received scant mention within and across API communities. This initial conference touched the tip of the iceberg in terms of exploring the complexity of sexual and gender dynamics. The organizers learned from that occasion that continuous dialogues are imperative to encourage and harness research and preventive intervention programs. The motivation behind Crosstalk II was to make links between activists, artists, service providers, and scholars in hopes of affecting social policy in relation to API sensuality and sexuality issues. Grounded in these premises and sensitive to the entanglement of knowledge and power, this anthology is a compilation of different forms of knowledge production—autobiographical accounts, humanistic research, community-based work, and artistic expression—by various members of Asian/American communities whose works are shaping and redefining Asian/American sensuality and sexuality.

Embodying Asian/American Sexualities builds specifically on several studies—most notably David Eng and Alice Hom's introduction to *Q&A*, Dana Takagi's lead essay in the *Amerasia Journal* issue "Dimensions of Desire," and Jennifer Ting's article in the inaugural issue of *Journal of Asian American Studies*—that have recently articulated the need to deploy LGBT and queer studies to rethink the heteronormative[64] and sometimes heterosexist discourses that have shaped Asian/American racial formation from the institutionalization of Asian American scholarship in the late 1960s through the mid-1990s.[65] In contrast to the multiple and useful thematic groupings in *Q&A* and "Dimensions of Desire," contributors to this anthology were asked to focus on embodiment or corporeality, because individual and collective Asian/American bodies may support, complicate, and/or defy attempts to make them legible. Although contributors responded differently to this request, we have endeavored in this introduction to suggest ways in which the various chapters engage this issue while situating the project as a whole within a larger history of U.S. racial formation as well as some of the critical genealogies that inform the chapters: Asian/American studies, women's studies, sexology, and queer theory. Our brief outline of these contexts, we hope, renders our initial discussion of the *Details* piece with which we began more meaningful. The stakes of the "Gay or Asian?" feature are tied to the fact that it is one iteration in a history of knowledge production and image-making. In this case, the site for that production is a nationally distributed magazine whose visibility and economic success suggest the capacity for wide influence. The letters to the editor in regard to the piece circulate around this point.

As a touchstone for *Embodying Asian/American Sexualities*, the *Details* page and the thoughts it provoked serve to remind us of the ongoing struggles around the representations of Asian/American bodies as they emerge through and in relation to categories of gender and sexuality. Since the production of representation is not only a political act but also an economic one, many of our contributors address modes of production. From the public domain of community organizing to the intimate exchange of letters, the chapters demonstrate how bodies emerge through different media. To further this point and to emphasize processes of embodiment, we have specifically included performance pieces in the volume (Alumit, Chan, and Irwin). We hope this will help to inspire students to engage with the material in visceral fashion. Beyond what we have chosen to include and the thematic frame of embodying, we have resisted the urge to organize the chapters in what would strike us the most useful pedagogical order. Instead, we list the chapters alphabetically by author, assuming that each reader or classroom will have different desires and needs with regard to the material contained herein.

A collaborative effort, *Embodying Asian/American Sexualities* is the result of a long process that now involves you as reader. We invite you to engage.

NOTES

1. Whitney McNally, "Anthropology: Gay or Asian," *Details* 22 (6) (March/April 2004): 52. Although we attempted to obtain permission from Conde Nast to reprint the image and text, the editors of *Details* have stated they do not wish to see the piece reprinted again for any reason.

2. "Teabagging" is a slang word for bouncing a scrotum on another person's head.

3. A reference to the film *The Karate Kid* and to masturbation.

4. Daniel Peres, "Letter from the Editor," *Details* 22 (8) (June/July 2004): 34.

5. Stereotype here means a generalized statement that associates particular characteristics with particular social groups or people. Here the stereotype would seem to benefit a dominant group in society, enabling easy and reductive categorization of minority groups.

6. Peres, "Letter from the Editor," 36.

7. Peres, "Letter from the Editor," 38.

8. "LGBT" is an abbreviation for lesbian, gay, bisexual, and transgender, terms we explore in detail later in this introduction.

9. Peres, "Letter from the Editor," 38. The first quotation comes from the published letter of Raymond Wong, national president of the Organization of Chinese Americans; the second quotation is from the published letter of California Assemblywoman, Judy Chu.

10. In this introduction, we use the term "Asian/American." By "Asian/American" we follow but modify the geographic contours of Asian/American discourses recently suggested by Gail Nomura (Gail M. Nomura, "Introduction: On Our Terms: Definitions and Context," in *Asian/ Pacific Islander American Women: A Historical An-*

thology, ed. Shirley Hune and Gail M. Nomura [New York: New York University Press, 2003]). Nomura defines Asian American quite expansively. (Page numbers indicated in the following refer to the citation above.)

Asian American generally refers to immigrants and those born in the United States of Chinese, Filipino, Japanese, Korean, South Asian (e.g., Indian, Pakistani, Bangladeshi, Sri Lankan, Nepalese, Burmese), and Southeast Asian (e.g., Vietnamese, Hmong, Mien, Laotian, Cambodian, Indonesian, Thai, Malaysian, Singaporean) ancestry and may "include 'peoples of Asian descent in all of the Americas' as well as 'peoples from the entire geographical region of Asia'" (16).

We also agree, although we use slightly different terminology, that Pacific Islander in this context refers to "indigenous peoples of Pacific Islands with a history of U.S. colonialism: the state of Hawai'i; the organized, unincorporated territory of Guam; the Commonwealth of the Northern Mariana Islands; the unorganized, unincorporated territory of American Samoa . . . as well as the three sovereign nations that comprise the Freely Associated States . . . [and] all Pacific Islander immigrants and their descendents born in the United States" (16).

However, we differ from Nomura in that we place a slash between "Asian" and "American." We place this slash, following the argument that David Palumbo-Liu set forth in *Asian/American: Historical Crossings of a Racial Frontier* (Stanford, Calif.: Stanford University Press, 1999). (Page numbers below refer to this citation.) Liu writes that the slash "instantiates a choice between two terms, their simultaneous and equal status, and an element of indecidability . . . as it at once implies both exclusion and inclusion" (1).

11. We use discourses here to mean discussions, talks, representations, and framings of issues by conflicting groups with differential power.

12. "Bear" is a term used to describe a type of gay male masculinity that often, but not always, corresponds to gay men whose gender presentation emphasizes dominant characteristics—such as body build and hair—that generally contradict the stereotypes of gay men as effeminate or "pretty boys."

13. Alonso Duralde, "Bear or Straight?" *The Advocate* 17 (August 2004): 44–45.

14. "Metrosexuality" refers to individuals who desire the opposite sex as their primary sexual object choice but whose look (choice of fashion, etc.) corresponds to dominant images of gay men.

15. The ability to detect if someone is gay, lesbian, or bisexual.

16. Duralde, "Bear or Straight?" 44.

17. Peres, "Letter from the Editor," 34.

18. Michael Omi and Howard Winant, *Racial Formation in the United States from the 1960s to the 1990s*, second edition (New York: Routledge, 1994), 62.

19. Many books tackle the subjects of slavery and abolitionism. For example, see David Brion Davis, *Inhuman Bondage: The Rise and Fall of Slavery in the New World* (Oxford: Oxford University Press, 2006).

20. Thomas Lennon, *Jefferson's Blood*, PBS, 1999.

21. See David Kazanjian, *The Colonizing Trick: National Culture and Imperial Citizenship in Early America* (Minneapolis: University of Minnesota Press, 2003).

22. Omi and Winant, *Racial Formation*, 63. For a good example, see Joseph Arthur Comte de Gobineau's (1853 to 1855) four volumes on *The Inequality of The Human Races*, republished by Howard Fertig in 1999. These volumes argue the superiority

of the white race. Adding to this differentiation and evaluation of human groups, Madison Grant's 1916 *Passing of the Great Race* (reprinted by Kessinger Publishing, LLC, in 2006 with a foreword by Henry Fairfield Osborn) not only assumes white/European superiority but differentiates within this category: the superior "Nordic race" from the inferior "Alpines and Mediterraneans."

23. Philip C. Wander, Judith N. Martin, and Thomas K. Nakayama, "The Roots of Racial Classification," in *White Privilege: Essential Readings on the Other Side of Racism,* ed. P. S. Rothenberg (New York: Worth Publishers, 2005).

24. Omi and Winant, *Racial Formation,* 183. Omi and Winant's footnote number 26 cited that in *The Mismeasure of Man* (New York: W. W. Norton, 1981), biologist Steven Jay Gould reexamined proslavery physician Samuel George Morton's collection of eight hundred crania from all parts of the world and suggested that the research data were deeply manipulated, though unconsciously, to agree with Morton's "apriori conviction about racial ranking."

25. Omi and Winant, *Racial Formation,* 64.

26. For an overview of this topic, see Amy Kaplan and Donald Pease, *Cultures of United States Imperialism* (Durham, N.C.: Duke University Press, 1993).

27. U.S. imperialist interest in China finally resulted in concessions from China during the second opium war. These were provided through the Treaty of Tianjin, ratified by China in 1860. For a history of the second opium war, see J. Y. Wong, *Deadly Dreams: Opium and the Arrow War (1856–1860) in China* (Cambridge: Cambridge University Press, 2002). On the significance of the opium wars in a U.S. context, see, for example, Curtis Marez, *Drug Wars: The Political Economy of Narcotics* (Minneapolis: University of Minnesota Press, 2004).

28. The U.S.-Mexican War occurred from 1846 to 1848 following the 1845 annexation of Texas.

29. Haunani-Kay Trask, *From a Native Daughter: Colonialism and Sovereignty in Hawaii,* rev. ed. (Honolulu: University of Hawaii Press, 1999).

30. Among the many useful books on the implications of 1898 and the Spanish-American War is Neil Smith, *American Empire: Roosevelt's Geographer and the Prelude to Globalization* (Berkeley and Los Angeles: University of California Press, 2004).

31. See, for example, Susan Koshy, *Sexual Naturalization: Asian Americans and Miscegenation* (Palo Alto, Calif.: Stanford University Press, 2004); Lisa Lowe, *Immigrant Acts: On Asian American Cultural Politics* (Durham, N.C.: Duke University Press, 1996); Ronald T. Takaki, *Strangers from a Different Shore: A History of Asian Americans* (Boston: Little, Brown, 1998).

32. Shirley Hune, "Rethinking Race: Paradigms and Policy Formation," in *Contemporary Asian America: A Multidisciplinary Reader,* ed. M. Zhou and J. V. Gatewood (New York: New York University Press, 2000).

33. This usage of the term intersectionality can be traced to Kimberle Crenshaw's article "Demarginalizing the Intersection of Race and Sex," published in 1989 in the *Chicago Legal Forum.*

34. Processes of racialization were complicated in the 1920s. For example, Neil Foley explained that while court decisions like *Ozawa v. United States* (1923) and *United States v. Thind* (1922) restricted definition of citizenship and whiteness to include only Caucasians from Europe, Mexicans through lobbying of the League of United Latin American Citizens were legally recognized as "Hispanic White"; the

qualifier also marked them to be treated as non-white. (Neil Foley, "Becoming Hispanic: Mexican Americans and Whiteness," in *White Privilege: Essential Readings on the Other Side of Racism*, ed. P. S. Rothenberg [New York: Worth Publishers, 1998].)

35. Takaki, *Strangers from a Different Shore*, 357.

36. For example, see John Okada's fiction, *No-No Boy* (Seattle: University of Washington Press, 1957).

37. In the late 1960s, images of Asians as the ideal minority emerged. News magazines started running articles about the success of Asians in the United States by looking at communities of Japanese people and Chinese people in terms of improving incomes, improving occupations, high educational achievements, low crime rates, etc. These articles explained and generalized the success of Japanese/Americans and Chinese/Americans to all Asian and Asian/American peoples. They argued that Asian/American communities were successful despite facing racial discrimination because of Asian cultures that stressed hard work, obedience, and education. Unlike Latinos, African Americans, and Native Americans, Asian/Americans were able to overcome their adverse conditions through their cultural values and practices. Source: Keith Osajima, "Asian Americans as the Model Minority: An Analysis of the Popular Press Image in the 1960s and 1980s," in *Contemporary Asian America: A Multidisciplinary Reader*, ed. M. Zhou and J. V. Gatewood (New York: New York University Press, 2000).

38. J. Philippe Rushton, *Race, Evolution, and Behavior: A Life History Perspective* (New Brunswick: Transaction Publishers, 1995).

39. Renee Tajima-Peña, *My America, Or Honk If You Love Buddha* (PBS National, 1997).

40. This position has been perhaps most forcefully articulated in the work of author Frank Chin.

41. Yen Le Espiritu's *Asian American Women and Men: Labor, Laws and Love* (Thousand Oaks, Calif.: Sage Publications, 1997) traces some of the historical precursors of this deviant sexuality. When immigration laws restricted Chinese and Filipino men from forming families by excluding immigration of Asian women, the Chinese and Filipino communities existed as bachelor societies. Because of these social, historical conditions, they were then imputed as "asexual." At the same time, there were laws against miscegenation and cases of lynching to control these men's sexuality in the frontier where white women were also few in numbers.

42. Note that Pacific Islander men's sexuality is constructed differently from Asian men's sexuality. Given the specific encounters of Europeans with Pacific Islanders whose sexuality was considered too open for the reserved Europeans, Pacific Islanders' sexuality is seen as more closely resembling that of Africans (i.e., hypersexual) than of Asians. Asian/American men's sexual images began to diverge from other men of color in the late 1960s.

43. William Hung, a celebrated failed contestant of the TV reality show "American Idol," epitomizes this nerdy misfit image. Fans of Hung created websites devoted to this "untalented" but earnest aspired singer and civil engineering UC Berkeley student and proclaimed him the "universal sex nerd" who amused them by his earnest renditions of pop songs of mega stars like Ricky Martin.

44. Emma Perez's *The Decolonial Imaginary: Writing Chicanas into History* (Theories of Representation and Difference) (Bloomington: Indiana University Press,

1999) suggests both that postcolonial and hegemonic theories and methodologies are inadequate in addressing concerns of mestizo/as in the United States and that a new theory and methodology of decolonization may be a better fit in addressing the complexity of resistance when a population is not politically, economically, and culturally independent from the colonizers.

45. May Joseph, *Nomadic Identities: The Performance of Citizenship* (Minneapolis: University of Minnesota Press, 1999).

46. Aihwa Ong, *Flexible Citizenship: The Cultural Logics of Transnationality* (Durham, N.C.: Duke University Press, 1999).

47. Lowe, 4 (original emphasis).

48. A useful text here is Dana Nelson, *National Manhood: Capitalist Citizenship and the Imagined Fraternity of White Men* (Durham, N.C.: Duke University Press, 1998).

49. Frank Chin, Jeffrey Paul Chan, Lawson Inada, and Shawn Wong, eds., *Aiiieeeee!: An Anthology of Asian-American Writers* (New York: Doubleday, 1975), xi.

50. Chin, et al., *Aiiieeeee!* xix.

51. Russel Leong, ed., *Asian American Sexualities: Dimensions of the Gay and Lesbian Experience* (New York: Routledge, 1996), 10.

52. Candice West and Don Zimmerman, "Doing Gender," *Gender & Society* 2 (1) (1987): 125–51.

53. Adrienne Rich, "Compulsory Heterosexuality and Lesbian Existence," in *The Lesbian and Gay Studies Reader*, ed. H. Abelove, M. A. Barale, and D. M. Halperin (New York: Routledge, 1993).

54. Monique Wittig, "One Is Not Born a Woman," in *The Lesbian and Gay Studies Reader*, ed. H. Abelove, M. A. Barale, and D. M. Halperin (New York: Routledge, 1993).

55. This term was used by Betty Friedan, president of NOW (National Association of Women) in 1969.

56. A. C. Kinsey, W. B. Pomeroy, and E. E. Martin, *Sexual Behavior in the Human Male* (Philadelphia: W. B. Saunders, 1948).

57. Alfred Kinsey and Institute of Sex Research, *Sexual Behavior in the Human Female* (Bloomington: Indiana University Press, 1953).

58. For information on ACT-UP, see www.actupny.org. For information on Queer Nation, see *Outlook: National Lesbian and Gay Quarterly* 11 (Winter 1991), and Lauren Berlant and Elizabeth Freeman, "Queer Nationality," in *Fear of a Queer Planet: Queer Politics and Social Theory*, ed. Michael Warner (Minneapolis: University of Minnesota Press, 1993).

59. Judith Butler, "Critically Queer," *GLQ* 1 (1) (1993): 17–32; Teresa de Lauretis, "Queer Theory: Lesbian and Gay Sexualities," *differences* 3 (2) (Summer 1991): i–xviii; Eve K. Sedgwick, "Queer Performativity: Henry James and the Art of the Novel," *GLQ* 1 (1) (1993): 1–16.

60. Michel Foucault, *The History of Sexuality: An Introduction*, vol. I (New York: Vintage Books, 1978). Foucault has produced a large body of work, and we cite here only the text most frequently cited in queer studies.

61. Gayle S. Rubin, "Thinking Sex: Notes for a Radical Theory of the Politics of Sexuality," in *The Lesbian and Gay Studies Reader*, ed. H. Abelove, M. A. Barale, and D. M. Halperin (New York: Routledge, 1993).

62. See, for example, Gregory Bredbeck, "The New Queer Narrative: Intervention and Critique," *Textual Practice* 9 (3) (Winter 1995): 477–502.

63. Organized by a group of scholars working at universities and activists working at several different venues in Los Angeles, we used the term "API," or Asian Pacific Islander, to be consonant with the term as it was used in social service circles.

64. Anything that makes heterosexuality normal and pervasive.

65. Much work has been done in literary and cultural analysis. For example, see useful summaries of gay and lesbian representation in Asian/American literature by Karin Aguilar-San Juan, "Landmarks in Literature by Asian American Lesbians," *Signs: Journal of Women in Culture and Society* 19 (4) (1993): 936–43; Alice Hom and Ming-Yuen Ma, "A Speculative Dialogue on Asian Pacific Islander Lesbian and Gay Writing," *Journal of Homosexuality* 26 (2–3) (1993): 21–51; and David Eng and Candace Fujikane, "Asian American Gay and Lesbian Literature" in *The Gay and Lesbian Literary Heritage: A Reader's Companion to the Writers and Their Works, from Antiquity to the Present*, ed. Claude J. Summers (New York: Holt, 1995): 60–63. More recently, Sau-Ling Wong and Jeffrey Santa Ana have published the most exhaustive review of gender and sexuality in Asian/American literature to date: Sau-ling Wong and Jeffrey Santa Ana, "Review Essay: Gender and Sexuality in Asian American Literature," *Signs: Journal of Women in Culture and Society* 25 (1) (1999): 171–226. In film studies, Eve Oishi has brought several little-known queer film- and videomakers to the fore. Her work supplements discussion of gay Asian/American filmmakers with more established reputations, such as Richard Fung and Quentin Lee.

1

The Rice Room

Scenes from a Bar

Noël Alumit

GEORGE

I had a very hard day. I wake up this morning with this raging headache. Pounding. Pounding. Pounding. My friend Greg tells me to meditate more often. So I try it. IT DOESN'T WORK! I find myself late to work, because I'm desperately trying to find my glasses. I look everywhere. I pass my hall mirror to discover they were on my face the entire time.

I work for this gay organization. I won't mention the name but they're very big and very influential. I quit my last job in marketing because I wanted to work in a less stressful environment and get away from my straight asshole of a boss. Now I work for a gay organization, the stress is still there, and no matter what anyone says, bosses are still assholes regardless of sexual orientation.

I get to work and phones were going off and the receptionist called in sick. I'm fielding calls left and right. I must have had thirty-two people on hold at the same time. And while all of this was going on, the only thought that kept going through my head was that at the end of the day, I would go to a bar and relax.

I walk into the Rice Room and I see him. Him. I don't know his name, I don't know what he does for a living. I don't know anything about him. I just know it's him. The man of my dreams. He looks like an Asian James Dean. A rebel. His hair is slicked back with pomade, grooves of hair pulled back, formed no doubt with the teeth of a black comb. Stunning. He's wearing a T-shirt, one size too small, so it's tight. From my view, I could see the muscles of his back tightly, firmly hug his ribcage. He turns around, and his one-size-too-small T-shirt looks like it's going to rip open from the sturdy

23

pecs of his chest. He lays back on the bar with his elbows resting on the counter. I see the outlines of little rectangles on his abdomen building and collapsing as he breathes in and out. He's wearing blue jeans, also one size too small. Levi's. Button fly. He's leaning back with one leg out like this, his foot resting on the heel of his black Tony Lama ostrich skin boots, looking like a 1950s matinee idol. I think to myself: It's him. The man of my dreams.

I could see it all in my head. Images popping in my head. Like paparazzi camera bulbs. I would walk up to him and say, "Hi." He would say, "How zit going?" He wouldn't say "How is it going" or "How are you?" He would say, "How zit going?" And I would look deeply into his eyes and say, "I had a shitty day, but since I've met you, my day and any other day from this point forward is a little brighter." And he would laugh, no chuckle, no smile, yeah, smile, and give a reverse nod. He would say, "You're cute, in a Clark Kent sort of way." And I would say, "You're gorgeous, in a way that is indescribable, incomparable, gorgeous in a way that you only possess and no one else." And he would see through my being, see through my soul, see through my glasses, that I'm the only man for him. We'll get married, start our life together, adopt two children from Korea, save money to send those two children to college, and they'll visit us in our home on a hill in Los Feliz, where we would spend the rest of our days until we die only minutes apart, then meet each other as cosmic light on the rings of Saturn where we would spend the rest of eternity traveling from one heavenly star to another . . . together.

So I'm at the far end of the bar. And I see him. I'm working on my third gin and tonic to build up the nerve to go over to this guy. Happy hour is in full swing now, and I think to myself: You idiot go over to him before someone else steals him away—before someone who doesn't even figure into our scheme of flying from star to star for the rest of eternity comes along and causes a cosmic imbalance where I would never meet this gorgeous guy in the first place. Go over. Go over. Go over! and meet him.

I take my drink napkin and dry off the sweat on my palms, I put my hands in my pocket to warm the coldness in my fingers. I get up from my barstool. But just before I go over, I pull out a pen and write a number on a napkin. I slowly walk over to him and say, "Hi." "How zit going?" he says, with a smile and a reverse nod. For a moment, I'm quiet. I don't say anything because he is more beautiful up close than from afar. I take my bar napkin with my scribbled telephone number on it, my name on the napkin is unreadable because the sweat from my palm dampened the paper, blurring the ink.

I say out loud, "Call me." But I pray to myself: God, please let him find me just somewhat attractive. Let him see through my being, see through my soul, see through my glasses, and see that I am the man for him. God please let him see that. I sit next to him. I order him another drink. "Bartender, another Scotch on the rocks." Like they say in the movies. I tell him my name. He tells me his. His name is Richard. Richard. We start to talk. He tells me he's from LA. I tell him I'm from LA. He tells me he loves to read Harold Brodkey. I tell him I love to read Harold Brodkey. He tells me he loves to watch old reruns of Laverne and Shirley. I tell him I love to watch old reruns of Laverne and Shirley. He's laughing and I'm laughing. And I'm thinking this is great. He tells me he only dates white guys—I tell him . . . all of a sudden I'm thinking of the two Korean kids we adopted and how they will never go to college. He tells me he has to go and wanders off to another part of the bar. He neglects to take the napkin with my blurred name and telephone number on it. He walks away. He stops. He turns around and smiles at me. My heart leaps, thinking that God answered my prayers and this gorgeous guy, Richard, finds me attractive after all. He's willing to leave his boyfriend because he can see my soul. And my soul possesses elements that transcend color lines. Adopted Korean kids, college here we come.

He looks at me. Richard looks at me, and says, "It was good talking to you. You're kinda cute in a Clark Kent sort of way." He shoots me with his finger. "Catcha later," he says. He leaves. He's gone. I sit at the barstool, for an hour or two. Go-go boys get on the stage and dance. While I sit here and watch.

RICHARD

(Pounding on the bathroom door) OPEN THE DOOR!!! I hate having to wait for the restroom. It seems the line to the bathroom is longer than the line to get into this place. All the scotch I drank is running right through me like water does a faucet. (To bathroom door) Listen, you little maggot. My bladder is about to fucking burst. If you don't get out real soon, you're gonna have a pee pond bigger than fucking Lake Superior. You got that asshole. YOU GOT THAT, FUCKING PIECE OF SHIT!

My friends tell me that I need to work on my communication skills. They say: "Richard, you gotta be more sensitive." Fuck sensitive. I'm mean. I like it that way. I like having people scared of me. They're less likely to fuck with you if they're scared of you. If they're not scared of you—you're nothing—dispensable.

Imagine: You're walking home. Minding your own business. Walking home from the gym, the Sport Connection, let's say. You're walking down Westbourne on your way to your house off Melrose. A house you got working as a personal trainer, let's say.

You notice a car behind you. It's driving really slow. You don't think much about it. Cars drive slow all the time, right? Plus you're only two blocks from your house and what could happen in two blocks? All of the sudden, the slow driving car passes you. You feel a sense of momentary relief. I say momentary because the car stops just ahead of you. Six guys—or was it five—it was six guys get out and start yelling at you: "Are you a faggot?" You try to walk a different direction. Once again: "Are you a faggot?"

You try to walk away, thinking they can't be talking to you, because you try really hard not to look like a faggot, I mean look gay. As you walk away they follow you. Then you run. And they run. One of them catches up to you, grabs you by the collar, and throws you down. You try to get up. But you feel this whack at the side of your face. Like someone just kicked you. Then you're out of breath because someone just socked you in the gut. Your try to fight back, but you can't. Two guys have your arms. They pulled it so far back that you think you're gonna snap in two. You feel this pain in your chest and stomach, because they're pummeling you. You try to scream but you can't get enough air into your body to do that because every time one of them punches you the wind is knocked right out of you. Until finally, between blows, you get enough air into your lungs into your gut to scream: "HEEEEEEELP!"

You notice off to your right, a light switches on in a kitchen window. A dim light, but bright enough to notice, bright enough for the guys kicking your ass to leave you alone and speed off. You wait for someone to come out of their house to help you. But you remember people don't do that anymore. So you make your way home. You want to cry, but a memory from childhood, a saying, a phrase—that someone said to you, but you don't remember who—reverberates in you head—big boys, men, real men don't cry. So you don't.

You want to call the police, but if you call them, you may have to tell them that you were attacked because you're gay. This was a couple of years ago, you're still in the closet, so you're not ready to do that yet. You don't call anyone. Instead, you wash yourself up, put alcohol on whatever part of you is busted open, and go to bed. In the morning you tell anyone who asks that you fell or got into a car accident.

For the next two years you try to figure out what happened, why it happened. You keep looking over your shoulder or rearview mirror to see if anyone is following you. You think: If I were straight, this wouldn't have happened. If I were a little scarier to them—if they thought I carried a gun, if they thought I were stronger, if they stopped seeing gay men or Asian men as wimpy or effeminate or weak—maybe they would have let me alone.

OPEN THE GODDAMNED DOOR!!! This guy was nice enough to buy me a drink, a couple drinks, actually. I'm sitting minding my own business. I'm thinking about how I got to get myself to the gym and workout. I have a forty-four-inch chest. I want to keep it that way. Plus, I'm training for a triathalon next month. I injured myself running. So I turn around to stretch my leg like this. Then I see him. Him. My worst nightmare. This Asian guy—Coke-bottle glasses, slouched over like he's afraid to be here. He is giving me this look, like he likes me or something.

I see this wimpy, effeminate, weak Asian guy in the periphery of my vision. He comes toward me. He says, "Hi." I say, "How zit going?" He sits right down next to me. He tells me his name is George. We get into this conversation. We're talking about weird shit, something about Laverne and Shirley. I wanna leave, but George keeps talking; I can't get a word in edgewise. George keeps yapping and yapping. How many Laverne and Shirley episodes can a guy talk about? George is really pissing me off. I think to myself: This guy's fucking clueless. He is the kind of guy who makes us look bad. The sight of him makes me sick. I think that it's guys like George that allows people to think that it's OK to bash the living daylights out of us on our way home. I get so mad, I say the one thing that I know would hurt him—hurt any Asian man: I only date white guys.

I feel victorious. Take that you faggot chink. Score one for the butch guy. And just before you walk away, you see the disappointed look on his face. Your feelings of victory go away. So you turn around and say: "Hey, you're kinda cute in a Clark Kent sort of way." In the back of your mind, you want guys like these to fall off the earth and die. "Catcha Later."

OPEN THE GODDAMNED DOOR!!!

*This is an excerpt from a larger work originally published in *Take Out: Queer Writing from Asian Pacific America*, ed. Quang Bao and Hanya Yanagihara (New York: The Asian American Writers' Workshop, 2000).

2

Pornography and Its Dis/Contents

A Roundtable Discussion with Anjali Arondekar, Richard Fung, and Sylvia Chong

Transcribed by Stacy Lavin

The following is an edited transcription of a conversation among three scholars, whose work deals with pornography, held at the Association for Asian American Studies annual meeting in April of 2005. Because it is a conversation (and one that has been edited for space), the point of the following pages is not to provide the student with fully elaborated arguments, but instead to offer provocative suggestions about pornography that will facilitate further discussion of the topic.

PARTICIPANTS

Anjali Arondekar (AA) is associate professor of feminist studies at the University of California–Santa Cruz. Her research engages with the poetics and politics of sexuality, colonialism, and historiography in South Asia. Her comments are excerpted from her book *For the Record: On Sexuality and the Colonial Archive* (2009).

Sylvia Chong (SC), assistant professor of American studies and English at the University of Virginia, works on film and the "Oriental Obscene" in the Vietnam era.

Richard Fung (RF), associate professor at Ontario College of Art and Design, is a filmmaker and writer, who has written seminal articles on pornography in relation to Asian/American representation.

Other participants indicated: SM = Sean Metzger (moderator); AUD = Audience member

Anjali Arondekar: I work primarily on questions of empire and sexuality in the nineteenth century. I'm currently writing a history of homosexuality in colonial India. And I work mainly on law, pornography, and anthropology. I want to discuss the identificatory relationship with past histories to present formulations of how we think, theorize, and script pornography.

We look to the past, as Carolyn Dinshaw has so eloquently argued, to find, touch, imagine, and materialize subjects of our own historical desire. Pornography requires—if you follow a vulgar formulation here—a savage-to-salvage approach, whereby pathologized, oversexualized, racial subjects are reimagined and rescripted in a cultural narrative that situates them within a larger context of pleasure, colonialism, immigration struggles, and so on.

As a literary form—and pornography *is* a literary form, regardless of how resistant you may be to that idea—pornography has shifted the very terms of where we situate our sexual politics. Our reading practices, especially within Asian and Asian/American studies, are directed toward recuperating and celebrating the lost subjects of pornography: the racialized bodies of multiply-gendered, immigrant, and colonized subjects, who incarnate the limits and possibilities of hegemonic containment.

What happens if the props and architecture of pornography become equal subjects of our archival desires? How do we make sense of pornographic objects, like the India rubber dildo—which I write about—whose colonial iconography is the primary space through which Indian male sexuality in the nineteenth century can be examined? What does it mean for a history of objects to provide a genealogy for an Asian and Asian/American history of sexuality?

Sean Metzger: Sylvia has a porn-theoretical background, but she talks about violence and the way that that is related to, say, how squirts of blood are like squirts of semen.

Sylvia Chong: Yes. Ejaculating blood, ejaculating semen. But my work is somewhat tangential to the study of hardcore pornography, sexual pornography. I've been looking at porn through the legal category of obscenity, which encompasses a larger body of texts than the purely sexual. For example, my work on extreme violence looks at the prevalence and emergence of forms of extreme violence in Hollywood as well as in independent cinema, and also the application of the term "obscenity" in general to the excessive, tactile space of the body.

One of the ways I define pornography is as a visual medium that calls upon its viewers or readers to respond in embodied form. The most obvious form, especially in violence and sexual pornography, is mimetic: a sort of "do as I do" or "do as I show." But another visual genre where the pornographic comes out—I'm thinking of Sau-ling Wong's idea of "food pornography" in Asian/American literature—is the cooking show, where there's a literal address to a reader to experience a sort of embodied response to the film.

And this definition opens up a lot of different ways of investigating pornography, so not only are you investigating the formal codes or the legal and formal hysteria around that which is represented, but you're also looking at a larger issue, which is how texts access the tactile, the bodily, the embodied. In the last ten years, people have started to categorize violence as legal obscenity, and that's where they're just starting to move the regulation of video games and videos into that legal realm of foreclosure.

Another example is child pornography, where recently one of the definitions of child pornography (struck down by the courts) was that representation of "child porn" is itself an act of child exploitation, whether or not you were exploiting actual children in its production. This raised a whole set of legal and theoretical issues: What do we do with animation, or computer-generated imagery, or montage that creates the illusion of child exploitation? Rather than seeing this case as law simply misunderstanding film, we can look at how law actually informs our conception of film and is itself a form of film theory.

Richard Fung: The first work I did was in Toronto at a time of anti-porn feminism on the one hand, and on the other hand, libertarianism among white gay men who saw it as inappropriate to critique any form of gay, sexual representation. For the first time you could make this stuff, so it was taboo to critique discourses within it. Right now the Canadian government is threatening to produce a new law that will delete artistic merit as a defense in porn cases. This comes out of the case of Robin Sharpe, a pedophile who was prosecuted in Vancouver for short stories he wrote depicting intergenerational sex. He was acquitted because literary scholars testified that what he had written was in fact art, that it had artistic merit. The government was very upset.

I've been organizing with artists in relation to this law, but as I do that, I am also very aware that it sets up a kind of elitist privilege in relation to sexual representation. So work that can't be passed off as art can't use that defense.

Also, when we're talking about porn and when we're talking about Asian/Americans or Asian Diaspora, we are actually talking about a lot of different categories—different kinds of porn, different kinds of people involved in porn, different kinds of interests, and different representations of different kinds of Asian/Americans within porn and within sexual representation. I always have to keep reminding myself of that because often I, too, can use those categories in large, sweeping ways that lose track of the complexity.

There are a number of films about sex workers: *Sex: The Annabel Chong Story; Girl Next Door* is another one, a whole bunch, not just on sex workers, but also on sexual practices, circuit parties, orgies, and stuff. And they follow a very similar arc. Because what you've got is a bad-talking, out-there, sexual practitioner. And in the course of the film the narrative arc works to humiliate them, in a way, to chasten them, to put them in their place. And this is what it does with *The Annabel Chong Story*, too, in which she makes all these claims she's doing this out of sexual pleasure, as a kind of feminist practice. She loves, you know, cock up her ass, and all this kind of stuff. And by the end of the film she comes off as pathetic.

The climax or turning point is where you see her slashing her hands; she revisits the site of her rape in London. And so her promiscuity is seen as pathological and caused by this. I see this arc in many of these films. And there's a way in which there's a mutually dependent, titillation/moralism factor that operates there. I think one of the things that's interesting about that film is that, at the heart of it, there is a sense, in general, that sex is degrading. That idea underlies a lot of the critique of porn, in fact.

Anal gay sex, specifically, was a factor in convincing judges in Canada to adopt what came to be known as the "Butler decision," whereby Canadian obscenity laws incorporated the notion that pornography can cause "harm" to society in general, and women in particular. So sexual representation would be OK, but not any depictions of sex that was "degrading or dehumanizing." The judges were having a hard time understanding how porn was harmful, and then the legal team of the Women's Legal Education and Action Fund (LEAF) working with Catharine MacKinnon apparently showed these heterosexual judges gay porn and asked them to imagine themselves as a participant in this, and it freaked them out, and that pushed them over the edge. This was triumphantly claimed, actually, by the people who pushed for this. So there's a way in which that kind of simmering and not always present or explicit sense of sex comes to the fore sometimes.

And the Abu Ghraib photographs illustrate this anxiety, the implication that sex, specifically gay sex, is degrading. And in *The Annabel Chong Story* there's a scene from one of her earlier films where she's acting out a screen test scenario. She's asked various questions, among them where is she from. She says that she's from London. The person says, "Oh you're from London town," and then, "And what's your nationality? Where are you *really* from?" And so Chong says she has Singapore citizenship. And that's the end. So there's a way in which that, even when it's not present, that the desire to place the Oriental, I think, haunts a lot of sexual representation.

And in former research around pornography—my sense it that some of the racial categorizations have become more calcified. Asian representation has become more of a kind of single fetish. So if you, say, look at Internet porn there are, in a gay context, bondage sites, fetish sites, foreskin sites, watersport sites, and Asian sites. So, that Asian, as a specialized category of desire, has become even more segregated. And I think porn and the representations in porn may be slightly anachronistic to what's actually happening on the ground, certainly among young gay men.

SM: It's interesting and useful to think about how much the colonial project depended and hinged on ideas of—or trajectories—of sexual desire. Also, popular culture always has to do with race and sexuality. What if we start to look at other kinds of cultural products as forms of pornography, not just as representational but also epistemological, the way we think about the emergence of that category applied as an analytic to different cultural products.

AA: There's a legacy of privileging indeterminacy that has come along with making pornography more capacious. Such indeterminacy emerges in the vagaries of the legal process, in the kinds of videos we can now purchase, or even the very contents of the archive. On the other hand, we're also committed to understanding the very determining structure of epistemic violence that undergirds pornography as a genre of representation—representation that includes pleasure and whatever the opposite of pleasure may be! When the space of empire is the very space of the pornographic, how do you produce bodies, or subjects, that exceed such a structure of representation? This is why I turn to these objects, like the India rubber dildo, which is the only place where you see native sexuality in colonial pornography, in a supplementary form. There are no Indian men; there are no Indian women, [but] there are dildos that perform a relationship that is about moving India rubber to India and the economic exploitation of that, being a way in which you have sexuality being coded in.

So I was curious about an object, which forces me to re-imagine how I do a history of sexuality within the period, which goes back to the production of dildos. In the nineteenth century in economic journals, you find references to "questionable goods" that are made out of India rubber, and, as it turns out, they are dildos. So there is a continuity here obviously; in the United States, dildos are sold routinely. We know that the plastic and all the materials that go into making sex toys don't happen here.

SC: Pornography is always cast, defended, or salvaged by the category of the artistic or aesthetic, because it is defined as that which lacks aesthetic value. But what do you do, then, with non-artistic expressions of sexuality? And in a way, it's as if any artistic expression of pornography, in some definitions, makes it not porn anymore. *Legally,* that may be a valid distinction—I support the right of artists to use the category of the aesthetic as a way of defending themselves from the law, but it does cast this dichotomy between artists who produce work that is sexualized and the pure sexual commodity. And it really destroys that middle place where many people are actually working to produce sexual texts.

And here's why it's interesting to recover that space where porn does intersect with violence. I'm starting a research project on the Abu Ghraib photographs and the execution videos from Iraq. And in Susan Sontag's article on Abu Ghraib, she labels those photographs as pornography as a shorthand critique, and instantly the sexualized aspect of those photographs becomes what is most horrifying about their existence. And then you stop any further analysis because the condemnation is so obvious.

On the one hand, you want to critique Sontag for her obvious collapse between sadomasochistic practices in real life and whatever's going on in Abu Ghraib, which condemns all SM as unethical. But on the other hand, you do want to acknowledge that perhaps the celebration of a "porn-utopia" and the absolute fluidity of identifications does really reach an impasse with the *racialized* body and the violence committed on that racialized body. Judith Butler raised a similar issue in her discussion about the fluidity of identification in Robert Mapplethorpe's photography. So in Abu Ghraib that fluidity has its limit case in question of "whose body is being violated?" So it's not the porn-utopia of "we're just all having an orgy and you can be on top sometimes and you can be on bottom at other times and it's all good." There is a clear "top" and "bottom" in the Abu Ghraib photographs. And this represents one of the problems porn studies has to deal with: finding a way through the impasse between sex negativity and sex positivity, to be able to discuss both in a critical stance.

RF: And it's not that one exonerates the other or condemns the other, but it's the existence of these different kinds of relations, different kinds of pornographies, and power relations within pornography existing simultaneously. It reminds me of the discussion around prostitution. Those people who say prostitution is exercising my right, it's liberated me, and then people like Sherene Razack, who do work about refugee women who are sold into prostitution, and then other people who come back and talk about the circulation of women, and the anxieties around women moving through space on their own. So different kinds of relations are happening at the same time.

AUD1: Whatever you link porn to—as literature and/or artistry, etc.—is there a point at which you make some kind of a judgment—can it do damage? I can't quite understand, since even if you pluralize it with all these different domains of people producing it and receiving it, unless you do a *porntopia* thing where sort of anything goes, I don't see how you would adjudicate damage. I mean that's moralistic. But I don't see how you would not—unless you're saying it's all literature.

AA: The political imperative is for some of us who do non-contemporary work, if you look at these spaces, they provide you with a genealogy. Right? So, the challenge is, what is this genealogy for? Is it to produce an already known script for the racialized pathologizations you see? Or is it about telling you something that you don't already know? Therein lies the rub. So I'm sort of not so much interested in whether it's *good* or *bad*, but more about what labor is lost in only foregrounding certain kinds of pathologization.

For example, some of the colonial pornography I look at is housed in the British Library in a rare-book collection curiously called "The Private Case." Any and all access to the books is carefully monitored, and reading has to be done under the careful gaze of the reference librarian. I am told that such precautions are warranted because the library has allegedly had problems with emissions!!

Now what's equally interesting about these books is not just their narrative content, but also their very materiality. Some of the pornographic texts I've looked at have soft velvet spines, and their pages are made out of delicate Japanese paper. Thus, the actual pornographic artifact is a perfect exemplar of colonial modernity. So, when you think about pornography, the kind of boundaries between what is being judged—the actual effect of touching the book is part of the pornographic experience.

SM: Pornography has a currency in the world. And it allows you to think about the body and its relationship to those kinds of discourses. And that becomes a medium, in some ways, of how you track the nexus of power relationships, through sex and money, right? And, although, it's interesting to think about what happens when the body falls out of that—you know, like, the question of "Can you have porn without bodies?" And, you can, of course. But then the question is: Okay, what does that mean? What do you do with that? Once you take the bodies out, what are you learning?

AA: Henry Giroux has an article called "Education after Abu Ghraib," which I find incredibly troubling, but he has a section where he says some of the army officials who reviewed the photographs said *the reason these soldiers indulged in this behavior is because they had been watching gay pornography.* The assertion here is that gay popular culture is somehow responsible for such deviant forms of conduct at Abu Ghraib. Even as such formulations of causality are completely arbitrary and not necessarily comprehensible, it's important that we don't substitute one form of problematic causality with another more progressive one. What is at stake here for us is that we keep our efforts at legal reform alive without surrendering to an easy language of causality. But then how do we have legal reform that doesn't rely on narratives of assimilable coherency? This is the crisis of law's relationship to sexuality.

SC: Often embedded in the legal language either defending or denigrating porn are large unexamined assumptions regarding sexual and racial minorities, and also regarding how film reception works. If you're going to legislate about something based a very unexamined or very reductive theory of how the body interacts with the text—*if there's gay porn out there that shows bodies in a stack, therefore we get prison abuse*—this has troubling implications for case law and for establishing legal precedents.

It's interesting that you're speaking about these dildos as being, taking the place of these bodies. There are legal arguments for treating pornographic texts as if they were material objects, like dildos—as tools used in actions, rather than as speech acts.

AA: In India, Section 377 is the anti-sodomy statute—usually it's limited to men having sex with men—so in the only case where two women are being sued for 377, the father who's bringing the case says they're using objects which replicate dildos or which replicate the penis; ergo, legally an object is being introduced that makes legal transaction of MSM possible, through an insertion of objects.

In other words, there are all kinds of ways in which a dildo is represented as simply doing the work of a substitute, which is not quite what it is in the texts I examine. In these pornographic texts, the dildo is not a substitute for anything; the dildo becomes what the women desire. They don't want men anymore; they want dildos. So the story is very funny. It's not just that Indian men are erased and supplemented by the presence of these India rubber dildos. Rather, there is a more ironic chain of supplements at work here—the ironic presence of a dildo that stands in for something that was never there to begin with. After all, we know that India rubber was often used to create prosthetic limbs for English men wounded during the Crimean War. So the rubber used to create prosthetic limbs is in the same India rubber used to manufacture dildos.

The most famous book is called *Venus and India*, and another one is called *The Story of an India Rubber Dildo*, which is actually part of a manual given to administrative officers who went to India. The manual is especially interesting because it speaks to the long history of the dildo, and explains how dildos used to be made of wood, metal (all excruciatingly painful descriptions). Given such a history, the arrival of the India rubber dildo seems very timely! And the idea is that we'll use these dildos of India rubber because they provide a smooth efficient motion. And so that's when you have all of these prosthetic limbs also being invented. There's a very close emphasis on the material.

SM: One of the questions that we had was about circulation and currency because all three of you have worked in different economic and cultural environments, in terms of the media you're working with and what constitutes pornography. What changes happen when your object constituting pornography moves from one locale to another?

AA: My book is really about the history of the archive and sexuality in India. I began this project when a friend of my father had passed away. He was a well-known scholar and his wife kindly extended me access to all the contents of his well-stocked library. I was in the first year of graduate school then—and generally interested in all things colonial—and so was surprised to find a dusty first edition of *Venus in India* among his collections. After reading it, I went to the state archives in Bombay in search of answers and histories of publication and circulation. The head archivist laughed when I asked him whether he had heard of the book, and laconically said: "Well, of course. It circulated more than the Bible in colonial times."

So I spent a lot of time tracking customs records, copyright records, trying to find out how these books move. Even as these books were explicitly written by Oriental bibliophiles, their consumption, circulation, and content exceeded the policing of race and empire. After all, the books depicted the sexual escapades of white men and women, sexual activities that were then read and consumed by brown men and brown women who gained access to these books in complex and untraceable ways. It becomes almost impossible to track the circulation records because there were no established copyright laws or publishers. So this circulation is really a cultural argument. The circulation of the colony to the metropole is very complicated because you find translations of *Venus in India* that are not attributed to any original. And also a lot of the pornographic texts in the nineteenth century were written by anthropologists. So Edward Sellon wrote a book called [*The*] *Ups and Downs of Life*, and he was an anthropologist who translated.

Pornography for earlier periods is interesting because it's also about making an intervention in what constitutes the colonial archive. To say that pornography is as important as Kipling is an important argument to make because it's about not just the importance of sexuality, but the importance of certain genres of texts. England was the largest importer and exporter of pornography in the nineteenth century, which changes the ways in which we look at the empire as well.

SC: I started out studying sexual pornography with Linda Williams, and then I got interested in the idea that violence can also be pornography, and I fixated on that construction because it didn't make sense to me as easily as it did to other people. Why is violence obscene? In my study on the Vietnam War, I deal with two sets of visual archives: One is the set of images that come to America about Vietnam through the news, and the other set are these movies that aren't about Vietnam, but are circulating from Japan and Hong Kong into America at the same time as the war. And the two sets of archives pose two different, interesting problems. One of the things I am trying to do with this book project— "The Oriental Obscene"—is to look at what violence does to actually orientalize a body—how race becomes legible through the body becoming a site of violence, either the perpetuator or the receiver, the recipient of violence. And with the Vietnam War, where you have an overwhelming number of real versus fictionalized images of violence, it is interesting to me that most of the images that are of actual violence feature Vietnamese bodies. All the famous images of death and violence, such as Ron Haeberle's photographs of the My Lai massacre, or Eddie Adams's photograph of the Saigon Execution, don't involve Americans in the image. When we think of the Vietnam War as a particularly violent period, we're not imagining about American soldiers, we're imagining Vietnamese civilians and soldiers killing or being killed. Like the circulation of pornography, these images are providing scripts for how to understand violence—thus, you have American films scripting the suffering of the American body based on how you've seen Vietnamese bodies suffer. And, as I argue in my article on *The Deer Hunter*, I think that ends up orientalizing the American body, such that in fictional Vietnam War films, we see all these American bodies imagining themselves being orientalized by their presence in Vietnam. And that's one form of circulation, of "actual" images of the East traveling into American culture and entering into a form of transit with other American cultural texts.

With the Hong Kong martial arts film, there's more of a vexed relationship between the history and the text—why did America find this set of films and started importing it right around 1973? We get this eroticized, Asian male body appearing in American cinema suddenly, and for the first time really eroticizing the *male* body of any race. 1973 marks an era where you start to see a lot of male torsos—Bruce Lee's torso first and foremost, nearly naked. You also see a lot of bodily performance, which I think somewhat parallels what's happening in hardcore pornography at the time. There are a lot of very acrobatic, "did-they-really-do-that?"/"let's-see-that-again!" types of performances in film. And that indirectly orientalizes the body, but from a different perspective, because soon afterwards, Chuck Norris and Steven Seagal and Sylvester Stallone start taking over that style of bodily performance and use it to animate their narratives of returning to Vietnam or being traumatized by Asians. So it's a different kind of circulation, where the texts are from another national cinema. But when they get brought over to America and become part of the American imaginary—if you think of them as American texts—they occupy a different position than when they stay inside those national boundaries. Suddenly, it's not an Asian diasporic audience watching Bruce Lee, but an American audience— a multiethnic American audience—watching Bruce Lee, and an American industry using the figure of Bruce Lee to signify different kinds of traumas, also Vietnam-related and otherwise.

AUD1: A lot of people I've come into contact with see certain Korean movies and say this is offensive, this is abusive to women—there's like beating scenes, abusive scenes, and then sex. And it's a judgment: That's saying it's bad, it's not good. Paul Willemen studied pornography made in Korea and said you just gotta change your discursive register, come up with a whole discursive regime of seeing that's very different. But, at the same time this thing comes out, there's a law in the government outlawing prostitution, so suddenly thousands of workers are displaced from their jobs with almost no support as I could understand from the pro-sex-worker side of the street. Whereas in Taiwan or Hong Kong there was a lot of support. So, at the same time that you have a huge proliferation of porn on the web and cable TV that's opening up, then you got the government crashing down on it.

SC: What bothers me sometimes about the work being done on Asian cinema in America is the discourse on cultural authenticity that's part of the fan discourse and of the scholarly discourse as well—that differences in forms of representation simply arise from cultural differences. This assumes that there is an authentic frame of interpretation for each national cinema, and we just have to find that authentic frame and then everything falls into place. This authenticity is fetishized by the fans as well. For instance, if you don't understand Hong Kong kung fu or Japanese pornography, if it seems wrong or dirty or low budget to you, you can simply change your frame of reference, and suddenly the films make sense. And I'm not sure that's a valuable direction to go, although the assumption of authenticity is a fascinating phenomenon to study. I think it's more interesting to think about what investments a non-Asian fan— a white American fan, a Western fan—has in a cultural object like Japanese porn, which even more than Korean porn has been fetishized in the marketplace, or Hong Kong martial arts. What investments do such fans have in maintaining the purity of racial other by positing a frame of reference that has no overlap with Western culture? Why are they interested in the purity of that racial or cultural difference, "the Japanese are just different, so . . ."?

RF: But it is like that "What is your nationality?" question in *The Annabel Chong Story*. There is a way that I thought what you were saying earlier about when something travels it actually becomes another object or a way. So that, for example, if it's Korean porn or a Hong Kong film, and it comes to the United States or Canada, it actually becomes in a sense another film. But also, it brings along traces—as you're saying in terms of fan discourse—of this extra knowledge too that people bring with it. That is the kind of expertise that people develop around what it really means and how it situates itself in its own context. I think that that's also kind of interesting, a sort of miscegenation of cultures and ideas that happen along the way. They both represent but also both spark, right. That happens with all cultural objects, I think.

SM: With pornography you get quite a lot of consumption across the board, where people assume that they know the codes already, because they're looking at the naked bodies. Then people are like, "Oh, I can consume this because I have the mastery of the codes that I need to access this text in some way."

RF: I think it goes two ways. I went to India in 1977 for the first time and took photographs of women construction workers in New Delhi. And I remember showing it to Canadians who said "Wow, women are working! They're doing manual labor." And they saw it actually in the framework of non-traditional workplace practices—women trying to become carpenters, for example. And they completely misread the code. So there's a way in which you can also have the assertion of cultural competence as well as these misreadings, and it's often quite mixed up.

When I was doing my earlier work I wanted to find Asian American–produced porn, or images of Asians in America as opposed to same-sex porn produced in, say, Thailand, to find something that was located here that was true to here, as opposed to something imported that was seen as less authentic in terms of what it said about sexual relations among performers.

AUD3: As writers in the discourse of pornography, how are you *pornofied* yourselves? How has that shifted as you move on? I'm interested in how you're condemned by your work, or . . . the cultural attachments to you doing what you do.

AUD1: You're turned into like a pornographer or a porn—something like that?

AUD3: Yeah.

SC: I am conscious of the fact that I am working on highly racialized, sexualized topics as I myself am a racialized, sexualized person in a very white university. I did my graduate work at UC Berkeley and then I went to University of Virginia, and these are two very different institutions. And so I do find myself at the nexus of a lot of [overdeterminations] that are beyond my control. And, I think, that's maybe where the pedagogy starts to overlap with the scholarship. Because I do try to—I don't teach classes on porn *proper*, but I teach classes in censorship and about violence, and the violence classes invariably have a limit text, like Pasolini's *Salo* or Oshima's *In the Realm of the Senses*. So you do find yourself both educating a mainstream that just needs to hear some of these things said in the first place and also a feminized activist or APA student activist space that has maybe been encouraged to go along with these very sex-negative, Catharine MacKinnon/Andrea Dworkin types of arguments, where the only way to speak about sexuality is as that thing which subjugates you. And there's no space right now for the reclamation of that. And I definitely feel that pressure as an APA scholar trying to give student activism a different kind of language to deal with racialized sexual harassment, and a way of talking about sexual abuse that isn't just anti-sex.

AA: One of the things I would say is the colonial pornography that I work on is actually very good. So this is an interesting question about affect and reading practices too. My interest in writing about this stuff is to thread that discourse of pleasure into how I'm working this out. That's definitely not something that I want to confess to as in "oh it's too bad it's good." What I'd like to do instead is understand what we designate as "good" pornography and trace its linkages to other kinds of colonial production. For example, there are a bunch of scholars in Philippine studies who have made the obvious but subtle point that it's important to understand why certain kinds of texts are written in certain ways and forms during moments of repression. Ergo, if colonial pornography sustains a resolutely pleasurable aura, it's important for us to consider why that is the case rather than simply writing it off as Orientalist fantasy. So I think the awkward but productive place of pleasure in this reading and writing and finding a way to pedagogically install these texts as part of the canon is attached to allowing students and allowing yourself to think about the narrative of pleasure in a way that allows for these incommensurate possibilities as something that you have to be happy with.

RF: My interest in dealing with pornography, gay Asian representation, and racialized scenarios came out of activism. It was not an academic project, originally. It came out of being part of a movement and having discussions with people about how they felt in bars, how they felt in the sexual marketplace, if I can use that term, and feeling a kind of exclusion. So my first work was actually in the early 1980s around the exclusions of Asian bodies in gay male pornography. And then, as I did that, I began to think about the terms of inclusion. And that's how I came to doing that work around "Looking for My Penis." From there it was driven by this idea of what is the relationship of representation and the realities that we lived? My interest in pornography has waned at that level, because I've seen that not much has shifted within pornographic representations, unfortunately. So change what you can change, and have the wisdom to know what you can't change. I'm waiting for something else to happen before I revisit it again. So there's a demand for increase in scholarship, and I'm interested in the different directions people are going. But I don't have that much more to add, though I have students working on pornography and sexual representation, and that's interesting—to engage with them on their work, which is coming from all different angles.

AUD4: A number of you have touched on this point about moralizing about pornography and always looking at it as bad or trying to see what part is good and what part is bad, what's art and what's not art. But is there anything in the literature coming out now that focuses on Asian/Americans producing whatever form of pornography that represents our own bodies, and is it a reproduction of the power dynamic of evil, dominant other vs. a subordinate Asian body? Or, even, for example, in your case, when you're doing archival research, did you find any kind of parallel in pornography made by Asian Indians about their own bodies?

AA: I wasn't really looking for that. The intriguing fact about pornography is that it's always anonymous, at least in the colonial context. . . . There is actually a canon in regional languages, which I look at, where there is pornography written in different Indian languages as well.

RF: I live in a city, which is incredibly cosmopolitan, very multicultural, with all kinds of relationships going here, there, and everywhere, and then you look at the porn that's available, and, as I say, if you're looking for Asians—if you're looking for any kind of miscegenation in porn—it's a kind of specialty item. So there's a way in which porn hasn't moved to reflect the way that people actually live. And of course there's a dialectical relationship between those two things. So what does that mean and what does it take to make the porn shift? And what is at stake in making the porn shift? I mean, do I *care* if the porn shifts? That's a question that I ask myself.

SC: I think I'll be curious to see—if Darrell [Hamamoto] produces more porn—that when there is a body of Asian/American porn that goes out there, what other themes emerge, because I feel like the first film [*Skin on Skin*] is simply too overdetermined by all the expectations placed upon it. And it has this troubling tension for me between the pro-ness of the female performer and the amateur-ness of the male performer, and I wonder if that will start to have interesting iterations in the future.

AUD5 (Darrell Hamamoto): Apparently there's a pretty big market for it because there have been any number of entrepreneurs who've approached me and want to make it a commercial enterprise. The market is Asian/American and Asian/American transnationalist. Overseas, thirties, forties, fifties people who live in the San Diego valley, Korea-town, Little Saigon, places like that. So there's different segments we're talking about. We're not talking about academic Asian/Americans, we're talking about community—North American Asian/Americans.

RF: The reason that I said that was because when I did that study, there were all of us demanding—a lot of people—demanding, particularly when AIDS was happening, that we have different kinds of representations in porn. And what I found was that when those representations were there the people who were interested in them weren't the people who demanded that they be reflected in the porn. And they weren't that interested in using it. So it may work differently in the heterosexual context, too.

REFERENCES CITED

Arondekar, Anjali. *For the Record: On Sexuality and the Colonial Archive*. Durham, N.C.: Duke University Press, 2009.

Butler, Judith. "The Force of Fantasy: Feminism, Mapplethorpe, and Discursive Excess." *differences: A Journal of Feminist Cultural Studies* 2 (2) (Summer 1990): 105–25.

Chong, Sylvia. "Restaging the Vietnam War: The Deer Hunter and the Primal Scene of Violence." *Cinema Journal* 44 (2) (Winter 2005): 89–106.

Dinshaw, Carolyn. *Getting Medieval: Sexualities and Communities, Pre- and Postmodern*. Durham, N.C.: Duke University Press, 1998.

Fung, Richard. "Looking for My Penis: The Eroticized Asian in Gay Video Porn." In *How Do I Look? Queer Film and Video*, ed. Bad Object-Choices. Seattle: Bay Press, 1991, 145–68.

Giroux, Henry. "Education After Abu Ghraib." *Cultural Studies* 18 (6) (November 2006): 779–15.

Hamamoto, Darrell Y. "The Joy Fuck Club: Prolegomenon to an Asian American Porno Practice." In *Countervisions: Asian American Film Criticism*, eds. Darrell Y. Hamamoto and Sandra Liu. Philadelphia: Temple University Press, 2000, 59–89.

MacKinnon, Catharine, and Andrea Dworkin, eds. *In Harm's Way: The Pornography Civil Rights Hearings*. Cambridge, Mass.: Harvard University Press, 1997.

Sontag, Susan. "Regarding the Torture of Others." *New York Times Magazine*. May 23, 2004: 25–29.

Wong, Sau-Ling. *Reading Asian American Literature: From Necessity to Extravagance*. Princeton, N.J.: Princeton University Press, 1993.

3

The One that She Wants

Margaret Cho, Mediatization, and Autobiographical Performance

Dan Bacalzo

"They'd never seen a Korean American role model like me before," says Margaret Cho. "I didn't play violin. I didn't fuck Woody Allen."[1] Bold, irreverent, and vocal, Cho has found out the hard way that conforming to other peoples' expectations can be damaging to one's own feelings of self-worth. In this chapter, I examine Margaret Cho's first full-length performance piece, *I'm the One That I Want*, analyzing the self-reflexivity inherent in autobiographical performance and the ways it may counter mediatized representation.[2] Issues of sexuality, race, and body image are addressed through discourses involving identity formation and theatrical presence.

With images of herself broadcast on TV, plastered on magazine covers, and denigrated in the tabloids, Margaret Cho's production of self through her first solo show can be seen as a battle to control her own representation. She employs her onstage presence to stake out claims to identity on her own terms, rather than those that may be expected of her. I use the term "identity" here to refer to a discursive formation, whose definition depends on how it is deployed. Early in her solo show, Cho tells a number of jokes centering around the gay community. "I love the word faggot, because it describes my kind of guy," she states. "I am a fag hag. Fag hags are the backbone of the gay community."[3] Through this declaration, Cho identifies with a marginalized community that is, significantly, *not* the Asian/American community. While the majority of *I'm the One That I Want* addresses her status as an Asian/American artist, it is to the gay community that she initially pledges an allegiance within her performance. Cho has a large gay fan base and was awarded a GLAAD (Gay and Lesbian Alliance Against Defamation) media award in 2000 for "making a significant difference in promoting equal rights for all, regardless of sexual orientation or gender identity."[4] Her

43

commitment to gay and lesbian issues extends to a discussion of her own same-sex experiences. Describing a time she had sex with a woman, she states: "I went through this whole thing. Am I gay? Am I straight? And I realized I'm just slutty. Where's my parade?"[5] While it's clear from the rest of *I'm the One That I Want* that Cho usually dates men, this early acknowledgement of an alternative to heterosexuality is important in the way Cho fashions her image. She is not the model Korean/American that many in the Asian/American community might wish her to be; instead, she is a queer, outspoken individual who refuses to be silenced.

Cho's choice to utilize autobiography in her work creates an immediacy that is grounded in the personal experiences of the live body the audience sees on stage. It presents the illusion of authenticity by producing a certain kind of truth. This truth is relational, dependent upon the trustworthiness of the autobiographical narrator. In Foucauldian terms, it is a "truth game" defined as "a set of rules by which truth is produced. It is not a game in the sense of amusement."[6] It is important to remember that in any discussion of Foucauldian truth games, there is a kind of multiplicity at play. Truth is not a fixed point; it is what is accepted to be true, what functions as the truth. By taking control of the production of truth through autobiographical performance, Cho positions herself as being able to intervene in existing discourses around representation.

The primary arc of *I'm the One That I Want* covers the period immediately before, during, and immediately after her experiences as the star of the short-lived ABC sitcom *All-American Girl* (1994–1995). The TV program promoted itself as being the first situation comedy to center on an Asian/American family. Although that is technically incorrect—that distinction belongs to the even more short-lived television program *Mr. T. and Tina*[7]—*All-American Girl* remains a watershed moment in the representation of Asian/Americans on television. Cho is highly conscious of this, and *I'm the One That I Want* makes clear both the joy of finally showcasing Asian/American talent in such a high-profile manner, as well as the burden of representation that was unfairly placed upon the show.

In her solo performance piece, the Korean/American comedian delivers the behind-the-scenes story of her shot at television stardom. When she first received the news that her sitcom was going to go to series, she was ecstatic. "I felt real, I felt alive, I felt for the first time in my life I was not invisible," she says.[8] In this statement, Cho demonstrates how conceptions of the self are often tied in with approval and acceptance from others—whether it be family, friends, employers, or the general public. The formation of self-identity is further complicated in our contemporary era by the emphasis society places upon mass media representation. "When I was growing up, I never saw Asian people on television," says Cho in *I'm the One That I Want*. After a brief pause, she continues: "Oh, except for on *M*A*S*H* sometimes.

Every once in a while on *M*A*S*H* you'd see an Asian person in the background unloading a truck."[9] Cho points out how Asians were literally kept
in the background in television programs, rarely developed into supporting
characters, and almost never in lead roles. The lack of substantial parts
given to Asian/American actors is further underscored by Cho's next example, *Kung Fu*. "But that doesn't really count because David Carradine, the
star of *Kung Fu*, was not Chinese," says Cho. "So, that show should not have
been called *Kung Fu*. It should have been called, 'Hey, that guy's not Chinese.'"[10] Although Cho does not mention it in her performance, this example is particularly apt in that *Kung Fu* was originally set to star martial arts
master Bruce Lee, but studio executives were nervous about producing a
show with an Asian protagonist and cast a white actor instead. By providing this lack of televisual representation as context, Cho frames the behind-
the-scenes story of *All-American Girl* within a discourse that is inclusive of
more than just her own story. While extremely personal in nature, Cho's
narrative is also a reflection of the way the hegemonic forces of mediatized
representation force those who appear different to conform to certain standards that are seemingly preestablished.

The term "mediatization" was first coined by Jean Baudrillard, and is now
used to describe the postmodern condition in which media and information technologies saturate our everyday lives.[11] The words and images with
which we are constantly bombarded through the media become part of a
self-perpetuating system reinforcing the status quo. Mediatization often de-
termines what is desirable, particularly in relation to body image. In her
1993 book, *Unbearable Weight*, Susan Bordo argues that popular culture imagery sends the message that we can "choose" our own bodies through diet,
exercise, or cosmetic surgery. However, such choices "efface, not only the in-
equalities of privilege, money and time that prohibit most people from in-
dulging in these practices, but the desperation that characterizes the lives of
those who do."[12] Bordo's point is aptly illustrated by Cho, whose performance documents how she was required to undergo rigorous diet and exercise regimes to please the network. After Cho's initial screen test, she reports
that her producer called her up. "Listen, there's a problem," she was told.
"The network has a problem with you. They're concerned. The network is
concerned. They're concerned about the fullness of your face."[13] Despite the
harshness of the comment, Cho tells the story with humor. "I always
thought I was okay looking," she states seriously before switching to a
lighter, more jovial tone. "I had no idea I was this giant face taking over
America!" Lifting up her arm to shield her eyes, she looks up and screeches:
"Here comes the FAAAACE!"[14] By taking the comments about her weight
and blowing them up to absurd proportions, Cho acknowledges the painful
nature of the remarks while simultaneously transforming the experience
into a joke that she has control over. In this manner, her performance is

able to reclaim an identity that was lost as a result of her experiences in television.

In his 1994 book, *Presence and Resistance*, Philip Auslander attempts to reformulate the relation of presence to live and mediatized performances. He analyzes a range of avant-garde performers and argues that their deconstructive strategies put the idea of presence into question. His primary contention is that their performances are always already mediatized, and their self-awareness of this fact is what enables them to mount a critique of an increasingly commodity-driven culture from within. This accurately describes Margaret Cho, who produces representations of self that result from the internalization of her relationship to her own mediatization. However, I strongly disagree with Auslander's assertion that as a result of this mediatization, autobiographical performers enact a "refusal of presence."[15] On the contrary, performers like Cho utilize their presence to stage interventions in the way their image has been controlled and regulated.

All-American Girl, although initially based on Cho's stand-up act, was never in the artist's control. This is clear from a story Cho relates about the first episode of the series in which her character makes fun of her family in a nightclub act, but learns by the end of the episode that she should not do so. In *I'm the One That I Want*, Cho gives the voice of reason to her boyfriend at the time, filmmaker Quentin Tarantino. "What the fuck was that?" he asked her. "You fucking live to publicly embarrass your family. They took away your voice. Don't let them do that to you."[16] This loss of voice is equated with the loss of a sense of self. Tarantino does not reference Cho's actual vocal abilities; instead he speaks metaphorically, identifying Cho's writing and performance talent as something unique to her. However, that same talent— Cho's "voice"—is something that must be guarded, for it can be taken away. As Cho remarks in her show, she "didn't get it."[17] However, in the act of writing and performing *I'm the One That I Want*, it is clear that she now does. By reflecting on past events, she learns the lessons from her experiences and fashions a new narrative that critiques her prior perception.

Following the failure of *All-American Girl*, Cho sank into a life of depression, alcoholism, drugs, and anxiety. She describes her sense of self in the following terms:

> I didn't know who I was at all. I was this Frankenstein monster made up of bits and pieces of my old stand-up act mixed with focus group opinions about what Asian/Americans should be. . . . I didn't know who I was. All I knew is that I had failed. And I had failed as somebody else.[18]

This idea that Cho "failed as somebody else" indicates that her own sense of self had broken down. This disintegration of the self is a direct result of the pressures from outside forces that try to fit identity into neat categories.

Sidonie Smith and Julia Watson, in a discussion of autobiography, state: "In telling their stories, narrators take up models of identity that are culturally available."[19] In other words, they must mediate between cultural forces that provide prescribed scripts for what constitutes a given identity. The stereotypes and mediatized representations associated with these identities thus become stumbling blocks for anyone who wishes to forge an alternative sense of identity. However, culturally constructed stereotypes—for example, Asian/Americans as the model minority—can also lure individuals into a false sense of security. Cho's descent into drugs and alcohol is a cautionary tale in relation to this.

"I always thought that I would somehow be saved by this stereotyped notion of what I'm supposed to be, like, because I'm an Asian/American, I have this inherently responsible nature that would exempt me from overdosing, becoming an addict, all of that," states Cho in an interview with *Noodle Magazine*. "Stereotypes can make us feel invincible in some ways and in other ways close us off. We have opportunities closed off for us because of what we think of ourselves."[20] In this quotation, Cho acknowledges the impact of stereotypes in determining personal identity, as well as their failure to account for individual lives. She notes how stereotypes can lead to the closing off of opportunities by placing limitations on personal behavior. Her solo performances, then, work as a counter to such limitations. By describing the restrictions that these stereotypes have placed upon her—both in the eyes of the public and in her own sense of self—she shows that she can go beyond such limitations. *I'm the One That I Want* is not just Margaret Cho's professional comeback; it also represents her staking claim to her own image. The title of the show reflects this idea, declaring that she wants to claim herself for herself, and not be beholden to the forces of media and the general public who try to fit her within certain models of identity.

I'm the One That I Want demonstrates the writer/performer's ease in staking out her own territory. Without the burden of conforming to what studio execs demand of her, she forges her own image that runs counter to the mediatized representation of herself that exists in *All-American Girl*, as well as the negative media coverage that followed in the show's wake. It is worth noting, however, that Cho's performance persona in her solo work must still be seen as a representation, and not as Cho herself. Performing in front of an audience, she is aware that she needs to make jokes, that there must be punchlines to tell her story.

Comparing the stage show of *I'm the One That I Want* to her written autobiography of the same title, one is immediately struck by the difference in tone and style. The book version is not only more detailed, it tells fewer jokes. Stories that appear in the stage show are treated with greater seriousness in the book, and the written work includes details—such as an abortion—that are not included in her performance. The book is an engaging read, but it is an entirely different writing strategy from the one Cho employs in her stage work. An oft-heard criticism of autobiographical performance is that it is merely confessional, and that there is no art to the telling of your own experiences. However, this brief comparison between these two modes of storytelling that Cho employs—her book and her performance piece—demonstrates how it is not the story itself that is of utmost importance, it is *the way that story is told.*

Autobiographical performance requires more than just relating a series of facts and events. Cho utilizes a range of performance techniques such as facial expressions, vocal inflection (including the use of accents), body language, pacing, timing, and more to tell her story. In other words, she makes the most of her theatrical presence, creating a direct relationship between her live performing body and the audience that comes to watch her perform. Cho listens and responds to her audience, taking in their laughter, and oftentimes letting such reactions dictate her own pace. She possesses the ability to stretch out a joke over an extended period of time, pausing to accommodate the audience's laughter and repeating bits and phrases that she knows will garner an enthusiastic response.

One of the more popular segments of *I'm the One That I Want* details Cho's visit to the hospital after her dieting and exercise regime caused one of her kidneys to collapse. While not a comical event, Cho manages to keep the audience in stitches by describing a nurse named Gwen, whose first words to Cho are "Hi, my name is Gwen. I'm here to wash your vagina." Cho, mimicking Gwen, pronounces "wash" as "warsh," highlighting the comic effect. The line, while funny, somehow grows in hilarity through the use of repetition. At one point, Cho acting as Gwen repeats the line over and over to a series of imaginary women as if in an assembly line. When she reaches the edge of the stage, she runs back to where she began and starts over again. Her manic energy and comic exaggeration transforms her pain into humor.

Cho's material is often extremely explicit in its graphic detailing of physical traumas that Cho endured, as evident from this particular sketch. As Sarah Hepola comments in the *New York Times*, "It seems she can bear any embarrassment, any indignity, except one: being told who she is, whether by her parents, the television industry or fans."[21] Cho does not try to be a role model in the sense of being overly conscious of the way she represents her gender, sexuality, race, or ethnicity. Her routines are far from politically correct. "I make fun of everything that happens to me," says Cho in an interview with the *Houston Chronicle*. "To be able to talk about race and ethnicity freely, in order to laugh and enjoy that aspect of it, is very important. If I went there and didn't address race, that would be odd."[22] Cho acknowledges all aspects of her life, and then re-presents them in a format designed to provoke both thought and laughter. It would be a mistake to consider autobiographical performance as merely documenting one's life; it is about transforming the memories and experiences of the writer/performer into stories that enact self and produce the truth (in a Foucauldian sense) about one's experiences without necessarily sticking to completely factual detail.

Cho's success has also given her a greater amount of flexibility in managing her career. She no longer needs to worry about changing her image or censoring herself for fear of offending TV execs or potential producers. "I have my own company," she states baldly in an interview with the *Atlantic Journal-Constitution*. "I have the freedom to say what I want."[23] In her autobiographical performance, she does just that. She is candid about her sexuality, the issues she's had with her weight, the ways in which her body is racialized, the perils of mass media coverage, and much more. Utilizing her wit, honesty, and presence as a performer, Cho engages in a "truth game" that does not limit the identity to which she lays claim. Instead, it opens up possibilities without ignoring the cultural forces that have shaped her sense of self.

NOTES

1. Margaret Cho, *I'm the One That I Want*, DVD release, Cho Taussig Productions, 2000.

2. For a different take on Cho's *I'm the One That I Want*, see also Rachel C. Lee's essay, "Where's My Parade: Margaret Cho and the Asian American Body in Space," *The Drama Review* 48 (2) (Summer 2004). Lee argues that Cho troubles the idea of distinct borders with the performer's own body signifying excess.

3. Cho, 2000.

4. See the GLAAD website (www.glaad.org).

5. Cho, 2000.

6. Michel Foucault, "The Ethics of the Concern For Self as a Practice of Freedom," in *Foucault Live: Collected Interviews, 1961–1984*, ed. Sylvère Lotringer (New York: Semiotext(e), 1996), 445.

7. This 1976 show starred Pat Morita as a Japanese inventor from Tokyo who relocates to Chicago, along with his family. It lasted only five episodes before being cancelled.

8. Cho, 2000.

9. Cho, 2000.

10. Cho, 2000.

11. Philip Auslander, *Presence and Resistance* (Ann Arbor: University of Michigan Press, 1994).

12. Susan Bordo, *Unbearable Weight: Feminism, Western Culture, and the Body* (Berkeley: University of California Press, 1993), 247–48.

13. Cho, 2000. The television series *M*A*S*H* ran eleven seasons from 1972–1983.

14. Cho, 2000.

15. In his analysis of the now-deceased autobiographical performer Spalding Gray, Auslander suggests that Gray enacts a "refusal of presence" by positing that the writer/performer is "always already mediatized" (Auslander 1994, 81). As evidence, Auslander cites the multiple formats that Gray's autobiographical narratives have appeared, including film, video, humor publications, and, of course, performance art. He also suggests that the style of Gray's performance mimics that of the television serial with Gray as central personality and that his presence "is on the verge of being subsumed within a cultural flow that renders the distinction between live and mediated performance virtually irrelevant." However, I would argue that Gray's live performance style does not eschew presence, but rather depends upon it. Auslander makes too much of the film and video adaptations of Gray's work, which are, of course, mediated. Yet in live performance the relationship between actor and audience is of quite a different nature. For example, in a 2001 remounting of *Swimming to Cambodia* that I attended, I was struck by the vulnerability that Gray's live performance allowed and which was not as evident in the video version of the same piece. Gray's presence as a performer was immediate and visceral, and there seemed no attempts to resist this direct relationship between author and audience.

16. Cho, 2000.

17. Cho, 2000.

18. Cho, 2000.

19. Sidonie Smith and Julia Watson, "Introduction," in *Getting a Life: Everyday Uses of Autobiography*, ed. Sidonie Smith and Julia Watson (Minneapolis: University of Minnesota Press, 1996), 9.

20. Quoted in Max Lau and Priscilla Otani, "Cho Fun, Our Favorite Noodle," *Noodle Magazine*, June 2002.

21. Sarah Hepola, "Margaret Cho Has Something on Her Mind: Herself," *New York Times*, 28 September 2003, 2 (4).

22. Quoted in Mike McDaniel, "Margaret Cho: Notorious and Loving It," *Houston Chronicle*, 9 January 2002.

23. Quoted in Rodney Ho, "Onstage: Free Style; From Sex to Politics, Raunchy Rebel Reigns," *The Atlanta Journal-Constitution*, 29 May 2003.

4

Novell-aah!

A Short Play

Eugenie Chan

CHARACTERS

MARLENE, Chinese, old
IZZY, Chinese, young
OLGA, the maid
EL LOCUTOR (voiceover), suave, male radio announcer

(House lights down. Stage black. The gushy music of a Spanish soap opera swells. El Locutor, a suave male radio announcer, in voiceover, introduces this evening's drama and players.)

> El Locutor (v.o.): Entre un mundo divinísimo, un mundo suave, delicado, y tremulante como la rosa. Una tierra en donde los hombres son caballeros y las mujeres—diosas. Un universo apasionado en donde sus deseos pueden ser realidad. Venga, esta noche, al mundo de NOVELAAAAAA. Aquí, con *name of actress playing Olga* haciendo el papel de *Olga, la criada. Name of actress playing Izzy* como *Isabela, la Chinita.* Y *name of actress playing Marlene* como *Marlene, la Mama China.* ** (See last page for translation.)

(Lights up on: A pink boudoir. With the satin and gloss of the 1940s. Potted palms waft. An elegant couple makes whoopee on the chaise. Izzy, young and dashing in a tuxedo, reclines succumbing to the pleasures of Marlene, an aging grand dame in peignoir and 'do. Izzy and Marlene are Chinese. Izzy's hair is slicked, Casanova-style. Marlene's is blonde. Izzy is played by an actress. Marlene covers Izzy with a light trail of kisses up the arm.)

Izzy: Teach me, Mami! Teach me, Mamacita! Ay! No no no.

Marlene: Sí, Papi! Sí sí sí. Sí, Papasote! Lose yourself in my musky heat. Grrr grrrr.

Izzy: Grrrr. Animal you. Gnash gnash gnash.

Marlene: So many roles. So many men. So many babies to diaper and roll. Say it, child. Say your lines.

Izzy: I adore you. The world adores you. My navel adores you. You are an origin.

Marlene: Perfect. Now the treat. (Marlene kisses him hard like a woodpecker.) Smack. In zee ear canal.

Izzy: Ay no! Not upside the head! You're torturing me. I hear violins. A string quartet is strangling my rhapsody in blue. You send me. I am deaf to no one but you.

Marlene: Smack on zee temple.

Izzy: Oh no. Not my peckerwood. You're getting to the source there. No fair. No hitting below the belt. You're cheating. You know you have total control down there up here. Here in my tierra del fuego.

Marlene: Then I attack. Smack. I blind you.

Izzy: Syphilis! Oh no! My Columbus, you conquer me!

Marlene: I love you. I love you deep. I love you hard. I love it when the blood rises in your eyes. I see red. Grrrrrr!

Izzy: You're scaring me, Mami.

Marlene: Grrrrrowl!! I could turn myself inside out for you.

Izzy: Oh my! (Izzy swoons.)

Marlene: Now get up and fix your face. You are my daughter, and you have a big date. You know what to do.

Izzy: I have a headache. Not now I have a headache. Not now I have a headache. Not now I have a headache. A headache. I have a . . . (Marlene smacks her.)

Marlene: Good. He'll want more then.

Izzy: Is he really coming? Or are you just faking it?

Marlene: I like you with your pert cheek, like your ass. Stuck up. I like you to coo. Shoulders back, arms twisted, boobs to the fore, cleavage aft, and south-ward down the tierra del fuego. Carlos likes that.

Izzy: I know. I know Carlos. Carlos is mine.

Marlene: But of course. It's all in the arrangement. Of course Carlos is coming, so I want you to come too.

Izzy: Me too. I want to come too. I want the wind in my hair. The door half-closed. The room finally still. And nothing. Nothing. Nothing. Only peace, only quiet. And only the sound of two crow's feet flapping from where you are.

Marlene: Don't enjoy yourself so much. It's not what you think it is. Moan. (Izzy does.) See?

Izzy: Nothing.

Marlene: Told you. Again, but louder. (Izzy moans.) How's that?

Izzy: Nada.

Marlene: Bueno. Otra vez. Pero fuerte. (Iz moans.) Más. (Again) Louder! (Again.) More. (Gasp.) And more. (Gasp.) And more. (Gasp.) And more. (She groans.) I mean a real convincing hellhole moan. (Iz screams at the top of her lungs, peaking, and thrashes about.)

Izzy: Yes yes yes yes yes. . . .

Marlene: Finally!!!!

(Izzy screams again, coming down. Olga, the maid, rushes in screaming too.)

Olga: Aaaagh! (She sees Marlene on top of Izzy.) Oh my lady! (She sees Izzy spent.) My lady! Ooo-lah-lah.

Marlene: What the hell is going on, Maria?

Olga: Olga. I am Olga. Maria is a Mexican. I am not.

Marlene: What are you then?

Olga: I am a generic, like you.

Marlene: I am a blonde. And don't you ever forget it. Now, what is the godforsaken problem?

Olga: Prepare yourselves. You and the Young You are not going to like this. Will not be equipped to like this. You are much too delicate and full of hope to like this.

Izzy: Spit it out, Olga. We don't have all day. I have to dress, powder, and pamper myself. Today is my wedding day.

Olga: Ay!! Jesús María. Congratulations. But, but, but . . .

Marlene/Izzy: WHAT?!!!!!

Olga: It is about Don Carlos. Don Carlitos. . . .

Izzy: Carlos?!

Marlene: What about Carlos?

Olga: Carlos, Carlos, Carlitos is . . . is . . .

Marlene/Izzy: WHAT?!!!!!!!

Olga: Carlitos is . . . stuck!

Marlene/Izzy: Stuck?!

Izzy: My Carlos, Stuck?!! . . . Stuck!!

Marlene: How can that be? Where? Whyfore? How now, Brown Cow?

(Izzy throws herself into a tantrum.)

Izzy: He's always stuck.

Olga: Bridge traffic. You know.

Izzy: Always late. Always never.

Olga: He called. "Sorry."

Izzy: Always always. He never touches me. Never never. He never touch me. No no not on your life no. Hey Carlos. Carlos. Come here. Come touch me. I've got a gold coin. (She rummages in her pocket and holds out a gold coin to Marlene.) Come here. Come touch me. (Marlene takes it and hands it to Olga.)

Marlene: Go out. Get the girl some chocolates for her heart. Quick. Now!

Olga: Yes, my doña. (Olga runs out.)

Izzy: I've got two coins. (Throws them at Marlene.) I've got three. (Throws.) Four. (Throws.) Five. Six. Seven. Eight. You know how you like the clink of gold hard cash. I can buy you anything. These are your own words. So just eat 'em, you pig! Come out come out wherever you are. Soo ee soo eee. You fucking cocksucking . . .

Marlene: Isabella!

Izzy: Non-fucking non-cocksucking non-sucking anything amoeba sea urchin sea horse android plasticine Romeo toy . . .

Marlene: Isabella, your language!

Izzy: Non-fucking thing. Here I sit alone. Molding. Waiting to eat a chocolate. A truffle, a Nestlé, a Hershey, a kiss!! I grow fat waiting for you to touch me. Carlos! Mami! You promised. I need something to eat.

Marlene: Have a panty, daughter.

Izzy: A cup of milk. I want a cup of milk.

Marlene: There is no more. Wait for the maid.

Izzy: I want it now!!

Marlene: Patience.

Izzy: Carry me on your back.

Marlene: You stand up and get in his car. You want it so much. (Pause.)

Izzy: Mami?

Marlene: Yes, darling.

Izzy: Can I borrow the keys to your hair? They say albinos have more fun. He might like it. It might be a turn-on. Bing! White-out.

Marlene: You touch one hair on this head and you're a dead girl.

Izzy: But it's so beautiful. I want to be an angel too.

Marlene: And so you are. I taught you to love your little black head.

Izzy: I do. But your hair, it goes so much better with satin. I want to wear satin too. I want to wear a dress. I wanna wear a dress like you.

Marlene: Wear pants. Be a man. It's cold outside. Today is a pants day. Tomorrow you'll get a dress.

Izzy: Today! I'm the bride.

Marlene: I'm the bride!

Izzy: I am!

Marlene: I am! I am the mom. I am the Mami.

Izzy: I am the daughter. I am the ingenue. I am the moon. I am the stars!

Marlene: I am the ocean!

Izzy: I am the lover! I am . . . CARLOS!!!

Marlene: CARLOS!!!

Marlene/Izzy: CARLOS!!!

(Olga runs in screaming.)

Olga: CARLOS! He calls. He is . . . SICK!!!

Marlene/Izzy: SICK?!

Olga: Sí! Sí, SICK. Too much stop and go, in and out. The traffic.

(Izzy throws herself on the couch again.)

Izzy: That washed up bag of seaspray!

Marlene: How, how, how, great becursed God. How in my splendid name—Marlene—did he get . . . sick?

Olga: He ate too much. Some black lace got caught in his throat. And then he . . . (Makes signs of throwing up.)

Izzy: Ahhh. My black lace with the pearls.

Marlene: My black lace with the pearls.

Izzy: Mine.

Marlene: Mine. I gave it to you.

Izzy: I asked you for it.

Marlene: It's your fault.

Izzy: Your fault!

(They stick their tongues out at each other viciously and noisily.)

Izzy: You castrating bitch!

Marlene: Whiner!

Izzy: Voodoo queen!

Marlene: Spoiled brat!

Izzy: Has-been wannabe!

Marlene: Baby!

Izzy: Mother! Fucker.

(Marlene lunges for Izzy's neck. The two strangle each other.)

Olga: Oh my God. I better get the police. I better get the men. Oh my God. Dios mio. Diós mio. (Olga runs out.)

Marlene: Where is Papa when you need him? He'd teach an ingrate brat slut like you. He'd wash your mouth out with Ivory Snow. If you hadn't led Carlos on your trail of Sodom and Gomorrah.

Izzy: Me. Me? Why I was just icing on the cake. Who was the one that egged me on?

Marlene: I'm only thinking of your future.

Izzy: I'm only thinking of yours.

(Marlene lets go. Izzy collapses.)

Marlene: I want to be left alone.

Izzy: You will be soon enough. When Carlos comes.

Marlene: When Carlos comes we will all be alone.

Izzy: Silly-billy. When Carlos comes you'll walk down that altar. You'll walk, you'll turn, you'll wave goodbye with a tremble of your elbow-length glove. Then you'll give me away. Like a Daddy, like a Papi. Mami, you will give me away. And your fans will cheer, and the chiffon in your gown will rise. Up, up, up you will float and you will be airborne. Cloud Nine. So don't cry. You'll muss your gown.

Marlene: I am tired. My bathrobe is getting wrinkly.

Izzy: Sleep. Lie down.

Marlene: Is it nighty-night time?

Izzy: Come, Mami. Come to me. I take you in my arms and sing you a song. (Marlene relaxes on top of Izzy. Izzy sings a full set of Brahms's "Cradle Song.") Lullabye and goodnight . . .

Marlene: What do you have in your pants?

Izzy: Pray tell, come by me again.

Marlene: What's that in your pants? I smell something.

Izzy: Well, check it yourself. You're the Mami.

Marlene: Unzip. (Izzy does.)

Izzy: Alright already.

(Marlene takes a look.)

Marlene: Aaaagh!!! Jockey shorts!!!!!? Dirty ones at that. Dirty pink smelly underones. You're not the daughter I raised. Where's the g-string? Are you a man? Or a mouse? If I've told you once, I've told you twice. Silk silk silk silk silk . . . (Izzy smacks her.) Silk is from China.

Izzy: Cotton is for virgins. Like me. Innocents who have known no such sullied moments. Baby's breath who tickle rosebuds pink with first blush of passion.

Marlene: Liar.

Izzy: Not! Ask Carlos. Ask him.

Marlene: Don't you ever lie to your mother!

Izzy: Carlos!

Marlene: I can see things. I am the third eye. Confess. Confess, or I'll take away your dowry.

Izzy: Carlitos! Come quick!

Marlene: Take away your crystal ball. Take away your cloak of darkness. Your ten steps to a total you.

Izzy: Carlos I need you.

Marlene: I'll wash that brilliantine glow of youth all down the drain. Your hair will go flat and what will you have left.

Izzy: Carlos.

Marlene: Carlos. (Beat.) Carlos (to Izzy, as if she were Carlos), you really don't need me.

Izzy: Carlos (to Marlene) I really don't need you. (Beat.) Carlos, I really do need you.

Marlene: Carlos, I really do need you.

(Olga walks in somberly.)

Olga: Carlos, Carlitos. I am so sorry, ladies. Carlos . . . your Carlos . . . is dead.

Izzy: Carlos is dead?

Marlene: Carlos is dead?

Olga: Yes, señoras. I apologize.

Izzy: Carlos is dead.

Marlene: Carlos is dead.

Izzy: My life is over.

Marlene: My life is over.

Izzy: Mami, what do I do?

Marlene: Pray. Pray for peace. Pray for a quiet space. A patch of sod. Pray.

Izzy: Our father who art in heaven, hallowed be thy name. Thy kingdom come, thy will be done. On earth as it is in this hellhole. I, for one, would like some fresh air, a little light in my eyes, a little mud between the toes, a bit of grass between the teeth. Is that asking too much?

Marlene: Yes, querida.

Izzy: Mami?

Marlene: Yes.

Izzy: Would you like to go for a walk? You're looking a tad bit peaked.

Marlene: You're asking me to go for a walk?

Izzy: Why yes. Of course.

Marlene: You're asking a bag of bones to hit the streets with you.

Izzy: Why certainly.

Marlene: You won't be embarassed by my glasses, my sunglasses, my wind hood, my visor, my parasol, my sunblock? I'm so ashamed. I think I'm peeling. My pancake is flaking.

Izzy: No, Mami. You look beautiful. I think some fresh air would do us some good. Would you care to take a turn round the floor?

Marlene: Certainement.

(Both women rise.)

Izzy: Your arm, Mommy dearest.

(Marlene hooks her arm in Izzy's.)

Marlene: Aren't you forgetting your hat, darling? It's cold outside.

Izzy: Oh yes. Olga. The white one, please. (Iz snaps her fingers. Olga scuttles under the chaise and pulls out a wedding veil. Iz puts it on.) My snow white hat. I've been waiting all day to wear it. Okay. I'm ready.

Marlene: Olga?

Olga: Yes, ma'am.

Marlene: Your lines, please.

Olga: Oh yes. Dearly beloved, we are gathered together to love, honor, and etcetera each other. You may now kiss, you may now etcetera the bride. Etcetera, etcetera, etcetera.

Izzy: This is my happiest moment. I'm celebrating! (Iz and Marlene kiss on the lips.)

Marlene: Till death do we part.

Izzy: Forever and ever. Happily ever after. Shall we dance, Mami? I'll lead.

Marlene: Certainement, darling.

Izzy: Olga? (Olga hums a waltz. Izzy and Marlene waltz around and around the floor. Marlene rests her head on Izzy's shoulder. They end up barely moving in one spot.) Ahhh! This is the best. The sun in my face. The wind between my toes. And you. And me. Don't you agree, Mami?

Marlene: Ahhh, yes.

Izzy: Ahhh.

Marlene: Ahhh.

Izzy: Ahhh.

END OF PLAY

** Translation of El Locutor's voiceover

El Locutor: Enter a divine world, a world as soft and delicate and tremulous as a rose. A world where men are men, and women—goddesses. A passionate world where desire is reality. Come, tonight, to the land of Novell-aaaaaaah. . . .

With *name of actress playing Olga* as Olga, the maid. *Name of actress playing Izzy* as Isabella, the little Chinese girl. And *name of actress playing Marlene* as Marlene, Big Mama China.

5

And the Crow Cries Before He Dies

A Brandon Lee Spoken-Word Soliloquy

Cathy Irwin

It can't rain all the time.

That was my line before a bullet entered my spine.

I died and people cried,
"IT'S HIS FAMILY'S CURSE!"

Perhaps the image of Bruce Lee fit
my American fans' fantasy of who I was.

Or was meant to be.

It's all there in the script that
my family and friends know by heart.

It's like my father's most famous scene,
when he enters a hall of mirrors.

He's the hunter and the hunted down.

Enter the dragon!

Are you ready to rumble?

What do you call style?

And the camera keeps rolling,
filming the image found in the mirror.

They cut across his body
magnifying the one into many

FISTS OF FURY.

Want to know the truth?
My father followed a script given to all Asian actors:
    1. Get in fight.
    2. Stand stunned.
    3. Taste your blood.
    4. GO BERSERK!
    5. Make animal sounds.
    6. Wipe out anyone who stands in front of you.[1]
Those mirrors marked my father's body as Chinese.
    Immortal.

        A legend.

An image of transcendent speed, light, and revenge
that no other man could ever match.

And those who watched him knew it.

JACHINSON W. CHAN—SCHOLAR

Linda Emery Lee's biography of her husband (Bruce Lee) offers evidence
that his identity was constructed through various racial and sexual negotiations. Lee fell in love with a white American woman despite her family's rejection of him. Symbolically, this marriage represented Lee's desire to be
part of mainstream America. However, Lee did not reject his Chinese heritage in this process of acculturation. As a Chinese American male, he
wanted to appeal to both Chinese and mainstream American audiences. In
Emery Lee's (1975) words: "Could he widen his international appeal without destroying his popularity on the Mandarin circuit?" (11). Through
Emery Lee's biography, she further describes Lee's difficulties and struggles
to excel over white American actors of the period, such as James Coburn,
Chuck Norris, and Steve McQueen. By competing with his white male
counterparts, Lee's fictive models of masculinity can be interpreted as a
project to redeem a Chinese American manhood.[2]

But I.
I've been trying to make my own way through this hall of mirrors.
Understand what I see in the reflection.

My father wasn't even 100 percent ASIAN!

Are you listening?

He was born in 1940 in San Francisco, for Christ's sake![3]
And his mother was Chinese-German.[4]
Maybe that's why my father
refused to teach martial arts

Only to Asians.

He got a lot of flack for that.

In movies, he would do a flying kick to smash signs that read
    "NO DOGS OR CHINESE ALLOWED"[5]
then teach gong fu to anyone who entered his school.

Maybe that's why he didn't flinch
when he fell in love with my white mother.

And maybe that's why I was born with blond hair
that turned brown as I got older.[6]

Is my body still cursed?

Is the camera still rolling?
Perhaps my family is part of a single script,

and the director keeps asking for

ACTION! ACTION! ACTION!

And I'm still on the set,
    with the house on fire
    and the crow on my shoulder.
And Funboy has shot the bullet
    that blasted through my stomach walls
    and into my spine.[7]

And the crew thinks I'm acting fine!

I saw a reflection of myself—
I was no longer my father; I was no longer my mother.

    —I left my body in 1993—

But the remains of my mixed-race family legacy:

    THEY STILL LIVE.

JEFF YANG—JOURNALIST AND CULTURAL CRITIC

Does it matter? He died.

Yes, it matters. Because for Brandon, and for a generation of Asian American men, Bruce was a figure to be claimed and shunned—his power was our power, but our identity was our own. Playground fights where we struck fear in others with Bruce's poses; chopsocky Chinamen taunts, when older, about prowess that we did not have. Brandon was buried by his family in a grave at his father's side. And perhaps the cult will rest. Perhaps, like *The Crow*, it will revive with vengeance in its eye—the story of Bruce's life,

Dragon, has been brought to screen; there is talk of finishing *The Crow* and releasing it, in Brandon's honor.

But we who wait, we wait for the story to end.

So we can mourn.[8]

And so I was raised from the dead,
a new body, a new head.
They turned me into something new and
I'm suddenly one among the few

GONE VIRTUAL

where the erotic meets the exotic in cyberspace.

They digitally composed my face onto a body

LESS THAN ONE AND DOUBLE.

And when I saw my face
superimposed onto my double,

I cried,
    as the image of me walked towards the window
    with the crow
    looking over my shoulder
    to someone no longer me.

I swear I wasn't looking for trouble.
But nothing prepared me for the afterlife.

I died and woke up a superstar!

Through computer generated images,
I finished *The Crow* and took over the big screen.

It was as if my double became the preferred me.

My photograph appeared next to the Keanus, Mariahs, and Johnny Depps.[9]

All I could do was look out from the mirror and
catch a glimpse of my face and body on posters and in teen magazines.

I could have sung my songs and taken part in the traffic of pictures.

But am I real?

Film is a world of pure surface and cunning PR
And by the time my father realized this, he was dead.

When he died in Hong Kong, I was only a child,
    who didn't understand his Chinese side.

I became a teenage rebel who refused to share.
And when I was kicked out of school,
        people thought I didn't care.

They thought I was troubled, disturbed,
an outsider living in a white, Anglo world.

I wanted someone to teach me how to be and what to do,

And that's when I got hooked on Hollywood too.

I wanted to be an actor,
    no matter how Asian or other I looked.

I learned by watching,
     listening;
  the scripts were feeding me my lines
  and yet I still felt like there were times
  when I didn't know how to be a man,
  White, Chinese, German, Swedish
  AMERICAN.

So I studied as hard as my father worked on his timing,
by going further, by doing my own miming.

If I was to be my father's keeper,
then I had to go deeper,
swallow my father's image and turn it into a show,
and that's why I did the film *The Crow*.

It was my turn to kick and sing and go with the flow—
I wanted to make love like any white, male hero.

It's all on screen.

I am a lover, friend, musician, fighter,
who takes my father's image somewhere higher.

  I take on bad guys
  and leave before the crow cries.

I know I've left way too soon.
But I can't escape the footsteps of my father's doom.
  This house is cursed
    and the crow.

The crow carried my soul back into the living

TO MAKE WRONG THINGS RIGHT.

JEFF YANG—JOURNALIST AND CULTURAL CRITIC

"He said he was going to relate the loss of Shelly"—Eric's fiancée in the movie—"to the loss of his father. He was going to try to use those kinds of emotions," says James O'Barr, author of the comic book on which the film was based. "We sat in his trailer one night and talked for about four hours. You know the first thing he said to me? A quote from *Blade Runner*: 'It's not an easy thing to meet your maker.'"

Nor it is easy to escape him. And that is the great tragedy of Brandon's passing, that in death, like in life, he is forever bound to the man who made him, whom he loved and was haunted by.

People are talking about curses. Robert Lee, Brandon's uncle, spoke to reporters about the curse of the Lee family—"Our grandfather was told that in our family, there would be death, there would be divorce. Conspiracy theory: Brandon was killed by his father's killers, martial arts mystics who envied Bruce's fame and swore vengeance on him for revealing secret techniques."[10]

I am still the son of Bruce Lee,
no matter where I work.
China, Hong Kong, Bangkok, Hollywood.
You would never believe the hype I got in New York—

I saw it,
but I still got caught in his shadow.

One night on stage, at an audition,
I asked the manager to turn off all the lights
        —except the ghost light
that haunted upper stage right.

I was wearing my black boots, black jersey and black jeans.
My eyes were lined with dark eyeliner
while my skin, caked in porcelain white powder,
lit up the stage.

I looked magnificent.

And as I walked down stage,
the director's face turned white from beige.

Later, he said he could not move
        —he almost had a heart attack—

because, to him,

BRUCE LEE WAS BACK.

Taller,
        whiter—

It was as if I'd stormed in from the sky.

He asked if I could fly.

Hell, I said, I can fly.
I threw myself into the air and
released a kick that was beyond compare.

I was playing with his mind.

My father had people eating out of his hand,
but I didn't know where my own cards would land.

Not in this business.

When I studied martial arts in Hong Kong,
I discovered that I could not hide:
I learned about America from my Chinese side.

I went to work with my father,
walked on the set of his action films,
and watched American fighters,
who were powerful in their own right,
looking for my father to stage a fight.

And he fought them all.

He fought them all.

And after he beat them,
these fighters,
dying to make others as helpless as he made them,
would take it out on other Chinese men.

RICHARD FUNG—FILMMAKER AND CULTURAL CRITIC

Because of their supposed passivity and sexual compliance, Asian women
have been fetishized in dominant representation, and there is a large and
growing body of literature by Asian women on the oppressiveness of these
images. Asian men, however—at least since Sessue Hayakawa, who made a
Hollywood career in the 1920s of representing Asian men as sexual threat—
have been consigned to one of two categories: the egghead/wimp, or—in
what may be analogous to the lotus blossom–dragon lady dichotomy—the
kung-fu master/ninja/samurai. He is sometimes dangerous, sometimes
friendly, but almost always characterized by a desexualized Zen asceticism.
So whereas, as Fanon tells us "the Negro is eclipsed. He is turned into a penis. He is a penis,"[11] the Asian man is defined by a striking absence down
there.[12]

And so I grew up wondering what would happen
if I walked out there into the bright light and showed
myself in my full power as a man.

How would people accept me?

The son of Bruce and Linda Lee,
an American of Swedish, Chinese, and German descent.

My sleek physique and exotic, alabaster skin
has become "the look" in fashion and film.

And yet I wonder if the script will ever change,
whether those of us who are mixed-race actors will have our day.

Like Asian male actors, we still have to prove we can do karate,
do yellowface for the entertainment of casting directors.

Could my father have changed things in Hollywood?
Could he have been more active in the civil rights movement?
Could he have done more for Asian Americans?
Could he have flaunted his mixed-race heritage?

Could he have done more?

What do you think?

Would you have taught *jeet kune do* to any man—
white, black, Asian, Latino—
who walked through your door, knowing that one day
he might want to fight you to your death?

Would you have married a white woman when there were still anti-miscegenation
laws?
Would you have studied Western philosophy?
Tried to become a star in Hollywood, when most Asian men were white people in
Yellowface?

I cannot fault my father for doing the things he did.

I mean, Hollywood wouldn't hire him,
so he had to go all the way to China to make movies![13]

How many other starving American actors did that in the 50s and 60s?

Yet, in the 1990s, I too had to take that long road:
The only movie that Hollywood would cast me in was *Kung Fu: The Movie.*[14]

I had to go all the way to China,
do Cantonese action films in order to get a job![15]
And then more martial arts films
with directors screaming,

ACTION! ACTION! ACTION!

And when it came time to tie the knot,
I too fell in love with a white woman.
She was my living dream,
until I got shot and threw in my lot.

Man, this was in the '80s and early '90s.

Things have changed.
A little.

At least I understand myself better.
Understand how I was manufactured to
be who I was.
How I was taught who to love and how to love,
who to be and how to be.

Should I be wandering around in the twenty-first century
moaning about the past?

After all, my stock has once again gone up and
I can proudly call myself a mixed-race star.
At last.

I still believe that true love never dies.
And it's still not an easy thing to meet your maker.

NEW YORK TIMES (28 DECEMBER 2003)

Ad campaigns for Louis Vuitton, YSL Beauty, and H&M Stores have all purposely highlighted models with racially indeterminate features. Or consider the careers of movie stars like Vin Diesel, Lisa Bonet, and Jessica Alba, whose popularity with young audiences seems due in part to the tease over whether they are black, white, Hispanic, American Indian, or some combination. "Today what is ethnically neutral, diverse, or ambiguous has tremendous appeal," said Ron Berger, chief executive of Euro RSCG MVBMS Partners in New York, an advertising agency whose clients include Polaroid and Yahoo. "Both in the mainstream and at the high end of the marketplace, what is perceived as good, desirable, successful is often a face, whose heritage is hard to pin down."[16]

Brandon Lee died on the movie set of *The Crow*, weeks before he was to marry his fiancée Eliza Hutton. The footage of Brandon Lee's death was destroyed.[17]

NOTES

*This dramatic monologue is 100 percent fiction. It does not denote or pretend to private information about actual persons, living, dead, or otherwise. Although the monologue uses the names of the "real" Bruce and Brandon Lee, these public figures are superimposed onto made-up characters in made-up circumstances. In places where the stuff of imagination is embellished or supported by other writers' ideas and biographical details of these public figures, the source is credited.

1. Adapted from material on Bruce Lee's "trademarks." See Leonard Maltin, "Biography for Bruce Lee I," *IMDb: The Internet Movie Database*, 1994, www.imdb.com/name/nm0000045/bio (28 December 2004).

2. Jachinson W. Chan, "Bruce Lee's Fictional Models of Masculinity," *Men and Masculinities* 2 (4) (April 2000): 373–74.

3. Because of anti-miscegenation laws, mixed-race marriages were not common before 1950. However, because of immigration laws during the early twentieth century, there may have been more interracial marriages among Chinese men. According to Philip Tajitsu Nash, the first published account of an interracial marriage that included someone with Asian ancestry was an 1857 *Harper's Weekly* article that described the marriage of Chinese men and Irish and German women. In 1960, the census reported 150,000 interracially married couples. By 1990, that number had grown to 1.5 million couples (four of every one hundred in the nation), resulting in an estimated four million interracial children. Among those of Asian and Pacific Islander, the proportion is higher than 4 percent, as a survey in California in 1990 found that 25 percent (one in four) of children with any Asian ancestry were the product of both Asian- and European-derived parents. ("Will the Census Go Multiracial?" *Amerasia Journal* 23 [1] [1997]: 17–18.)

4. See Maltin, "Biography for Bruce Lee I."

5. Maltin, "Biography for Bruce Lee I."

6. See "Biography for Brandon Lee," *IMDb: The Internet Movie Database*, 1994, www.imdb.com/name/nm0000488/bio (28 December 2004).

7. See R. E. Payne, "The Death of Brandon Lee: The Untold Story," *Caught in the Crossfire: The R.E. Payne Story*, www.repayne.com/brandonlee.html (28 December 2004).

8. Jeff Yang, "Shadow of a Crow," originally printed in *A.* magazine, 1993. Reprinted at *Bruce and Brandon Lee: Lives Worth Remembering*, www.bruceandbrandon .info/library/print/brandon/shadow/html (28 December 2004).

9. Mixed-race performers of interracial descent became popular in the 1990s, suggesting the acceptance of mixed-race individuals into popular culture. As Houston and Williams write: "Even in pop culture, the presence of Asian-descent multiracial individuals has increased." Perhaps the apogee of this "mainstreaming" occurred when two of America's favorite pop icons, Superman and Madonna, were portrayed by Asian-descent multiracial actors, Dean Cain and Terumi Mathews, respectively. In addition, Tiger Woods, the golf superstar, graces the covers of sports magazines and Ralph Lauren Polo model "Tyson" boasts in *Essence* magazine that his eyes are a "gift from his Chinese grandmother." Independent fictional and documentary films by Asian-descent, multiracial artists have flourished, such as *Enryo Identity, Banana Split, None of the Above, And We are Whole*, and *Two Halves Make a Whole*. Filmmaker Reggie Life, who produced and directed the critically acclaimed *Struggle and Success: African Americans in Japan*, has produced another film, titled *Doubles: Japan and American's Intercultural Children*, about binational, biracial Japanese and American individuals. (Velina Hasu Houston and Teresa K. Williams, "No Passing Zone: The Artistic and Discursive Voices of Asian-Descent Multiracials," *Amerasia Journal* 23 [1] [1997]: viii–ix.)

10. Yang, "Shadow of a Crow."

11. Frantz Fanon, *Black Skin, White Masks* (London: Paladin, 1970), 120.

12. Richard Fung, "Looking for My Penis: The Eroticized Asian in Gay Video Porn," *Asian American Studies: A Reader*, ed. Jean Yu-Wen, Shen Wu, and Min Song (Piscataway, N.J.: Rutgers University Press, 2000), 340.

13. See Jachinson W. Chan's "Bruce Lee's Fictional Models of Masculinity," *Men and Masculinities* 2 (4) (April 2000): 371–87.

14. See "Biography for Brandon Lee," 28.

15. Michael Lipton and John Griffith, "Son of Bruce Breaks Loose," *People Weekly* (online), www.people.com/people/archive/article/0,,20108562,00.html (7 September 1992); *Arwen's Brandon Lee page*, 2000, www.geocities.com/brangillee/people (28 December 2004).

16. Ruth La Ferla. "Generation E.A.: 'Ethnically Ambiguous.'" *New York Times*, 28 December 2003, 1.

17. See "Brandon Lee: Biography," *Bruce and Brandon Lee: Lives Worth Remembering*, www.bruceandbrandon.info/library/print/brandon/shadow/html (28 December 2004).

6

Queer Theory and Anti-Racism Education

Politics of Race and Sexuality in the Classroom and Beyond

Ruthann Lee

As a queer-identified, racialized activist and student in the academy, I've been thinking a lot about the queer classroom and the anti-racist classroom and the ways in which queers of color negotiate their identities and politics in these spaces. I believe the tensions I have felt and continue to feel within these spaces as a politicized Asian[1] (sometimes Korean) Canadian dyke/queer[2] reveal the ongoing difficulties in both theorizing and engaging politically with the concept and reality of intersecting and interlocking identities and oppressions. The question I am asking myself in this paper is: What are my political responsibilities and/or possibilities as a queer, racialized subject in the academy? As an Asian Canadian dyke? I seek to understand this by looking at both the connections between and limitations of queer and anti-racist theories in educational practice. What happens when studies of sexuality and race are compartmentalized as academic disciplines? How do these theoretical frameworks reflect the way that the dynamics of race and sexuality are played out in the contemporary realities of the classroom? More importantly, what are the potentialities for transformative educational practice in examining the paradoxes and uncertainties of these categories?

My interest in mediating these theoretical perspectives arises out of the frustration and confusion I have often felt at certain moments and discussions in my queer and anti-racism courses. Frequently, when race and sexuality are mentioned simultaneously in these respective spaces the conversation shuts down, generating awkward silences and unresolved tensions. Questions remain unasked and unanswered. Too often it appears that we, as students and pedagogues, don't want to "go there" because it seems too difficult, too painful. (Indeed, even now I find it painful to recall and articulate

73

those moments of disjuncture.) But those constructed silences, obscurities, and tensions have meaning—whether they come from a place of not knowing, not wanting to know, or not knowing *how* to talk about what we think we know.

How, then, can we interpret silence when the concept of intersectional identities arises? I am aware that being racialized as "Asian" in a North American context complicates my relationship to notions of silence and the act of self-silencing.[3] For example, my reluctance to be an "in your face" queer frequently conflicts with the stereotype of the "mysterious, silent, and passive" Asian and reflects my ongoing struggles with internalized racism and homophobia. Consequently, I am somewhat ambivalent about my participatory role in creating those moments of silence and tension. However, like Mona Oikawa, who interrogates her position in the academy as a Japanese Canadian lesbian, "I want to look at my own self-silencing practices in sites that are of crucial social, political, and emotional importance to me."[4] I wish to revisit and critically interrogate those moments because conversations about race and sexuality must continue in order for us to better understand how differences are played out in the everyday realities of identity and subjectivity. By situating these experiences, I attempt to foreground larger systemic challenges by looking at how queer and anti-racist theory cohere for transformative thinking and practice in education.

SILENT EPISODE #1

I remember attending my first "Queer Theories" class, a new course offering at the Ontario Institute for Studies in Education at the University of Toronto. There was much dialogue throughout the various academic departments in anticipation of the course. I was particularly excited about the prospect of aligning queer studies with my interests in the field of anti-racism education.

As I walked into the room on the first day of class and glanced around, my heart sank. White, white, white. . . . I breathed in deeply and quickly caught the eyes of two other (and for me, the only visibly racialized) Asian students in the room, both of whom I knew previously as acquaintances. We smiled faintly and waved at each other. Almost immediately the three of us sat together, an unspoken but oh-so-obvious affiliation. I felt a flicker of relief at our mutual recognition but it seemed enormously apparent that other bodies were missing.

In my home department of anti-racism studies, I had become accustomed to attending classes inhabited predominantly by brown, black, and yellow bodies—spaces where "people of color" were in the majority. In this queer classroom, students were presumably united by our queerness—but the dominance of white bodies in the space overwhelmed me. The internalized phobia/mantra of "queer=white" began to echo in my head. As students introduced themselves to each other, I became hyperconscious of how I was to represent myself. Although no one was staring, I was suddenly struck by childhood memories of my family being gawked at by white families and staff at restaurants in rural parts of Ontario. I was reminded of how disconnected I have felt in feminist collectives in my earlier days at university and in most gay and lesbian bars on Church Street—how alien.

In the predominantly white queer classroom, I was confronted by my Asian-ness. Within that space my racial identity, my Asian-ness, became hyper-visible. Consequently, I felt pressured to take on a responsibility. I introduced myself to the other students on the first day of class by firmly stating that my interest in taking the course was to make connections between theories of race and theories of sexuality. However, as the term progressed, I felt myself becoming less confident and comfortable mentioning race. For example, I recall a moment during a small group discussion when I was asked to speak about my experience of racism by a white classmate. I remember following through with this request and later regretting doing so: "having to present our experiences *as* knowers of racism, or *as* people of colour, produces and reproduces those categories . . . the telling of experience may circumscribe us, for example, as victims of racism or resources on racism."[5] After that experience, I more carefully guarded my comments and reactions to the statements made in class. Whether or not I chose to engage in discussion depended on how I felt I was being racialized in that "queer" classroom space.

It should be of no surprise that the queer class I attended was filled mainly with white bodies. In part, the absence of bodies of color in the queer classroom can be attributed to the dilemmas of institutionalization—particularly when considering the separation of academic disciplines that are compartmentalized and structured around categories of identity.[6] Since queer theory is primarily situated within the domain of studies in sexuality, the category of sexuality is privileged and other axes of identity are frequently ignored. More specifically, whiteness remains centered—and this is reflected in the space and dynamic of the queer classroom.

Additionally, the lack of racial diversity in the queer classroom reflects a complex and often contested relationship that many people of color have with the term "queer." For example, who is represented as "queer"? Who (can) identify as "queer"? As Chantelle Nadeau has pointed out, "queerness is naturalized through the production of capital and the erasure of specificity."[7] In now-globalized media images, the trendy, desirable, and hip "queer" is rich, white, and gay. The marketing of the "alternative" or "queer" lifestyles adopted by affluent, white North American and European gays and lesbians by mainstream media complicates the way in which people of color choose to identify with definitions of queerness. Silenced in both heterosexist environments of racialized communities and the white queer communities of North America and Europe, queers of color often reinvent themselves with new words and names of identification.[8] The relevance of the categories "queer," "lesbian," "gay," etc., for many people of color may thus be fraught with ambivalence.

Gloria Anzaldua's reflection on the terms "lesbian" and "queer" describes a similar relationship to the one I hold with the term "queer" when applied as a category of identity.[9] I choose to define myself as a Canadian-born, Korean dyke/queer—I too have refused to name myself as "lesbian" because it forces me to define myself more obviously on terms of the dominant culture (white, middle-class). However, both politically and historically, the terms "dyke" and "queer" remain inadequate in describing my experience and location. Having a racialized body complicates my relationships to the terms "dyke" and "queer" since they have arisen out of a Euro-American history and linguistics. However, what other labels could I use? And could I (or anyone else, for that matter) ever be truly satisfied?

Attempting to create and/or define a queer culture or community runs into all sorts of problems because hierarchies of gender, race, and class are reproduced within that definition. We can read silence in the queer classroom as indicative of the limits of assuming political affiliations and understandings based on shared identities. Despite being united by "queer" in terms of identity, it remained difficult for students in the queer classroom to acknowledge and account for white privilege and racism apparent in that space.[10] Here, it becomes crucial to make distinctions between the politics of queer *identity* and the politics of queer *theory*.

Our silence in the queer classroom frequently illustrated how very differently situated we are in our experiences and histories. However, certain aspects of queer theory help us to understand and work through these conflicts in a more comprehensive way. For example, queer theory emerges out of poststructuralist theories in which "the notion of identity as a coherent and abiding sense of self is perceived as a cultural fantasy rather than a demonstrable fact."[11] One of the central principles of queer theory is an opposition to the understanding of identities as fixed. Queer theory seeks to resist the normativity inscribed in binary propositions, particularly the oppositional divide between the categories of "hetero/homo." Queer theory seeks to denaturalize the notion of essential and primordial sexualities. Although the boundaries between the definitions of homo- and heterosexuality are quite blurry, the apparent fixity of these categorizations remains because identities are constantly being articulated and (re)produced through acts of repetition—what Judith Butler has termed "performativity."[12] In a way, then, queer theory attempts to transgress, subvert, and disrupt the regulatory boundaries and constraints of identity.

Additionally, however, queer theory does not claim for itself any specific materiality or positivity and instead emphasizes the relationality of identities. It is thus often deployed to indicate a critical distance from identity politics. Notably, because it is difficult to predict how acts and notions of transgression, subversion, and disruption of norms operate, queer theory appears to lack a strategic approach to politics.[13]

By contrast, anti-racist theory is more explicitly action-oriented and geared toward institutional and systemic change to address racism and the interlocking systems of social oppression. In the context of education, for example, George Sefa Dei articulates that "anti-racism is a critical discourse of race and racism in society and of the continuing racializing of social groups for differential and unequal treatment."[14] Anti-racist theory seeks to name race and social difference as issues of power and equity rather than as matters of cultural and ethnic variety. Importantly, anti-racist theory acknowledges the historical processes of European colonization, cultural and political imperialism, and the enslavement of indigenous and non-white peoples that have resulted in world systems of racial domination. Rather than justifying racism and difference with simplistic explanations of "natural" difference, anti-racist theory attempts to foster deeper understandings of how current processes of racialization manifest themselves in postmodern societies. How does this theoretical approach play itself out in the anti-racist classroom?

SILENT EPISODE #2

In the anti-racist classroom, moments of silence and tension have similarly arisen following conversations that have referred to sexuality and race simultaneously. I recall one particularly painful episode in which a white student called attention to a black student's comments about the "black community" and the "gay community"—a remark that implied that the communities were mutually exclusive and hence implicitly heterosexist. Our professor quickly chastised the white student for calling the black student on her heterosexism. As a racialized subject, the professor's reprimand appeared for me to stem from the viewpoint that the white student, the dominant body, had no place in "correcting" or "teaching" the black student, the subordinate body, due to the historically constituted, colonial power relations of racism operating in the room. However, as a queer subject, I felt frustrated that the heterosexist implications of that conversation were not addressed. Instead, the dialogue was cut short and replaced by an awkward tension for the remainder of the class.

Why did the topic of queer and racial identities get closed off in that conversation? How did heteronormativity surface in that episode and operate to shut down a potentially transformative and productive moment in theorizing intersections? Richard Friend argues that the systematic exclusion and silencing of accurate and affirmative messages regarding homosexuality, coupled with the systematic inclusion of negative and oppressive ideologies, reflects and reinforces heterosexist beliefs and attitudes in schools.[15] And to echo Kevin Kumashiro, "many people of colour coalesce in the name of anti-racism but fail to address their own complicity with other oppressions."[16] This power dynamic revealed itself during that uncomfortable silence in the anti-racist classroom.

If anti-racist theory emphasizes the importance of validating embodied knowledge, is there not room for discussions about desire and pleasure in the anti-racist classroom? Deborah P. Britzman has proposed that queer theory may offer ways of rethinking the very grounds of knowledge and pedagogy in education by refusing "the unremarked and obdurately unremarkable straight educational curriculum."[17] How can theories of sexuality become relevant for those who do not identify as queer? The application of queer theory in the anti-racist classroom could have helped us to support and understand, for example, the contemporary claims of transgendered Asian Canadian sex workers organizing for rights in Toronto. However, this discussion was not taken up because we could not even discuss transgenderism in that "anti-racist" space. Kumashiro has further noted that "the achievement of an identity and the progress of a movement should never come at the expense of another category of people, especially those who are a part of that identity and movement."[18] By applying queer theory and conceptual frameworks to the analysis of race and racism, the term "people of color" can be critically interrogated. We might better comprehend the instability and uncertainty in—but also affirm—identities such as transgenderism and mixed-raciality. We might more conscientiously identify the differences within and among people of color by discussing gender and sexuality and thus (re)organize our politics accordingly. Merle Woo maintains that integrating queer theory into discourses of anti-racism will, for example, enable the rethinking of power relations relating to racial struggles over epidemiology, scientific research, public health and sex education, and immigration policies.[19]

Furthermore, if racism is rooted in systems of colonial domination and if the establishment of heteronormativity was foundational to the Western colonial project (under the guise of Judeo-Christian morality claims), it would appear crucial to interrogate the ways in which homophobic, heterosexist, and erotophobic paradigms sustain and legitimate racist systems and practices. Additionally, queer theory has illustrated how the institutionalization of marriage and the nuclear family are fundamental to the view of sex and sexuality solely as sites of reproduction and procreation. This has been a key component of racist arguments that purport the notion of race as natural and the fear of white racial contamination.

At another level, addressing the topic of sexuality and the production and regulation of sexual identities in the anti-racist classroom could open up discussions about the different ways in which people of color are racialized and positioned—and more importantly, how they are systematically affected and targeted in different ways. As Monteiro and Fuqua argue in their preliminary and specific study of African American gay youth, "the breadth of experiences represented by 'people of color' is too immense."[20] Historically, representations and stereotypes of "people of color" are gender-specific and subsequently regulate their sexualities in distinctly different ways. Gendered and sexualized norms operate very differently for black women and men than they do for Asian women and men: "[R]acist caricatures by the European-Americans have exaggerated both the hypermacho, sexually crazed images of the African-American male, as well as the nurturant, emotional, 'feminine' males."[21] Most commercialized "Asian" representations are informed by Orientalist ideologies that reinforce contradictory "model minority" and "yellow peril" stereotypes in which Asians are considered admirable yet threatening to the white ruling classes.[22] Such representations repeatedly fall within heterosexual paradigms—where the "otherness" of Asian sexuality reinforces the norm of white heterosexuality.[23] More specifically, Asian men are caricatured as "wimpy asexual nerds, crazed martial artists, gangsters, comic sidekicks, mystical 'orientalized' backdrops . . . and the 'faceless enemy.'"[24] By contrast, Asian women are portrayed as, on the one hand, hypersexual, exotic, and evil, and, on the other, passive victims who are bound to sexual enslavement in need of saving.[25] These stereotypes are centered on the normalization of heterosexuality and function to justify historically racist, exclusionary immigration policies and policing practices.

I want to note that, conceptually, both queer theory and anti-racism education share an understanding that all knowledge is partial, asking questions such as, what is knowledge? How do we know what we know? Thus, they are both critical discourses that do not purport and promise any guaranteed political outcomes.[26] Anti-racist theory refuses, for example, to present itself as an imperialist project in making claims to a discourse with guarantees. Along related lines, queer theory is "sensitive to an open-ended construction of politics, since it represents itself as unfixed, and as holding open a space whose potential can never be known in the present."[27]

By instituting disciplines of sexuality and ethnic studies in anti-racism, the organizational structures of the academy have been set up to regard such identities as separable from one another, making it extremely difficult to theorize and understand (and educate about) the complex intersectionality of identities, subjectivities, and oppression. Because of this compartmentalization, it is a great challenge to think outside of these divisions and even harder not to reinforce them as we work within them. The difficulty in understanding differences and theorizing intersections manifests itself when conversations about race and sexuality result in silencing practices and constructed silences in the classroom. However, relating aspects of queer and anti-racist theory and practice enables us to rethink and imagine new and useful ways of analyzing and understanding racialized and sexual subjectivities and identities.

SILENT EPISODE #3

I choose to revisit a final moment of silence in order to further illustrate how queer and anti-racist theory can work constructively to illuminate the limitations of multiculturalist policies in Canada and pose challenges to exclusionary and restrictive forms of nationalism and patriotism. This particular episode of silence occurred in the queer classroom and arose after a debate around the possibilities of (re)imagining a queer nationalist movement in Canada. Students were asked to consider how "queer" fit into definitions of Canadian nationalism and state politics. In small group discussions, we reviewed dominant constructions of Canada's national identity and identified the characteristics of the national citizen-subject: white, Anglo-Saxon, male, heterosexual, middle-class, English- or French-speaking, able-bodied with strong "family values." We began to review the limits of queer nationalist movements. Some of us noted that historical attempts at establishing queer nationalist campaigns such as Queer Nation[28] and Pauline Rankin's more recent attempt to advocate for Canadian lesbians in a reimagined queer nationalism tended to evade the topic of race as it related to citizenship claims.[29] In both cases, there were no accounts for the exclusions of racialized sexual minorities in nationalist campaigns—exclusions that are constituted through the historical legacies of colonial domination. We thus identified ways in which nationalisms tend to reproduce the dominant hierarchal structures of heteropatriarchy, colonialism, and sexism.[30]

In broaching the topic of multiculturalism in Canada during our class discussion, we began to identify how multiculturalist policies affected queer people differently—in particular, queers who are racialized. Suddenly, a white student exclaimed in frustration, "but I love queer because it's all-inclusive!" An awkward silence ensued and the conversation shut down. I silently reflected on this idealistic remark. All-inclusive to whom and on whose terms?

In Canada, national identity and citizenship is predicated on the values of white, heterosexual males: "[T]he nation-building project [has] produced a legacy of homophobic, racist and sexist public policy."[31] This is reflected in multiculturalism, as both an official state policy and a pervasive cultural ideology, which is a key component of Canadian nationalism. As various anti-racist practitioners have illustrated, Trudeau (via recommendations of the Royal Commission on Bilingualism and Biculturalism) created the Multicultural Act to address the French/English controversy in 1971, focusing the debate on (white) Anglo/Francophones.[32]

Multiculturalism thus denies the impact of colonialism, imperialism, and other forms of cultural hegemony. In Canada, the term multiculturalism is very much a euphemism—enabling those who use it to avoid naming the power relations that distinguish and hierarchically organize the multiple cultures that constitute the nation. Through claims of inclusivity and the rhetoric of tolerance, the logic of multiculturalism fails to problematize historically sedimented relations of power. By claiming to "celebrate" difference, it disregards the ways that difference has been valued historically. For example, in the context of the mainstream public educational system, history is taught in a way that denies the violent cultural and racial genocide of First Nations people. Through discourses of "tolerance," "acceptance," and "colorblindness," notions of plurality result in token acknowledgments and representations of marginalized communities—the most obvious examples being the creation of black history and Asian heritage months.

Multicultural policy in Canada appeared to appease large numbers of citizens in the 1960s when immigration was on the rise as a result of decolonization. The Multiculturalism Act states that Canada will "foster the recognition and appreciation of the diverse cultures of Canadian society and promote the reflection and evolving expressions of those cultures." But for whose eyes is such recognition important? While multiculturalist policies claim to protect and include ethnocultural minorities in Canada, they allow those groups to participate in predefined ways.

For example, official policies of multiculturalism in many ways predetermine how minoritized groups challenge oppressive organizational structures through their collective claims to citizenship. Unfortunately, these *minoritized* groups rarely get to self-define. As Himani Bannerji explains:

> The all-pervasive presence of diversity in our [Canadian] public discourse has created a situation where even those who are not entirely comfortable with its discursive constellation use it in its various guises in an unconscious submission to what is around, and for reasons of intelligibility. Being effective with funding proposals means translating our needs and concerns into the discourses of multiculturalism. This means speaking in the language of cultural communities and their diversities, of ethnicities and women of colour and visible minorities—both male and female. Otherwise our funders or the state do not hear us.[33]

Federal policies and funding procedures in Canada thus seemingly accommodate but actually constrain "special interest groups"—groups based on preformed identity categories—by charting difference in ways that emphasize exclusion. The fight for recognition among differently marginalized groups promotes hostility and competition, particularly as groups tend to hold great investment in their collective identities. The act is thus designed to benefit white Canadians, reflecting the ways in which white ruling classes attempt to control ex-colonials, and it does not seriously pose challenges to white hegemony.[34]

Anti-racist theories help illuminate the weaknesses of multiculturalist arguments. By considering how multiculturalism functions to regulate citizenry participation of immigrant and non-white ethnocultural groups in limited and specific ways, they can account for the ongoing exclusion and devaluation of racialized minorities both within the Canadian nation and the imagining of a queer nation. For instance, by acknowledging the legacies of European colonialism that continue to pervade Canada's legislative policies and practices, we can address the limits of attempting to establish a queer nation within Canada, a movement that will likewise mirror and reproduce the dominant social hierarchies of race, class, and gender.

On the other hand, queer theory helps to illuminate how multiculturalist paradigms enforce and sustain heteronormative definitions of community. Asian communities in Canada are frequently described, for example, as heterosexual communities and are exclusively associated by blood-family ties.

Anti-racist scholar Polly Pagenhart argues for the (re)examination of the language and logic of multiculturalism "because the rhetoric of cultural pluralism—deeply flawed though it may be—is . . . cunning; for it has been the most effective means of placing large endeavours to study oppression in mainstream institutions."[35] She further contends that there is a growing awareness and inclusion of sexuality as a power-laden signifier in North America. In other words, just as discourses of multiculturalism have become palatable to the mainstream, queer has become trendy. There is cultural and hence political currency with the term "queer," so strategically it seems relevant and necessary to mobilize and seize that opportunity in education: "[T]he advent of queer studies in the academy at this historical moment—after ethnic studies and women's studies—provides a rare opportunity for this new antioppressionist field to learn from the exclusionary mistakes made by its predecessors. Their early underpinnings have been based on an un- or underinterrogated sexism or racism (and for both, heterosexism), reinforced by inadequate constructions of identity."[36]

By simultaneously theorizing queerness and race in relation to the Canadian nation, queer and anti-racist theory may help to disrupt hegemonic understandings of the Canadian national narrative as white, masculine, and heterosexual. Perhaps more importantly, by drawing attention to constructions of citizenship as both historically and presently constituted, queer and anti-racist theories may pose challenges to norms around ideologies and practices that define who can and cannot belong to the nation.

Furthermore, because queer theory works to unpack the notion of fixed identity, it lends itself to anti-racist strategies in theorizing identities as socially constructed—by demonstrating how identities are produced through discursive and institutionalized structures of representation—and not inherent or essential. The corresponding anti-racist argument contends that notions of racial difference—and the orders of power associated with perceived differences—are transformable.

CONCLUSION

In her essay on Asian/American sexualities, Dana Y. Takagi maintains that examining the silences around the topic of sexuality may enable us to better comprehend political identity formations: "[O]ne way that homosexuality may be seen as a vehicle for theorizing identity in Asian America is for the missteps, questions, and silences that are often clearest in collisions at the margins."[37] She further contends that "marginalization is no guarantee for dialogue,"[38] but emphasizes the political importance of attempting to establish a constructive dialogue between positions of difference—especially when "difference meets itself—queer meets Asian, black meets Korean, feminist meets Greens, etc., at times, all in one person."[39]

In the different spaces of queer and anti-racist classrooms, moments of silence, silencing, and self-silencing are often generated by the difficulties of conceptualizing the interconnections between race and sexuality. Mona Oikawa remarks on the contradictory position of "visibility/invisibility" that many racialized queers experience in different spaces. She contends that "identities become fragmented and marginalized in settings when they are treated as minority, exotic, unique, even perverse. This is done through processes that either render them invisible or render them as larger than life, where only part (or parts) of us are called upon to be seen or to speak."[40] Consequently, this can affect how racialized queers discuss certain parts of our identities in different contexts. For example, a queer Asian may not feel safe to address heterosexism and homophobia in the Asian Canadian community and feel resentful of the expectation that a queer person of color should instruct white queers with a comprehensive analysis of gender, race, class, and sexuality.

For me, racism and heterosexism become glaringly apparent in these different classroom spaces according to the identity I feel is not being recognized. However, I must recognize that I too have been blinded to other marginalized aspects of identity that I do not share and that have undoubtedly contributed to the silencing of others. I must also assume that knowledge is not neutral but influenced by human interests, that all knowledge reflects the power and social relationships within society, and that an important principle of knowledge production is to help people improve society.

In order to address my responsibility as a transformative academic scholar, as an anti-racist, queer activist, and an Asian Canadian dyke, I must keep questioning, taking risks, and pushing the boundaries of silence. If, following Anzaldua's claims, "naming myself is a survival tactic,"[41] there is a clear political strategy in naming a more specific identity as an Asian Canadian dyke/queer; I face the responsibility of interrogating the inter-connected and complex relationships between race, nation, and sexuality.

In this chapter, I have thus attempted to reexamine my position around the constructed silences that arise during conversations about race and sex-uality, and through this process, I have tried to continue those conversa-tions. I have interrogated the concepts of queer identity, queer theory, and anti-racist theory, pointing to the limits and exclusionary tendencies of both queer and racial identity formations and politics. I argued that anti-racist theories help illuminate the ways in which queer ideologies and po-litical strategies fall in line with the logic of multiculturalism in Canada and, in doing so, lead to more nuanced and complex understandings of dif-ference and exclusion. As such, the mediation of queer and anti-racist the-ories enable transformative ways of approaching and envisioning anti-oppression education both in the classroom and beyond.

NOTES

*I would like to thank the editors, Heather Sykes, Richard Fung, and Cassandra Lord, for their encouraging feedback and suggestions on this chapter. Of course, all limitations and oversights remain my own.

1. Let me clarify my use of the term "Asian" here. In this paper, I use "Asian" to re-fer to racialized peoples of East and Southeast Asian descent who are socially and po-litically constructed and perceived as "yellow" in Canada. Richard Fung describes the geopolitical specificities associated with the term "Asian" in various diasporic contexts. He contends that while in Britain, "Asian" is more commonly taken to refer to people of the Indian subcontinent and Sri Lanka, in North America and particularly in Canada, many have chosen to organize explicitly as "South Asians" while "Asian" groups draw mainly from East and Southeast Asian communities. See Richard Fung, "Seeing Yellow: Asian Identities in Film and Video," in *The State of Asian America: Ac-tivism and Resistance in the 1990s*, ed. Karen Aguilar-San Juan (Boston: South End Press, 1994), 163. From a national perspective, I use the category "East and Southeast Asian" to include but not limit reference to descendants of Cambodian, Chinese (Hong Kong, China), Japanese, Korean, Filipino, Laos, Thai, and Vietnamese countries. My claim to the category "Asian," although problematic, is politically strategic.

2. In this limited investigation, I make broad references to the term "queer" by aligning it with a form of theory and as an umbrella term encompassing the sexual identities "lesbian," "gay," "bisexual," "transgendered," "transsexual," and "inter-sexed." See Annamarie Jagose, *Queer Theory: An Introduction* (New York: New York

University Press, 1996). This chapter largely seeks to distinguish between the understanding of "queer" as an identity (where it is employed by individuals and institutions to categorize a broad range of non-heterosexual identities) and "queer" in its theoretical sense.

3. Dana Y. Takagi has described the fraught relationship that Asian/Americans have with the concept of silence. She argues that in popular understandings of Asian/American identity, silence has functioned as a metaphor for the assimilative and positive imagery of the "good" (model) minority. However, Takagi further explains, "analysis of popular imagery of the 'model minority' suggests that silence is understood as an adaptive mechanism to a racially discriminatory society rather than as an intrinsic part of Asian American culture." See Dana Y. Takaki, "Maiden Voyage: Excursion into Sexuality and Identity Politics in Asian America," in *Asian American Sexualities: Dimensions of the Gay and Lesbian Experience*, ed. R. Leong (New York: Routledge, 1996), 26.

4. Mona Oikawa, "Exclusion/Inclusion," in *Privileging Positions: The Sites of Asian American Studies*, ed. G. Y. Okihiro et al. (Pullman: Washington State University Press, 1994), 267.

5. Sarita Srivastava, "Song or Dance: The Performance of Anti-Racist Workshops," *Canadian Review of Sociology and Anthropology* 33 (3) (1996): 300.

6. Teresa de Lauretis, "Queer Theory: Lesbian and Gay Sexualities: An Introduction," *Differences: A Journal of Feminist Cultural Studies* 3 (2) (1991): iii–xviii.

7. Chantelle Nadeau, "Between Queer-and-Lesbian: Translated Politics," *Concerns* 27 (Winter 2000): 57.

8. See Wesley Crichlow, "Buller Men and Batty Bwoys: Hidden Men in Toronto and Halifax Black Communities," in *A Queer Country: Gay and Lesbian Studies in the Canadian Context*, ed. T. Goldie (Vancouver: Arsenal Pulp Press, 2001), 69–85.

9. Gloria Anzaldúa, "To(o) Queer the Writer—*Loca, escritora y chicana*," in *Living Chicana Theory*, ed. C. M. Trujillo (Berkeley, Calif.: Third Woman Press, 1998), 263–76.

10. At the same time, however, the vast majority of us in the queer classroom *were* likely united along the lines of class privilege. Class status cannot be argued to be solely determined along the lines of race or other singular axes of social difference. Importantly, the positioning of queers of color is shifting, various, and contradictory in the constant (re)organization of the global economy. In this regard, I acknowledge that as graduate students, most of us will benefit materially from the social mobility and cultural currency that comes along with the ability to navigate the higher educational system in Canada.

11. Jagose, *Queer Theory*, 82.

12. See John C. Hawley, "Introduction," in *Postcolonial, Queer: Theoretical Intersections*, ed. J. C. Hawley (Albany: State University of New York Press, 2001), 3.

13. Studies have pointed to additional limitations of queer theory in addressing, in particular, issues that pertain to transgendered and transsexual communities. The theoretical and practical tools that have attempted to address the realities of transgendered and transsexual experiences have largely been additive and inclusive in approach. As Inderpal Grewal and Caren Kaplan contend, "the binary gender model is so pervasive and universalized that it has become naturalized. In most queer studies in the United States [and Canada, as I argue], destabilization of gender binarism seems to remain in the zone of gender permutation or diversity" (see Inderpal Grewal

and Caren Kaplan, "Global Identities: Theorizing Transnational Studies of Sexuality," *GLQ: A Journal of Lesbian and Gay Studies* 7 [4] [2001]: 667). My chapter does not sufficiently acknowledge nor challenge these limitations. I thereby posit that future research must deepen our understanding of the way that sex and gender binaries operate and the ways in which they intersect with and are simultaneously constituted by and through racial categorizations. See also Vivane K. Namaste, "'Tragic Misreadings': Queer Theory's Erasure of Transgender Subjectivity," in *Invisible Lives: The Erasure of Transsexual and Transgendered People* (Chicago: University of Chicago Press), 9–23. Namaste argues that queer theory considers only certain cultural and literary objects appropriate for examination—transsexual people are ignored and eclipsed in this paradigm. Namaste thus considers the rejection of queer theory based on the political argument that it exhibits insensitivity to the substantive issues of transgendered people's everyday lives.

14. George Sefa Dei, "Basic Principles of Anti-Racism Education," in *Anti-Racism Education: Theory and Practice* (Halifax, UK: Fernwood Publishing, 1996), 25.

15. Richard A. Friend, "Choices, Not Closets: Heterosexism and Homophobia in Schools," in *Beyond Silenced Voices: Class, Race and Gender in United States Schools*, ed. L. Weis and M. Fine (New York: State University of New York Press, 1993), 209–35.

16. Kevin Kumashiro, "Queer Students of Color and Antiracist, Antiheterosexist Education: Paradoxes of Identity and Activism," in *Troubling Intersections of Race and Sexuality: Queer Students of Color and Anti-Oppressive Education* (Lanham, Md.: Rowman & Littlefield, 2001), 5.

17. Deborah P. Britzman, "Is There A Queer Pedagogy? Or, Stop Reading Straight," *Educational Theory* 45 (2) (1995): 151.

18. Kumashiro, "Queer Students," 16.

19. Merle Woo, "Forging the Future, Remembering Our Roots: Building Multicultural, Feminist Lesbian and Gay Studies," *Tilting the Tower: Lesbians Teaching Queer Subjects*, ed. L. Gerber (New York: Routledge, 1994), 163–67.

20. Kenneth P. Monteiro and Vincent Fuqua, "African-American Gay Youth: One Form of Manhood," *The Gay Teen: Educational Practice and Theory for Lesbian, Gay and Bisexual Adolescents*, ed. G. Unks (New York: Routledge, 1995), 159.

21. Monteiro and Fuqua, "African-American Gay Youth," 169.

22. See Gina Marchetti, *Romance and the "Yellow Peril": Race, Sex, and Discursive Strategies in Hollywood Fiction* (Berkeley: University of California Press, 1993).

23. David L. Eng and Alice Y. Hom, eds., *Q & A: Queer in Asian America* (Philadelphia: Temple University Press, 1998).

24. Jachinson W. Chan, "Bruce Lee's Fictional Models of Masculinity," in *Men and Masculinities* 2 (4) (2000): 371.

25. Lynne Lu, "Critical Visions: The Representation and Resistance of Asian Women," in *Dragon Ladies: Asian American Feminists Breathe Fire*, ed. S. Shah (Boston: South End Press, 1997), 17–28.

26. George Sefa Dei, "Critical Issues in Anti-Racist Research Metholodology: An Introduction," in *Critical Issues in Research Methodologies*, forthcoming.

27. Jagose, *Queer Theory*, 107.

28. For a more elaborate description of the successes and pitfalls of the Queer Nation movement in North America, see Jagose, *Queer Theory*, 108–9; and in the Canadian context, see Pauline Rankin, "Sexualities and National Identities: Re-Imagining

Queer Nationalism," *Journal of Canadian Studies* 35 (3) (2000): 176–97, and Tom Warner, *Never Going Back: A History of Queer Activism in Canada* (Toronto: University of Toronto Press, 2002).

29. Rankin, "Sexualities and National Identities," 176–97.

30. See Anne McClintock, "Family Feuds: Gender, Nationalism and the Family," in *Feminist Review* 44 (1993): 61–80.

31. Rankin, "Sexualities and National Identities," 179.

32. See Augie Fleras and J. L. Kunz, *Media and Minorities: Representing Diversity in Multicultural Canada* (Toronto: Thompson Educational Publishing, 2001); Ouida M. Wright, "Multicultural and Anti-Racist Education: The Issue of Equity," in *Weaving Connections: Educating for Peace, Social and Environmental Justice*, ed. T. Goldstein and D. Selby (Toronto: Sumach Press, 2000), 57–98; and Marilynne Boyle-Biase and M. Gillette "Multicultural Education from a Pedagogical Perspective: A Response to Radical Critiques," *Interchange* 29 (1) (1998): 17–32.

33. Himani Bannerji, *The Dark Side of the Nation: Essays on Multiculturalism, Nationalism and Gender* (Toronto: Canadian Scholars' Press, 2000), 40.

34. Rinaldo Walcott, ed., *Rude: Contemporary Black Canadian Cultural Criticism* (Toronto: Insomniac Press, 2000).

35. Polly Pagenhart, "The Very House of Difference: Toward a More Queerly Defined Multiculturalism," in *Tilting the Tower: Lesbians Teaching Queer Subjects*, ed. L. Gerber (New York: Routledge, 1994), 177.

36. Pagenhart, "Very House of Difference," 183.

37. Takagi, "Maiden Voyage," 29.

38. Takagi, "Maiden Voyage," 30.

39. Takagi, "Maiden Voyage," 30.

40. Oikawa, "Exclusion/Inclusion," 265.

41. Anzaldua, "To(o) Queer the Writer," 264.

7

The Anxiety over Borders

Fiona I. B. Ngô

In response to the specter of racial mixing at a dancehall on Sixth Avenue, journalist Marion Carter indulged in literary hysterics: "Police can do nothing in this obvious menace of young white girls with young Orientals."[1] Carter responded to the spectacle of interracial sexuality to convey the shock and horror of her own sound moral sensibilities. At the beginning of her article, Carter baited her readers:

> A langorous [*sic*] and fragile blonde floating gracefully in the arms of a Filipino! A little black haired flapper in the close and questionable embrace of a Chinaman! A Negro orchestra blaring out jazz tunes. All around, Orientals— Filipinos, Chinamen, Japanese dancing with white girls for ten cents a dance! The only white men in the place the three managers.[2]

In this passage, Asian/American men embodied a powerful threat over white women and, by extension, white men. This description of white women exaggerated their weakness, described as "languorous," "fragile," and "little." In contrast, the article posed Asian/American men as active sinners, holding white women in their arms and initiating "questionable" embraces. Neither white women, portrayed as helpless victims, nor Asian/American men, constructed as sexual menaces, fared well at the hands of the author. Denigrating both as immoral and lascivious, Carter's exposé upheld those racial and gender hierarchies that located both white women and Asian/American men as morally inferior to white men, as well as those sexual norms threatened by the pairing of white women with Asian/American men. The danger of interracial sexual unions was brought to public attention to reinforce these norms and the racial and

89

gender order, and in doing so perpetuated the heightened eroticism and thrill of forbidden encounters.[3]

Police, vice investigators, and newspaper reporters closely monitored racial mixing in jazz-filled dancehalls and nightclubs. The discourses and documents created by intense surveillance addressed themselves to complex configurations of Asianness, whiteness, and blackness; morality tales about gender, sex, and sexuality; and anxieties about national borders. This chapter concentrates on these sexualizing stories about racial mixing in New York City at the end of the Jazz Age, roughly 1929–1932. Much of this racial mixing was spurred by the spread of U.S. economic and imperial powers, particularly in the Pacific, the Caribbean, and Latin America, over the second half of the nineteenth and into the twentieth centuries. This vast empire saw waves of immigration from U.S. possessions such as Hawai'i, Guam, the Philippines, Cuba, and Puerto Rico, as well as spaces of U.S. intervention like China and Japan, to the United States in general and, in this instance, to New York City in particular. The global reach of the United States' new empire had pervasive and often perverse implications for the national imaginary writ large and for the constitution and regulation of public urban spaces.[4] Spaces of urban nightlife drew attention to the anxieties caused by the breach of national borders accompanied with unsettling crossings of gender and sexual boundaries. Press, police, and vice investigators patrolled the borders of public spaces that served as microsites of imperial logics made intimate and dangerous. For example, newspapers in New York City published regular stories about the "yellow peril" meant to define and contain the danger posed by the sexual threat of immigrant and racialized men. To monitor the public sexual contact between Asian/American men and white women, state and civil interests framed these encounters as a moral contagion that threatened to corrupt both white femininity and white masculinity. Produced by but also contributing to national debates about imperialism and immigration, the stories told about racial mixing and those efforts to control local boundaries describe a battle over the mobility and access of particular bodies to the public space of the city and, by extension, the country.[5]

While these stories sought to curtail racial mixing and argue for the exclusion of Asian/American men from public and *national* space, these same stories also demonstrated the prevalence of uncontained racial mixing. Spaces of nightlife, understood as contact zones between Asian/Americans, whites, Latinos, African Americans, and black Caribbeans, prompt the emergence of new discourses of racialization that do not just describe power relationships between white people and people of color.[6] A more complex understanding of power between racialized groups was coded in the syncopated jazz music that flowed from the bandstand to accompany sexualized movement within multiracial clubs. These were spaces of possibility and negotiation tempered by limitation. The co-presence of so many differently racialized people in clubs and dancehalls did not point to equal access to public space because racialized borders and other forms of power continued to operate. Documents such as vice reports narrated how bodies inhabiting spaces of nightlife challenged borders and were violently policed. In order to explore these arrangements of racialization, sexuality, and power, this chapter examines documents generated by press and vice investigators to trace the cultural hybridities of multiracial public spaces in general, and of Asian/American nightspots in particular. The argument then moves to a discussion of Wallace Thurman's rendering of New York City nightlife in his novel *The Blacker the Berry* . . . to further explore the use of nightclubs as a site of possibility. These profoundly dissimilar archives address the limitations of policing cross-racial sexual activity, and gesture toward histories of complex negotiations between racial identities and national borders. As important responses to the Asian/American presence in the city and in the United States, these archives foreshadow a future in which public cultures could be controlled.[7]

MULTIRACIAL NIGHTLIFE

In order to begin exploring constructions of Asian/American masculinities in these spaces of public amusement, it is important first to understand how jazz, the defining music of the age, sexualized and racialized nightclubs, dancehalls, and cabarets. Jazz itself was directly associated with blackness, and through blackness with sex and sexuality. The spaces in which jazz was played were racialized and rendered sexually licentious. The promise of sexual looseness looped through the racialization of jazz and back again. The racial coding of the genre deployed ideas about an aggressive and/or primitive black sexuality that could then be mapped onto the music and its imagined effects. Ideas about the sensual sensibilities of jazz could also be remapped onto blackness. The importance of jazz in encouraging a sexual atmosphere in these nightclubs is illustrated in the language used to describe it against other modes of dance music. One investigator reported his experience at a dancehall:

> While dancing with Helen a second time a waltz was suddenly struck up by the orchestra and I observed about 25 men leaving the floor. I said "What is the matter, the dance is not over is it?" She replied "No, the cops are here." I said "How do you know that?" She said "That's the signal. Just as soon as they come we get that and we are ordered to immediately break into a waltz."[8]

According to the report, the "six piece colored orchestra" had been playing fox-trots before breaking into the waltz at the sudden arrival of the police. Because of its reputation for overt sexuality, the hot jazz that provided the rhythm for the foxtrot was intentionally arrested under their unwelcome surveillance.

Much of the surveillance and thus visibility of Asian/American men was due to their participation in dancehall cultures in cities across the country. Bruno Lasker, a researcher from New York City commissioned by the American Council of the Institute of Pacific Relations to address the issue of Filipino immigration, noted that it was "widely conceded, among those whose business it is to watch their behaviors, that the Filipinos are unusually considerate in their dealings with women." This, it was explained, is why Filipino men had so much success in the dance halls. But Lasker downplayed this success, arguing that the women who frequented the dance halls were by and large prostitutes or women only interested in Filipino men for their money.[9] Lasker pointed out that "in several cities dance halls have been closed, not so much because their patrons were in danger from immoral Filipinos, but because professional prostitutes invaded these places in large numbers attracted by the presence of unsophisticated Filipino patrons, who are known as lavish spenders."[10] This formulation served a dual purpose. First, it constructed Filipino sexual fortune as the result of an irrational impulse, spending too much on women. Second, it identified white women in relationships with Filipino men as prostitutes.[11] This formulation served as the moral grounds for white women to stay away from Filipino men, lest they be confused with prostitutes. This type of report then sought to limit the activities of both men of color and white women.[12]

Lasker's findings were echoed in vice reports as well. Regarding a night out at the Cathedral Ballroom in Manhattan, a vice investigator noted there were "25 Chinese and Japs, among them 3 sailors. There were 15 Philipinos [sic] and Spaniards and the only white men in the premises besides myself were bouncers, and lobby guys who are not considered as patrons."[13] His description of the racial mix of the dancehall divides and groups the Chinese and Japanese together; the Filipinos and, most likely, Cubans and Puerto Ricans; and white men. Though this was a multiethnic space, and any of the male patrons could be seen as threatening the authority of white masculinity, the investigator singled out the first group for particular scrutiny.[14] He surmised: "A white man has very poor standing here, the instructresses ignore them and prefer the Chinese or Japs who spend quite some money on tickets, drinks, and besides tip the girls."[15] The investigator revealed his anxiety that these "Chinese and Japs" had been able to afford access to white women, who, as in earlier days of working-class dancehall encounters, were variously interested in making money, getting men to buy them drinks, and otherwise enjoying the attention.[16] The fact that Asian/American men had to spend a much larger sum of money in order to win the company of these women seems not to have been entirely lost on the investigator, but this did little to relieve his anxiety.

This anxious discourse centered on ideas of proper and improper sexualities. "Some of the dancing instructresses laid full length on the benches here," reported the investigator, "and some of the Orientals fooled with them while they were in that position. Also improper dancing was observed by girls and men rubbing bodies imitating the act of sexual intercourse."[17] The investigator made the stakes clear in this particular vice investigation: White women were having sex with men of color in a space where white men were virtually ignored by women. Though this might seem to be merely a case of competition, the sexualities on display at the dancehall were classified as outside of respectable norms. The Asian/American men were cast as sexual aggressors willing to go to extreme (financial) lengths to fulfill their desires, whereas the white women were branded as simply money-hungry. Though they were not thought to be immediately attractive, Asian/American men were rendered as hypersexual and white women as available for their appetites in spaces like these multiethnic, multiracial dancehalls. The evidence cited in the report points to the sinister success of Asian/American men in seducing or being seduced by white women. As such the report produced Asian/American masculinity as simultaneously threatening *and* thrilling.

While these investigative accounts give us a sense of who frequented dancehalls and how Asian/American men in particular embodied an intoxicating danger, the style in which these "facts" were reported does not offer much insight about how the racial mixing and related transgressions might themselves be the allure of dancehalls. More colorful newspaper articles, like the one penned by Marion Carter, were written in response to the dilemmas introduced by the increasing presence of Asian/American men in dancehalls and in nightclubs. One such 1929 article centered on the Bamboo Inn, a Harlem nightspot owned by a Chinese man by the name of Lee Shu, and which reportedly boasted a significant base of Asian/American patrons.[18] The article described the establishment as a "transplanted bit of Mott St. whose oriental setting seems strangely out of place in the center of the capital of colored America."[19] The Bamboo Inn was purportedly adorned in an Oriental motif, and the presence of Asian/American men among both patrons and management certainly added to the unusual feeling of the space for the white reporter.

Though the space may have appeared exotic by design, it was the racial mix that the reporter thought newsworthy. He noted: "Men of the mysterious lands of the Far East—Hindus, Japanese, Chinese, Malays—rub elbows on the dance floor with West Indians and colored folk from all parts of America . . . a man of any color may walk in accompanied by a woman of any color—or with no woman at all."[20] The author's amazement concentrated on unusual sexual pairings—not necessarily queer pairings, but especially pairings that challenged racial boundaries. This challenge was also a challenge to those racial hierarchies that identified white men as the sole agents of masculine agency and sexual power. Though the article did not condemn the Harlem nightclubs described, and instead illustrated their pleasures, the author nonetheless orientalized the space of the Bamboo Inn through such scenes of exotic sexuality. In articulating the differences between this nightclub and what might be considered a respectable establishment, he reiterated powerful racial hierarchies and sexual norms. In other words, by making the clubs seem all the more foreign for the social transgressions occurring there, the author reiterated that whiteness defined moral measure and proper culture, and that the Orient and racial mixing disrupted this social order.

MIXED-RACE METAPHORS

The black writers of the Harlem Renaissance were also interested in the implications of racial mixing in the public city. Wallace Thurman addressed some these questions in his creation of the multiracial character Alva in his novel *The Blacker the Berry* . . . (1929). Thurman was particularly interested in the play of social and cultural identities in the rapidly shifting racial environment of New York City, and the presence of racial mixing and Asian/Americans in spaces of nightlife was not lost on him. Thurman adopted orientalist themes and Asian/American issues in two of his novels, *The Blacker the Berry* . . . and *Infants of the Spring* (1932).

Thurman belonged to a younger generation of artists to emerge as part of the Harlem Renaissance who, historian Martin Summers argues, "constructed and performed their gender subjectivity through the elevation of the physical and sexual potency of the body, consumption and self-gratification, and an individual self-expression that was not confined by the black bourgeoisie's standards of propriety."[21] Exploring these new ideas about the embodied performance of black masculinity, Thurman's work interrupted sexual, racial, and gender debates in important ways. Though much of the debate about race in Harlem focused on black/white relations, he pushed to include Asian/Americans.[22] Interested in the changing meanings of public space as Asian/Americans changed its demographics, he turned discourses about miscegenation away from a strict dichotomy. He further troubled the dialogue about miscegenation by introducing queer sexualities into these predominantly heteronormative conversations.[23]

Thurman pursued these interruptions in part through the metaphors modeled by mixed-race characters to examine the interplay of race in urban space.[24] And while deploying mixed-race identities to represent the racial and national borders that were being drawn and redrawn in the city, he also used these to pry at borders of gender and sexuality. The construction of de-

sire does not happen separately from histories of imperialism and colonialism. These histories necessarily reveal what Gayatri Gopinath calls an
"erotics of power."[25] At the point of the inclusion of Asian/American masculinity into national discourses and imperial structures of racialization
and sexuality, Thurman created a kind of queer space marked by the troubling erotics collapsing the distance between racial categories. In these
works, the metaphor and materiality of mixed-race identities was doubled
to describe the transgression of distinct sexual identities as well. This mapping of border logics did not stop here. The cultural logic that Thurman enacted in his novels was also trebled to create gender-queer characters. For
Thurman, the mixed-race metaphor became an embodied mode for expressing the anxiety of, as well as the challenge to, multiple (spatial, social,
and sexual) borders.[26]

Thurman addresses the implications of racial mixing in a fictionalized rendering of Small's Paradise, one of Harlem's most popular nightclubs. Referencing contemporary discourses about Asian/American men in the spaces of
nightlife, Thurman illustrates the allure of mixed-race men to women out for
an evening on the town. Of the first encounter between the main characters
of *The Blacker the Berry . . .*, Thurman describes Emma Lou's initial attraction
upon meeting Alva: "Some one touched her on the shoulder, and she looked
up into a smiling oriental-like face, neither brown nor yellow in color, but
warm and pleasing beneath the soft lights."[27] Alva's racial unintelligibility is
both pleasing and perplexing. When Alva asks her to dance with him,
"Emma Lou was confused, her mind blankly chaotic. She was expected to
push back her chair and get up. She did. And, without saying a word, allowed herself to be maneuvered to the dance floor."[28] In this passage, Alva's
appeal is evident, due in large measure to the erotic exoticism of racial mixing he embodied as person and promise. At the same time, this mixing in-
spires both confusion and chaos in Emma Lou. Through Alva, the novel's
main antagonist, Thurman explores a number of racialized, gendered, and
sexualized border crossings; Alva is fleshed out through complicated configurations of queerness, hypermasculinity, multiracial ambiguity, and gender
and class transgressions. Further, the character of Alva does not simply represent the precarious social position of a mixed-race man; his multiraciality
also operates as a metaphor for race relations in the city. In other words, he
stands for both a racially phenotypical and a multivalent cultural admixture.
Rather than stage his mixed-race characters as wretched or miserable, Thurman introduces a more ambivalent reading of identity. In place of the familiar trope of the tragic mulatto, Thurman imagines racial mixing as both
productive *and* destructive. He accomplishes this by portraying racial mixing
as a crucial index of gender and sexual norms and their transgression.[29]

Thurman's *The Blacker the Berry . . .* is most often studied for the color
consciousness that occurs among African Americans themselves, a practice

that Thurman abhorred.[30] Like Rudolph Fisher's "The City of Refuge" or the writings of the New Negro intellectuals, Thurman's novel works to destabilize the notion of a unified and coherent black identity for Jazz Age Harlem.[31] By interrogating the way that skin tone operated as a marker of status in black America, he argues that racialized identities were constructed according to demonstrably fallible categories.[32] This issue, however, is more complex than simply questioning those forms of racialization occurring within black communities. In his novel, Emma Lou Morgan grew up in a small black community located in Boise, Idaho, that valued light skin as a sign of status. In this community, much of the discussion around race revolved around the effort to make "good" marriages, defined by an acceptably light-skinned heterosexual partner. Emma Lou herself is the daughter of a light-skinned mulatto woman and a dark-skinned black man—a pairing that this community and Emma Lou's extended family deemed inappropriate. Emma Lou's feelings about sexuality are shaped and guided by a black and white dichotomy, color hierarchies, and heteronormativity. Worried about appearing too dark and finding a suitable partner, Emma Lou is attracted to the fairer-skinned Alva. But, of course, Alva is not just a light-skinned black man; rather, he is multiracial. As Thurman describes Alva, many of the transgressions that occurred at nightclubs like Small's are etched onto both his corporeal body and complex personhood:

> Alva's mother had been an American mulatto, his father a Filipino. Alva himself was small in stature as his father had been, small and well developed with broad shoulders, narrow hips and firm well modeled limbs. His face was oval shaped and his features were more oriental than Negroid. His skin was neither yellow nor brown but something in between, something warm, arresting and mellow with the faintest suggestion of a parchment tinge beneath, lending it individuality. His eyes were small, deep and slanting. His forehead high, hair sparse and finely textured.[33]

In this description, Alva's ambiguous racial and sexual characteristics are clear. These complexly anxious qualities, traversing formerly stable categories, foreshadow Alva's queer acts, divulged later in the novel.[34] Alva's queerness is composed at the intersections of unsettled and upset categories, and though his queerness is disparaged by the novel's narrative structure, his liminal status nonetheless affords him access to all the identifications implicated in his particular ambiguity. Alva is a mobile figure, able to accommodate a range of settings from highbrow intellectualism to falling-down-drunk, abject poverty, from heterosexual cohabitation and fatherhood to gay bachelorhood.[35] In many ways, Alva is the most compelling character of the novel, capable of both movement and dialogue with so many disparate peoples and places.

In Thurman's description, Alva's complicated racial mix, a mother who was mulatto and a father who was Filipino, also produces layered unease.[36] Alva embodies a troubled triangulation of race and racialization: part white, part black, part Asian. Thurman further identifies him as "neither yellow nor brown but something in between," though this in-betweenness is not demonized here. Rather, he uses this racial ambiguity to illustrate Alva's allure; his skin was "warm" and "arresting." In Emma Lou's first encounter with him, she notes the "pleasing foreignness of his face."[37] This blend, however, is ultimately unsuccessful and undesirable. Though from the outset it is clear what kind of man Emma Lou is looking for (a worry heightened by the "poor" marriage her light-skinned mother made with her dark-skinned father), Alva's light skin proves to be misleading and ultimately inadequate. For Emma Lou, intent on pursuing men who were lighter-skinned than she, Alva nonetheless is not an appropriate candidate. Though Emma Lou herself was a product of mixed-race couplings, her multiraciality is legible, unlike Alva's multiraciality. Alva's "parchment tinge" betrays the racial otherness that has metastasized throughout his body, the blood contamination—a failure to be black, white, or even mulatto—of all the known and legible terms.[38] Accordingly, the introduction of the Orient into a black and white equation signals corruption. Furthermore Alva's Asian-ness marks his moral and sexual depravity as neither black nor white, saving both from the horror and blame of Alva's despicable actions. Thurman deploys Asianness as a character flaw to demonize Alva, even perhaps to demonstrate that lighter was not always better. On the other hand, Alva's exotic ambiguity is rendered appealing to some (albeit dangerous) degree. Though he is not recuperated by the story, Alva's allure is relayed through his considerable knowledge and mobility as a charming guide to Harlem nightlife.

Alva's racial ambiguities cannot be separated from their gendered and sexualized dimensions.[39] The visual markers of his racial otherness are also implicated in emergent sexological discourses and its scopophilia. This new language of sexual science, as Siobhan Somerville argues, "conceptualized sexuality through a reliance on, and deployment of, racial ideologies."[40] Sexological discourses created gender, racial, and sexual classifications determining what was normal and abnormal, healthy and pathological, which Thurman employs within this novel as scenes of tension. In a textual caress, he characterizes Alva as "small in stature" with "small and well developed broad shoulders, narrow hips and firm well modeled limbs,"[41] deliberately confusing Alva's biological sex categorization as the origin of his sexual aberration, even before the novel's revelation of Alva's queer acts. Where notions of dimorphic sex often occurred through descriptions of masculine strength and bulk in contrast to feminine softness and slenderness, Alva is described as having shoulders that are simultaneously "small" and "broad," hips that are both "narrow" and "firm." Troubling the ordering mechanisms of gender and sexual categories, these sex-ambiguous physical characteristics function to prompt further anxieties about Alva's moral character, and foreshadow the disclosure of his queer sexuality near the end of the novel.[42]

Though Alva's gender transgressions can be understood as the trite feminization (or emasculation) of Asian men, Alva retains a threatening, even controlling, masculine agency that necessitates a more complicated reading of gendered power and its relationship to race and sexuality. While Alva and Emma Lou are married, Alva continues to have sexual relationships with many other characters in the novel, including bisexual Geraldine, heterosexual Marie, and queer Bobby.[43] In the climactic scene of the novel, Alva is with his male lover Bobby. In this last relationship, Alva asserts a confident and vigorous (queer) masculinity, as Bobby appears to be the more docile partner, even doing Alva's laundry for him. While Alva's queerness certainly blurs the borders of femininity and masculinity, his sexuality does not work to emasculate him. Instead, he retains a forceful and domineering masculinity. Though critics like Frank Chin and Elaine Kim might perceive homosexual acts as a means to feminize and degrade Asian/American men, this argument cannot account for queer behaviors that substantiate hierarchies of gender difference and sexual power.[44] In the novel, Alva is still considered a sexual threat despite, or perhaps because of, his deviant masculinity. He has sex with men and women, and both sets of sexual relations are undergirded with domination. His relationship with Emma Lou provides him monetary resources while his relationships with Geraldine, Marie, and Bobby function as narrative devices reinforcing his power over Emma Lou.

As Ann Laura Stoler argues, imperial orders have focused on ambiguous identities and the anxieties these created, precisely because their features do not cohere in stable or clear categories after all.[45] In much the same way that necessarily malleable social but also legal categories of blackness transformed the racial composition of the nation, Alva's transgressions confuse those discourses of gender and sexuality, racial thinking, and national boundaries that seek to locate physical and moral attributes according to a precise order. His ambiguous identities then can only be read as problematic given the conclusion of the novel. Though Alva's racial difference is at first regarded as pleasing and seductive, by story's end this difference is the key to his pathology. Portrayed as being rotten to the core, the origins of his despicable nature can be discerned in Thurman's initial physical description, in the maddening ambiguity of his visual and corporeal markers. Alva fails to be black or even mulatto; his Asianness, as his *other* queer quality, taints his character and his actions from the outset. Alva's racial excesses gesture toward and otherwise guarantee his sexual excesses. His sexual persona is marked as aberrant because he is both a shameless philanderer, repeatedly breaking his marital vows, and also queer. His dangerous unintelligibility, identified as evasive and deceiving because it cannot be indexed properly, furnish the reason why he cannot be a proper lover for Emma Lou, the novel's heroine. But to understand this danger, the tensions and outright hostilities produced by Alva's ambiguities must be read back against the empire, through which racial and sexual classifications emerged as ordering mechanisms. Those cultural and epistemic categories of race and sexuality, changed by encounters in multiple contact zones elsewhere, proliferated also at the microsites of national and cosmopolitan identity. These forms of racial thinking indexed Harlem nightlife as adventurous and stimulating because they were strange and erotic, but also unsettling and dangerous; in these sites of nightlife, the racial mixing, the presence of women, and the subsequent sexualizing of public spaces upset the social order.

While the narrative outcome prescribing Alva's Filipino blood as treacherous is consistent with the dangers associated with "yellow peril," and his mixed-race identity echoes elements of the "tragic mulatto" (both elements common to racial thinking for the era), Alva's reception and relations with other characters in the novel are more complicated and suggestively ambivalent. Though the prevalence of "yellow peril" stories might indicate that these orientalizing discourses sought to merely control and limit those subject to them, the character of Alva nonetheless hints at another mode of being in the world. Identified as threat and menace, even so Alva offers a portrait of a life lived, if not beyond then *beneath*, the stifling social order. Likewise, stories about Asian/American men in dancehalls and other spaces of public amusement illustrate anxieties about the changing demographic of the nation as it sought to extend its imperial reach. Though these stories sought to cut short the potential of those multiracial publics, the haunting presence of empire's consequence in those spaces were not, and should not, be forgotten. This kind of reading interrupts the whiteness of the American national imaginary to bring into focus histories of colonial and imperial rule and all their racial and sexual dimensions. What is offered instead is a view of the United States as a modern state defined by its imperial ambitions and domestic struggles, and of those resulting challenges and ambiguities that blur, resurrect, and create new identities from them.

NOTES

1. Marion Carter, "Fragile Blondes Float over Dance Floor in Arms of Filipino Partners," *New York Evening Journal* (28 January 1930), Committee of Fourteen Papers.

2. Carter, "Fragile Blondes."

3. Roderick A. Ferguson argues that in the contemporary moment of globalization, "the regulation and transgression of gender and sexuality are the twin expressions of racial formation." Arguably, the same was true in this earlier time period, even if the expression and structure were different. Ferguson, *Aberrations in Black: Toward a Queer of Color Critique* (Minneapolis: University of Minnesota Press, 2004), 145.

4. For example, the Johnson-Reed Immigration Act of 1924 was created in an attempt to control the population of the United States, favoring peoples from Western Europe over peoples from these imperial sites. For more on how legislation works to create national and racialized identities, see Lisa Lowe, *Immigrant Acts: On Asian American Cultural Politics* (Durham, N.C.: Duke University Press, 1996); Ian F. Haney López, *White by Law: The Legal Construction of Race* (New York: New York University Press, 1996); and Lisa Marie Cacho, "The People of California Are Suffering: The Ideology of White Injury in Discourses of Immigration," in *Cultural Values* 4 (4) (2000): 389–418.

5. Following the logic of Hazel V. Carby's arguments about the use of the figure of the mulatto as a "narrative device of mediation" in *Reconstructing Womanhood*, Siobhan B. Somerville argues that writings about interracial sexualities can function as "literary vehicles for exploring culturally specific structures of racialization, sexuality, and power." Siobhan B. Somerville, *Queering the Colorline: Race and the Invention of Homosexuality in American Culture* (Durham, N.C.: Duke University Press, 2000), 80.

6. I borrow the term "contact zone" from Mary Louis Pratt, though here, instead of challenging frontier mythology, I want to understand the way that the nation is continuously created through racialized and sexualized contact, even within national borders because those national borders are created from within as well as from without. Mary Louis Pratt, *Imperial Eyes: Travel Writing and Transculturation* (New York: Routledge, 1992).

7. Asian/American masculinities were not constructed the same in every time period; rather, constructions of masculinity are time and place specific. For more on understanding histories of masculinities, please see Gail Bederman, *Manliness and Civilization: A Cultural History of Gender and Race in the United States, 1880–1917* (Chicago: University of Chicago Press, 1995); Brian Klopotek, "'I guess your warrior look doesn't work every time': Challenging indian Masculinity in the Cinema," in *Across the Great Divide: Cultures of Manhood in the American West*, ed. Matt Basso, et al. (New York: Routledge, 2001); and Martin Summers, *Manliness and Its Discontents: The Black Middle Class and the Transformation of Masculinity, 1900–1930* (Chapel Hill: University of North Carolina Press, 2004).

8. Anonymous, Committee of Fourteen Papers, report dated 3 January 1931.

9. Bruno Lasker, *Filipino Immigration to Continental United States and to Hawaii* (Chicago: University of Chicago Press, 1931), 99. For Filipino participation in dance-hall culture, see also 120 and 139; Carlos Bulosan, *America Is in the Heart: A Personal History* (1946) (Seattle: University of Washington Press, 1973).

10. Lasker, *Filipino Immigration to Continental United States and to Hawaii*, 99.

11. Rhacel Salazar Parreñas argues that the points of difference used to marginalize these two groups were race for the Filipino men and class for the white women. Rhacel Salazar Parreñas, "'White Trash Meets the Little Brown Monkeys': The Taxi Dance Hall as a Site of Interracial and Gender Alliances between White Working

Class Women and Filipino Immigrant Men in the 1920s and 30s," *Amerasia Journal* 24 (2) (1998): 115–34. Kevin J. Mumford calls the dancehalls the "quintessential border institution" because they hosted a homogenous group of racialized men, including Chinese, Japanese, Filipinos, blacks, and whites. Kevin J. Mumford, *Interzones: Black/White Sex Districts in Chicago and New York in the Early Twentieth Century* (New York: Columbia University Press, 1997), 53–71. Ronald Takaki also writes about this type of marginalization, particularly in his recounting of Carlos Bulosan's days in the dancehalls on the West Coast. Takaki, *Strangers from a Different Shore: A History of Asian Americans* (New York: Penguin, 1989), 339–40, 347–48.

12. For a much more hopeful reading of racial mixing in dancehalls, see Matt Garcia, *A World of Its Own: Race, Labor, and Citrus in the Making of Greater Los Angeles, 1900–1970* (Chapel Hill: University of North Carolina Press, 2001).

13. Anonymous, Committee of Fourteen Papers, report dated 2 December 1927.

14. Though Filipinos were sometimes considered Asian, they were also sometimes considered black, or white, or Spanish, depending on who was viewing them. As an illustration of the confusion over racial categories at the time, Bruno Lasker noted in 1931 that "[u]ntil lately, there has been much uncertainty concerning the Filipino's 'official' race in states that impose restrictions upon marriages between Mongolians and white. Marriages between Filipinos and white women were frequent, and it was left, apparently, to the discretion of county clerks in issuing licenses to decide on the racial membership of applicants. . . . The majority of officials seem, without any recourse to science at all, to have married Filipinos indiscriminately with white and with Japanese and Chinese girls, thus exposing themselves to the possible charge that if Filipinos should through some court decision be declared to be white, then their marriages to the Asiatic girls would be illegal." Lasker, *Filipino Immigration to Continental United States and to Hawaii*, 118.

15. Anonymous, Committee of Fourteen Papers, report dated 2 December 1927.

16. Kathy Peiss, *Cheap Amusements: Working Women and Leisure in Turn-of-the-Century New York* (Philadelphia: Temple University Press, 1986); Parreñas, "White Trash Meets the Little Brown Monkeys," 115–34.

17. Anonymous, Committee of Fourteen Papers, report dated 2 December 1927.

18. Frank Dolan, "Spider Web Lures Old Harlem Fans," *Saturday News* (2 November 1929), Committee of Fourteen Papers. The Committee of Fourteen Papers confirmed the ownership as being held by a Chinese man. Committee of Fourteen Papers, report dated 17 May 1928.

19. Dolan, "Spider Web Lures Old Harlem Fans."

20. Dolan, "Spider Web Lures Old Harlem Fans."

21. Martin Summers, *Manliness and Its Discontents*, 152.

22. The canonical historiographical texts for this time period also portray race relations in the city as being strictly between blacks and whites. See Nathan Huggins, *The Harlem Renaissance* (New York: Oxford University Press, 1971); David Levering Lewis, *When Harlem Was in Vogue* (New York: Vintage, 1979); Ann Douglas, *Terrible Honesty: Mongrel Manhattan* (New York: The Noonday Press, 1994); and Lewis A. Erenberg, *Steppin' Out: New York Nightlife and the Transformation of American Culture, 1890–1930* (Chicago: University of Chicago Press, 1981).

23. Thurman also provides a break in the African American literary canon by being explicit about his queer characters. Sharon Patricia Holland notes that African

American literature and literary criticism often marks a disappearance of queer identities. Sharon Patricia Holland, *Raising the Dead: Readings of Death and (Black) Subjectivity* (Durham, N.C.: Duke University Press, 2000), 104.

24. Hazel Carby notes that the figure of the mulatto generally served two
purposes—a way of understanding interracial contact and an expression of that
contact. Hazel V. Carby, *Reconstructing Womanhood: The Emergence of the Afro-
American Woman Novelist* (Oxford: Oxford University Press, 1989), 89.

25. Gayatri Gopinath, *Impossible Desires: Queer Diasporas and South Asian Public
Cultures* (Durham, N.C.: Duke University Press, 2005), 1–2.

26. Part of what is at stake in the policing of borders is the creation of safe spaces
for people of color, queers, and queer people of color within the nation. Lisa Marie
Cacho presciently argues that "imagined boundaries and arbitrary borders" can be
used to legitimate violence in the creation of a national imaginary. Lisa Marie Cacho, "Disciplinary Fictions: The Sociality of Private Problems in Contemporary California" (dissertation, University of California, San Diego, 2002), 1–2.

27. Wallace Thurman, *The Blacker the Berry* . . . (1929) (New York: Collier, 1970),
106–7.

28. Thurman, *The Blacker the Berry*, 107.

29. For more readings of the "tragic mullato" narrative, please see Carby, *Reconstructing Womanhood*; Somerville, *Queering the Colorline*; and Sterling A. Brown, "Negro Character as Seen by White Authors," *Journal of Negro Education* 2 (1933):
179–203.

30. For example see, Sterling A. Brown, "The American Race Problem as Reflected
in American Literature," *The Journal of Negro Education* 8 (3) (July 1939): 286; De-
von W. Carbado, Dwight A. McBride, and Donald Weise, eds., " Wallace Thurman,"
in *Black Like Us: A Century of Lesbian, Gay, and Bisexual African American Fiction* (San
Francisco: Cleis Press, 2002), 63; and Amritjit Singh and Daniel M. Scott III, "Ex-
cerpts from the Novels," in *The Collected Writings of Wallace Thurman*, ed. Amritjit
Singh and Daniel M. Scott III (New Brunswick, N.J.: Rutgers University Press, 2003),
442–44.

31. Rudolph Fisher, "The City of Refuge," in *The New Negro* (1925), ed. Alain
Locke (New York: Atheneum, 1968); Alain Locke, "The New Negro," in *The New Negro* (1925), ed. Alain Locke (New York: Atheneum, 1968).

32. For more on the logic of the construction of false categories, see Denise Riley
"Am I That Name?" Feminism and the Category of "Women" in History (Minneapolis:
University of Minnesota Press, 1990). See also Judith Butler's use of Riley in *Gender
Trouble: Feminism and the Subversion of Identity* (New York: Routledge, 1991).

33. Thurman, *The Blacker the Berry*, 97.

34. Siobhan Somerville notes that at the turn of the century, sexological texts often connected the figure of the mulatto with deviant sex categories, that "[t]he mixed-
race body evoked the mixed-gender body." Somerville, *Queering the Colorline*, 80.

35. Lillian Faderman rightly points out that Thurman displays a certain ambivalence in regards to discussions of homosexual writing because of the way he demo-
nizes male homosexuality in particular, even though he was himself queer. Lillian
Faderman, *Odd Girls and Twilight Lovers: A History of Lesbian Life in Twentieth-Century
America* (New York: Columbia University Press, 1991), 69–70. The confluence between characters in the novel and Wallace Thurman himself is also pointed out by

Mae Gwendolyn Henderson and Eleonore van Notten, who both note that, like Emma Lou, he had moved from a western town to attend the University of Southern California, then, later, moved to Harlem. Eleonore van Notten also notes that Thurman shared biographical similarities with both Alva and Truman Walter, an intellectual doppelganger. Mae Gwendolyn Henderson, "Portrait of Wallace Thurman," in *The Harlem Renaissance Remembered*, ed. Arna Bontemps (New York: Dodd, Mead & Company, 1972), 155–56; Eleonore van Notten, "Wallace Thurman's Harlem Renaissance" (Ph.D. dissertation, Leiden University, 1994), 223–40.

36. Alva is misidentified by historian Lillian Faderman as being "a black bisexual who is a scoundrel," and again by literary critic Marjorie Garber through a quotation of Faderman. This misidentification again points to both the power of blackness and the seeming invisibility of Asians in New York within the literature pertaining to the Harlem Renaissance. Lillian Faderman, *Odd Girls and Twilight Lovers*, 69; Marjorie Garber, *Vice Versa: Bisexuality and the Eroticism of Everyday Life* (New York: Touchstone, 1995), 124. An exception to this type of misidentification comes from Eugene Arden, "The Early Harlem Novel," *The Phylon Quarterly* 20 (1) (January–March 1959): 30.

37. Thurman, *The Blacker the Berry*, 128.

38. Even in contemporary scholarship, it is relatively new to speak about mixed-race pairings beyond black and white. Christine C. Iijima Hall and Trude I. Cooke Turner, "The Diversity of Biracial Individuals: Asian-White and Asian-Minority Biracial Identity," in *The Sum of Our Parts: Mixed Heritage Asian Americans*, ed. Teresa Williams-León and Cynthia L. Nakashima (Philadelphia: Temple University Press, 2001), 81.

39. Kieu-Linh Caroline Valverde and Cynthia L. Nakashima have written more on the sexualization of mixed-race individuals, particularly women. Kieu-Linh Caroline Valverde, "From Dust to Gold: The Vietnamese Amerasian American Experience," *Racially Mixed People in America*, ed. Maria P. P. Root (Newbury Park, Calif.: Sage Publications, 1992), 158; and Cynthia L. Nakashima, "An Invisible Monster: The Creation and Denial of Mixed-Race People in America," *Racially Mixed People in America*, ed. Maria P. P. Root (Newbury Park, Calif.: Sage Publications, 1992), 168–69.

40. Somerville, *Queering the Colorline*, 17.

41. Thurman, *The Blacker the Berry*, 97.

42. My reading of Alva's body comes from the recent literature devoted to intersexuals, transgendered people, and transsexuals, perhaps the fastest growing fields in gender studies. Through the theories of sex and gender produced in these sites, it is possible to view Alva's body as sexually ambiguous at a physical level and to think through the meanings of that ambiguity and how they point to the possibility of many sexes. For more on intersexuals, see Anne Fausto-Sterling, "The Five Sexes" and "How to Build a Man," in *The Gender/Sexuality Reader*, ed. Roger N. Lancaster and Micaela di Leonardo (New York: Routledge, 1997), 244–48; Cheryl Chase, "Hermaphrodites with Attitude," *GLQ* 4 (2) (1998): 189–212. For more on transsexuals, see Kate Bornstein, *Gender Outlaw: On Men, Women, and the Rest of Us* (New York: Vintage, 1993); Bernice L. Hausman, *Changing Sex: Transsexualism, Technology, and the Idea of Gender* (Durham, N.C.: Duke University Press, 1995); Holly Devor, *FTM: Female-to-Male Transsexuals in Society* (Bloomington: Indiana University Press, 1997); Sandy Stone, "A Posttranssexual Manifesto," in *Body Guards: The Cultural Politics of*

Gender Ambiguity, ed. Julia Epstein and Kristina Straub (New York: Routledge, 1991), 280–304. Related work on the transgendered community can be found in Del Lagrace Volcano and Judith Halberstam, *The Drag King Book* (London: Serpent's Tail, 1999); Judith Halberstam, *Female Masculinity* (Durham, N.C.: Duke University Press, 1998); and David Valentine, *Imagining Transgender: An Ethnography of a Category* (Durham, N.C.: Duke University Press, 2007).

43. Though Alva might be considered queer because his sex acts were non-normative, he may not have been considered homosexual because homosexual acts were not necessarily connected to homosexual identities. In other words, simply because Alva had sex with men did not mean that Alva was considered homosexual. As George Chauncey notes, in early twentieth-century New York, effeminate men may have been labeled as "fairies" and considered homosexual, but if men behaved in a masculine manner, they were not necessarily considered homosexual. George Chauncey, *Gay New York* (New York: Basic Books, 1994).

44. Frank Chin, "Come All Ye Asian American Writers of the Real and Fake," in *The Big Aiiieeeee! An Anthology of Chinese American and Japanese American Literature*, ed. Jefferey Paul Chan, Frank Chin, Lawson Fusao Inada, and Shawn Wong (New York: Meridian, 1991); Elaine Kim, "Asian Americans and American Popular Culture," *Asian American History Dictionary*, ed. Robert H. Kim (New York: Greenwood Press, 1986), 99–114. Works on Asian/American masculinities that critique these positions, particularly Chin's, are Richard Fung, "Looking For My Penis: The Eroticized Asian in Gay Video Porn," in *Asian American Sexualities: Dimensions of the Gay and Lesbian Experience*, ed. Russell Leong (New York: Routledge, 1996), 181–98; David L. Eng, *Racial Castration: Managing Masculinity in Asian America* (Durham, N.C.: Duke University Press, 2001); and Daniel Y. Kim, *Manhood in Black and Yellow: Ralph Ellison, Frank Chin, and the Literary Politics of Identity* (Stanford, Calif.: Stanford University Press, 2006). For work on queer Filipino men in the later twentieth century, see also Martin F. Manalansan IV, *Global Divas: Filipino Gay Men in the Diaspora* (Durham, N.C.: Duke University Press, 2003); Victor Bascara, "'A Vaudeville Against Coconut Trees': Colonialism, Contradiction, and Coming Out in Michael Magnaye's *White Christmas*," in *Q&A: Queer in Asian America*, ed. David L. Eng and Alice Y. Hom (Philadelphia: Temple University Press, 1998), 95–114; Gil Mangaoang, "From the 1970s to the 1990s," in *Asian American Sexualities: Dimensions of the Gay and Lesbian Experience*, ed. Russell Leong (New York: Routledge, 1996), 101–11.

45. Ann Laura Stoler, *Carnal Knowledge and Imperial Power: Race and the Intimate in Colonial Rule* (Berkeley: University of California Press, 2002), 144.

8

An Interview with Pauline Park

Based on interviews conducted August 22, 2004, and January 3, 2005

*What does transgender mean? Can you distinguish between transgender and gay/
lesbian/bisexual for the reader?*

"Transgender" is an umbrella term that refers to a diverse population. The
transgender community includes a number of different subgroups, such as
transsexuals, cross-dressers, and gender-queers (gender-variant individuals
who may not identify with either gender). Some (including many but not
all transsexuals) will seek sex reassignment surgery while others will not;
some will present fully in the gender opposite their birth sex at least part of
the time (transgendered people), while others will not; but in its most general sense, "transgender" refers to those individuals who "transgress" gender boundaries in some sense and to some degree. The most important
point is that gender identity and sexual orientation are two entirely different phenomena; the common misconception that all transgendered people
are gay is belied by the fact that many (perhaps most) transgendered people are heterosexual, though many are lesbian, gay, or bisexual as well. Gender identity has to do with how one feels about one's gender (whether one
feels oneself to be a boy or girl, man or woman), while sexual orientation
has to do with whom one is attracted to.

*Given that this anthology addresses issues of "embodiments," could you comment
on what "embodiments" means for you as a transgender person?*

Like every other human being, I am "embodied" in that I occupy a physical
body. Many transgendered people are uncomfortable in their bodies or
even alienated from them. Some who identify as transsexual seek to alter

their body through hormones and surgery. Unlike some other transgendered women, I am comfortable occupying a male body, and I see no contradiction between being male-bodied and identifying as a woman. For me, sex and gender are two very different things.

Please narrate your "coming out" as a transgender person. Did religion impact your coming out process? If so, how?

I was born in Korea and adopted by American parents of European descent who were Christian fundamentalists and who had homophobic attitudes and very conservative views on gender roles. Transgender issues were never discussed. To that extent, my coming out as gay (at the age of seventeen) coincided with my rebellion against my mother's religious and political views (my father died when I was twelve going on thirteen). I had my second coming out at the age of thirty-six and have been living as an openly transgendered woman since then. But while my public coming out as a gay boy preceded that as a transgendered woman by nearly twenty years, in fact, I realized I was transgendered at the age of four, long before I began to identify as gay, and I always knew that the gay male identity that I adopted was a tentative and incomplete one that did not fully address my gender identity. I first began to "cross-dress" regularly in public at the age of twenty-one, but I went back in the "tranny closet" two years later and so my gender transition was far less linear and far more complicated than my gay "coming out" narrative.

Could you elaborate on what a "tranny closet" is? How is it different from the "gay closet"? Were there differences being in the "tranny closet" within gay versus straight communities? For example, what were the reasons for staying in the closet among those different groups?

The "tranny closet" is somewhat different from the "gay closet" insofar as transgender identity generally has more implications for one's public presentation. After all, a gay man is probably going to still present as a man, and a lesbian as a woman, even though they may be somewhat gender-variant. But a transgendered man or woman may significantly or even profoundly alter his/her gender presentation. So to that extent, "tranny closet" may literally involve what is in one's clothes closet. But in a less literal and a deeper sense, the alteration of identity may be more profound and life-altering for many transgendered people than for non-transgendered LGB (lesbian, gay, bisexual) people. Because of this, the process of "coming out" of that "closet" may be more complex for the transgendered. In my case, for example, my coming out as a gay male was much simpler and more linear than my coming out as a transgendered woman. There are some differences between coming out in the LGB community versus coming out in straight society; while there is still some prejudice within the LGB people, the transgenderphobia in straight society is much more pervasive and much more intense. It was partly for those reasons that I remained in the "tranny closet" as long as I did. I was particularly concerned about the potentially deleterious impact on my professional career.

Could you elaborate on the different issues of "coming out" versus "passing"? How are such issues different for a transsexual person versus a gay/lesbian person versus a gender-queer person versus a cross-dresser?

The term "passing" originates in the experience of light-skinned African Americans who could "pass" for white and would live as if they were born white, concealing their black racial and cultural origins. "Passing" for a transgendered person refers to the experience of being perceived as gendernormative. In other words, a transgendered woman "passes" when everyone around her regards her as a female-born woman without realizing that she is transgendered (i.e., was born male).

"Coming out" and "passing" are very different experiences, and, in some circumstances, they may even be opposed to each other. For example, there is a certain proportion of post-op transsexuals who live "stealth," concealing their transgender identity and living in their chosen gender as if they were born into that sex. In other words, a post-op MTF (male-to-female) may pretend that she was born female and conceal from neighbors, co-workers, and others the fact that she was really born male, or an FTM (female-to-male) transsexual may live as a man without revealing to others that he was actually born female.

For me, "coming out" means living as an openly transgendered woman, not in any way attempting to conceal my male birth and anatomy. That does not mean, of course, that I always alert strangers to my transgender identity; on the street, I do not wear a button saying, "I'm really male," or anything of that sort. Safety is important to me, as it is to everyone, but as long as my personal security is not at risk, I am very open about my being transgendered.

For part-time cross-dressers, by definition, it is not a question of living as transgendered women. But there is still an issue of disclosure, as spouses, family members, friends, and colleagues usually would not know unless told. Many, if not most, cross-dressers are closeted, and some are completely closeted (i.e., they only cross-dress alone, in the privacy of their own homes).

"Passing" for lesbians and gay men would mean passing as "straight." Some lesbians are sufficiently feminine, and some gay men sufficiently masculine, that they can pass relatively easily; others may be sufficiently gender-variant that it would be difficult for them to pass, and others may assume that they are gay based on their gender variance.

What led you to create the New York Association for Gender Rights Advocacy (NYAGRA) and what is its function?

NYAGRA is the first statewide transgender advocacy organization in New York. We founded NYAGRA in June 1998, because at the time there was no such organization and none that was involved in the legislative arena at the state or local level. NYAGRA's mission is to advocate for freedom of gender identity and expression for all; we do so through public education and public policy advocacy. Our public education efforts include public forums on transgender and intersex issues and transgender sensitivity training for social service providers, AIDS agencies, government agencies, and community-based organizations. But we are best known for our legislative work—in particular, for having led the successful campaign for Int. No. 24 (Local Law 3 of 2002), the transgender rights bill that passed the New York City Council in April 2002. NYAGRA was also instrumental in negotiating inclusion of gender identity and expression in the text of the Dignity for All Students Act, a safe schools bill currently pending in the New York state legislature that would prohibit discrimination and harassment in public schools throughout the state. In 2004, NYAGRA partnered with other LGBT (lesbian, gay, bisexual, transsexual) organizations in mounting a series of public forums on discrimination and harassment in schools based on gender identity and expression, held in cities throughout the state (Nyack, Albany, Syracuse, Ithaca, and Poughkeepsie). NYAGRA was a founding member of the coalition working to educate members of the New York state legislature on the need for the Dignity for All Students Act. NYAGRA also co-founded the coalition supporting the Dignity in All Schools Act, a safe schools bill passed by the New York City Council in June 2004 and enacted when the council overrode Mayor Bloomberg's veto of the bill in September 2004. The NYC law prohibits harassment in public and (non-religious) private schools in the five boroughs, and features a definition of gender that includes gender identity and expression.

California passed Assembly Bill (AB) 537, the California Student Safety and Violence Act, in 2000. One of the continuing struggles for the coalition that worked to pass and now to enforce this legislation is the inclusion of transgender issues. Please elaborate on NYAGRA's work with the DASA coalition. What, if anything, did you learn from other local LGBT activist organizations around the country, such as Seattle's Safe Schools Coalition (which started in the late 1980s) and the

Los Angeles Unified School District's Project 10 (which started in the mid-1980s), who have dealt with similar struggles? How did national efforts such as the Human Rights Watch "Hatred in the Hallways" study or the work of GLSEN (Gay, Lesbian, Straight Education Network) inform activist activities in New York?

We in NYAGRA try to keep abreast of developments in other states, including California, but the only thing that I can recall influencing our thinking working on the New York state DASA bill was our recognition that the California state legislature was able to include gender identity and expression in their safe schools legislation without mentioning that language explicitly simply by referencing protected categories already included in California state law through its state hate crimes statute; we were not able to consider that possibility in New York because the New York State Hate Crimes Bill Coalition was not willing to hold up that hate crimes bill to include gender identity and expression in that legislation. GLSEN is one of the member organizations in the NYS DASA Coalition, and NYAGRA has worked in partnership with GLSEN on our series of public forums on the issue of gender identity and expression in the NYS DASA bill. But GLSEN's support for the safe schools bill introduced in Congress in late 2004 by U.S. Rep. John Shimkus of Illinois (R-19th) raised questions within the LGBT community about GLSEN's commitment to full transgender inclusion in safe schools legislation at the state and federal levels.

Regarding the NYS DASA bill, it was NYAGRA that negotiated inclusion of gender identity and expression in that legislation so that it became the first fully transgender-inclusive bill ever introduced into the New York state legislature when it was reintroduced in 2000. Persuading the NYS DASA Coalition to support a transgender-inclusive bill was not easy. Both the Empire State Pride Agenda and GLSEN (which co-coordinated the coalition through 2004) initially resisted inclusion of the definition of gender in the bill. But we were eventually able to persuade the Pride Agenda and then GLSEN, and through the Pride Agenda we were able to persuade the prime sponsor of the bill in the assembly, assembly member Steve Sanders, chair of the assembly education committee. Ever since then, the coalition has stood by full transgender inclusion, though in the spring of 2004, there was some interest on the part of ESPA and GLSEN in exploring compromise language similar to that in the Florida DASA bill, which we in NYAGRA do not regard as being sufficiently transgender inclusive. That bill puts the phrase "identity or expression of" before the list of protected categories (including gender) but does not include a definition of gender or any other transgender-explicit language.

Do you foresee joining forces with other transgender groups to form a national organization for transgender people?

There already is a national organization: the National Center for Transgender Equality (NCTE). While we don't have a formal coalitional relationship with NCTE (NCTE is not a coalition or a national organization with state chapters), NYAGRA has co-sponsored events with NCTE, including a forum in New York City in December 2002 (co-sponsored by NGLTF [National Gay and Lesbian Task Force]).

Do you work with gay/lesbian organizations in New York? What about national gay/lesbian organizations like HRC (Human Rights Campaign) or NGLTF? In other words, where do you see your organization fit into other queer movements and efforts? Is the trend toward a merging of queer movements to fight for freedom on gender and sexual expressions? Or do trans and gay/lesbian have such different issues that they will remain separate organizations?

We work with a wide range of lesbian/gay and LGBT organizations in New York City and state. Our primary partner to date has been the Empire State Pride Agenda and (on education issues, including safe schools legislation) GLSEN. We have also had some limited opportunities to work with both HRC and NGLTF, both of which supported our campaign for Int. No. 24 (the transgender rights bill passed by the NYC Council in April 2002, enacted as Local Law 3 of 2002). But we also signed onto a letter from the Task Force in December 2004 that was highly critical of HRC for suggesting that it might support social security privatization in exchange for support from the Bush administration and Republican majorities in Congress for movement on LGBT rights legislation.

We in NYAGRA see ourselves as part of a larger LGBT community, and we have played a significant role in the shift toward greater transgender inclusion here in New York. For example, NYAGRA is a key part of the Coalition for Unity and Inclusion (CUI), which successfully lobbied the Lesbian and Gay Community Services Center to change its name to LGBT Community Center (aided significantly by the internal work on transgender inclusion by center staff). NYAGRA and CUI also successfully persuaded Heritage of Pride to change the name of the NYC Lesbian and Gay Pride March to "LGBT Pride March." And we were successful in persuading the NewFest to change the name of the New York Gay and Lesbian Film Festival to "LGBT Film Festival." Beyond nomenclature, since its founding in 1998, NYAGRA has contributed significantly to the shift in consciousness in New York City and state toward transgender inclusion. When we were founded in June 1998, few lesbian and gay organizations in New York City included the "T" in their names, much less included transgender in their mission statements, their programming, or their thinking more generally; now, most do in name as well as in practice.

But we in NYAGRA also see ourselves as part of a larger progressive movement for social justice and social change; not all LGBT organizations share that philosophy.

What are the particular challenges facing transgender Asian/Americans and Pacific Islander/Americans?

Transgendered Asians and Pacific Islanders (APIs), like many other transgendered people of color, face multiple oppressions based on race, ethnicity, citizenship status, and language. Many transgendered APIs are recent immigrants and have limited English-language proficiency and cultural competence. Some are undocumented and face problems related to their immigration status. Others would like to marry U.S. citizens of the same sex as their birth sex but cannot because of laws and state constitutional amendments prohibiting same-sex marriage. Others face problems changing their legal sex designation on documents issued either by U.S. government agencies or by government agencies in their country of birth (such as birth certificates issued by their municipalities of origin). Some transgendered API women—especially those who are undocumented—are forced into sex work and face heightened risk of HIV infection and other sexually transmitted diseases. Many transgendered APIs lack health insurance and/or full access to quality health care. Many transgendered APIs are reluctant to approach social service providers in their ethnic communities for fear of discrimination or being "outed," but those with limited English-language proficiency and cultural competence may find it difficult to access services through LGBT community centers and other LGBT social service providers. Given the centrality of the family in API communities, one of the biggest challenges for transgender APIs is gaining acceptance from their families of origin. Religious institutions also figure prominently in many API communities, but few are transgender-affirming. Christian churches in the Korean American community tend to be socially conservative and are often homophobic and transgenderphobic. The Roman Catholic Church is also a central institution in the Filipino community, with implications for transgendered Filipinos. For transgendered immigrants from predominantly Muslim countries (Pakistan, Bangladesh, Malaysia, Indonesia), the increasing influence of Islamic fundamentalism has further complicated their lives, already difficult because of the sex segregation and gender oppression of their immigrant communities and cultures of origin.

The API transgender issues are diverse. Is there a common issue that the majority of API transgendered people share that distinguishes them from non-API transgenders? We see, in Los Angeles for example, gay/lesbian groups splintering into smaller racial, gender, and ethnic groups. Is the trend similar in the transgender communities (between FTMs and MTFs; transsexuals who identify as straight versus gay/lesbian or bisexual, etc.)?

I think this question raises the larger issue of what is often referred to as "identity politics." There is certainly a trend throughout the LGBT community toward narrower and narrower focus in organization-building based on identity formations. The right wing is enamored of the term "Balkanization." I think the use of this term shows an ignorance of the need of marginalized groups to address the specificity of their oppression. Clearly, transgendered APIs have in common both being transgendered and being API, but transgendered API women in particular also have the commonality of being "fetishized" as "exotic" objects of sexual interest by straight "tranny chasers"; they also share the other multiple oppressions of queer APIs that relate to race, ethnicity, and citizenship status; and they share heightened risk for HIV/AIDS and other STDs. And yet, of course, transgendered APIs are individuals who are very different in other respects as well.

What resources are available for transgender Asian/Americans?

The resources available for transgendered APIs (as distinct from resources available to the transgender community as a whole) are virtually all housed in AIDS agencies serving API communities, including:

- Asian and Pacific Islander Wellness Center (San Francisco), www.api-wellness.org.
- Asian Pacific Islander Coalition on HIV/AIDS (APICHA, New York), www.apicha.org.
- Asian Pacific AIDS Intervention Team (APAIT, Los Angeles), www.apait online.org.
- AIDS Services in Asian Communities (ASIAC, Philadelphia), www.asiac .org.

Which texts (books, films, etc.) do you find particularly useful for educational purposes?

There are all too few resources on transgender and queer API issues currently available. Among the few that I find useful are:

- David L. Eng and Alice Hom, eds., *Q&A: Queer in Asian America* (Philadelphia: Temple University Press, 1998).
- Kevin K. Kumashiro, ed., *Restoried Selves: Autobiographies of Queer Asian/ Pacific American Activists* (New York, London, Oxford: Harrington Park Press, 2003).

- Franklin Odo, ed., *The Columbia Documentary History of the Asian American Experience* (New York: Columbia University Press, 2002).
- Ann Thomson Cook, *Made in God's Image: A Resource for Dialogue about the Church and Gender Differences* (Washington, D.C.: Dumbarton United Methodist Church, 2003).
- *Georgie Girl* (P.O.V. documentary about the life of Georgina Beyer).
- *Boys Don't Cry* (feature film).

9

Public Agendas and Private Struggles

Khmer Girls in Action

Sora Park Tanjasiri, Cynthia Choi, Sophya Chum, Phiravy Chung, Que Dang, Mary Anne Foo, Ra Pok, and Diep Tran

The politics of gender and power occur at many levels—between individuals, individuals and their social groups, and groups and larger organizations—with devastating or empowering impacts on those involved. We focus on processes and effects that occur between public organizations and the communities of color that they purport to represent and serve. Power plays between such groups are not often displayed in the public arena, since organizational and community unity is often needed to push larger advocacy agendas and actions, particularly when organizing involves women of color issues.[1] But dissention "within" is a natural aspect of community organization processes, with empowerment starting only after oppressed people define, act against, and reflect upon the root problems that affect their lives. According to Paulo Freire, such a "conscientization" process rejects "assistencialism" (the attack of symptoms rather than causes of social ills) in order to create challenges by subordinate groups over their subordinators.[2] Thus, tensions between organizational advocacy agendas and community needs provide the opportunity for such action and reflection, leading to the self-determination of people against their "advocates."

In this chapter, we chronicle the gender and power relationships that unfolded between a statewide Asian advocacy agency in Oakland, California, and a local community of Cambodian girls in Long Beach, California. California is home to the largest Asian population (4.56 million in 2003) in the continental United States, while Long Beach is home to the largest population of Cambodians outside of Cambodia (20,065 were counted in 2000, although unofficial community estimates are more than double).[3] Cambodian/Americans in Southern California possess low levels of formal education (with 54 percent having less than a high school degree) and high

115

poverty (with 36 percent below the federal poverty level); many are not only linguistically isolated but also illiterate in their own language (Khmer).[4] The birthrate among teens age fifteen to seventeen years in Long Beach is two times higher than the state, and Cambodian girls are at high risk due to not only poverty but also the lack of hope and ability to overcome their many community challenges.[5] While several published accounts exist of the advocacy agency's work on behalf of the Cambodian girls in Long Beach,[6] none have captured the gender-related power struggles between the agency and the community that ultimately led to the creation of a new, empowered, and self-determined organization of and for Cambodian girls.

THE PUBLIC EVOLUTION OF
COMMUNITY ENGAGEMENT AND ADVOCACY

Throughout its history, this Asian/American advocacy agency had many incarnations, as evidenced by different agency names, changing lead staff and board members, and, most importantly, divergent theories of how to best promote progressive advocacy agendas in both Asian Pacific Islander (API) ethnic and mainstream communities. Asian Pacific Islanders for Choice (APIC) began in 1989 as a group of politically progressive Asian women who recognized the need to mobilize women in the API community to support women's reproductive right to legal abortions. In its early years, APIC's many volunteers engaged with ethnic and mainstream organizations to define a frame for their work. In 1992, APIC changed its name to Asian Pacific Islanders for Reproductive Health (APIRH) and established itself as an advocacy agency with paid staff and a broader mission: promoting social and economic justice for API women and girls through collaborations, outreach, education, research, advocacy, and organizing.

Throughout its first decade of operation, APIRH achieved many organizational successes, including the opening of an office in Northern California in 1995, a convening of 150 women to create a health agenda for API women and girls, and the conduct of seminal research on API reproductive health in 1991, 1995, and 1997.[7] The 1997 needs assessment study surveyed four hundred Asian girls and boys age ten to twenty-two years old in primarily Contra Costa and Alameda counties of northern California. Results highlighted many pressing reproductive-related needs, including low knowledge of self-health behaviors (such as breast self-exams and STD prevention), high rates of sexual activity, low levels of contraceptive use, and several instances of teenage pregnancies and sexual abuse.

In response to the many needs of API women and girls, APIRH undertook some new organizational efforts. The APIRH leadership identified and recruited new board members and hired a new executive director. The reorganized agency brought about the sharing of new beliefs that advocacy approaches for APIs must be grounded in leadership development for, and community engagement with, women and girls. APIRH developed a training curriculum titled the "Health, Opportunities, Problem-Solving, and Empowerment (HOPE for Girls) Curriculum." HOPE for Girls used popular education approaches to develop adolescent girls' leadership, mentorship, and organizing skills among Southeast Asian girls. Paulo Freire (1970) developed such an approach that relies on the active involvement of participants in gaining control over their lives by identifying root causes of social and community problems,[8] with empowerment achieved when individuals and communities not only question forms of power but also take back control over their health and their lives.[9]

With this curriculum, APIRH staff sought opportunities for partnership with local communities to test their leadership development and community organizing approaches. APIRH staff initiated two local training efforts involving the HOPE for Girls Curriculum. The first began in 1995 and partnered with a neighboring agency, Asian Pacific Environmental Network (APEN) in Richmond, California, to educate APEN's group of Laotian girls. With federal funding from the U.S. Department of Health and Human Services, APIRH sought to develop collaborative research methodologies to promote environmental justice in this underserved community. APIRH's component involved training ten to twelve Laotian girls, age thirteen to fifteen years old, on reproductive health and rights issues within the context of their personal growth and development, the demands of being bicultural, and their roles as "cultural ambassadors" in their homes. A qualitative evaluation of the first HOPE summer training program indicated that the curriculum was successful in increasing girls' awareness about body functioning and health, self-confidence, and self-esteem; developing a cohesive and ongoing group of engaged girls; and igniting the group's interests and capacities as participants in social justice efforts.[10]

With their first agency success in community engagement, APIRH spearheaded their own effort in 1998 to work with Cambodian girls in Long Beach, California. This latter project required APIRH, headquartered in Oakland, California, to hire and supervise local staff in Long Beach (nearly five hundred miles away) to facilitate the many trainings and discussions that were integral to the girls' empowerment and leadership development. One such discussion among the girls about sexuality led to the disclosure by two of the HOPE girls that they were the targets of inappropriate, racially, and sexually offensive remarks made by their high school social science teacher regarding their participation in APIRH's meetings with state legislators about the health needs of API women and girls. The teacher told the girls that they were "tricked" into going on the field trip and were "stupid" for participating, that "if these girls would only keep their pants on" there wouldn't be any need for teen pregnancy programs, and that the program was "anti-white" and how would the girls feel if he started a program that "eliminated Asians." Throughout this incident, the teacher used profanity and sought to embarrass and shame the students in front of their peers.[11]

Using the Freirian popular education approach, the APIRH staff led the HOPE girls through a series of discussions on racism and sexism in order to understand the power dynamics of the incident and how they fall under the larger rubric of sexual harassment. The HOPE girls eventually identified sexual harassment as a regular occurrence in their lives for which they often blamed themselves rather than the larger power structure that perpetuated poverty, racism, classism, and sexism.[12] The result of these analyses was a campaign to decrease sexual harassment in their schools, and included the following actions and activities[13]:

- A letter of protest written by an API umbrella organization, of which APIRH was a member, to the principals of the high school asking for a meeting to discuss an administrative resolution to the incident (which subsequently occurred but failed to bring about any actions against the teacher);
- A needs assessment survey spearheaded by APIRH and the HOPE girls to determine the scope of sexual harassment at the high school, which found that 87 percent of the four hundred girls surveyed had experienced some form of sexual harassment, 16 percent by a teacher or school staff person;
- A community forum on school safety organized by APIRH and HOPE to share survey results and recommend student and staff trainings on prevention and grievances;
- Passage of recommendations by the school board for mandatory sexual harassment trainings for teachers and students, student-friendly grievance procedures, and posters in every classroom defining sexual harassment and hotline information.

Throughout the two-year campaign, APIRH as an agency continued to grow and evolve in its understanding of community engagement and advocacy, and slowly began shifting away from the girls' leadership development to the use of broader community organizing goals and processes.[14] APIRH once again hired a new executive director and recruited board members who were experienced in social action organizing in order to take their analyses of reproductive health and justice issues into more direct grassroots actions for change. The selection of social action organizing was based upon interviews with board members and APIRH's organizational allies (to the exclusion of local, community-based leaders and members) and raised such politically charged issues as welfare reform, immigration, domestic violence, and occupational/environmental hazards for Southeast Asians. Despite the absence of local community members in this needs assessment, APIRH described their work as based in "participatory action research" (PAR) strategies, defined as involving community members and researchers collaboratively and equally in a process of not only co-learning, but also capacity building to improve participants' control over their lives.[15] PAR is well documented in the research literature, and was seen as ideally suited to the empowerment work promoted by APIRH for the HOPE girls in both Richmond and Long Beach. Unfortunately, many of these organizational decisions were made without adequate input from either local staff (in Long Beach) or HOPE girls, and thus contributed to a slow and growing schism within the agency and the community it purported to advocate for and serve.

BEHIND THE SCENES: ORGANIZATIONAL VERSUS MEMBER POWER IN GENDER-BASED PROGRAMS

By 2000 APIRH had defined and embraced an advocacy agenda that called for the launching of "winnable" community campaigns at the local level. APIRH's organizational success at facilitating the HOPE girls through the mobilization and implementation of the sexual harassment campaign bolstered the agency's commitment to this agenda. However, underneath the organization's exterior, evidence of turmoil grew as the same HOPE girls who participated in the campaign found themselves without the power to make organizational decisions about their own programmatic needs and destinies. The first evidence of this turmoil occurred in December 2000 with the departure of APIRH's Long Beach community organizer after only one year of service. In her letter of resignation to the APIRH executive director and board of directors, she highlighted key areas of conflict between the local (Long Beach) HOPE girls and staff, and the APIRH administrative staff in Oakland, including the lack of an organizational communication structure to facilitate collaborative and timely decisions about local organizing efforts; lack of local input into organizational personnel policies and procedures, including the hiring and firing of local staff; and a conflict-driven model of organizing that was neither appropriate nor respectful of decisionmaking within the local Southeast Asian refugee communities. Regarding the latter, one unexpected outgrowth of the sexual harassment campaign was a considerable amount of burnout among HOPE girls, several of whom simultaneously experienced disapproval from their parents and families throughout their involvement. These parents were refugees under the Khmer Rouge regime in Cambodia, and were the survivors themselves of torture and killings in their homeland. To them, family survival in the United States rested on the success of their children in obtaining the education needed to secure employment to support their parents. These parents realistically feared retribution by the school administration against their daughters, and thus believed that conflict should be avoided in order to obtain longer-term aspirations. The local APIRH community organizing staff worked as best as possible with girls' parents and community leaders to allay fears, although they had many questions about "empowerment for whom?" and "empowerment at what community costs?"

In early 2001, APIRH's leadership reasserted their vision of social change organizing that would move beyond community service programs (such as the HOPE for Girls projects) into more political arenas requiring solidarity building among constituencies toward winning strategies for institutional change. Such campaigns would be directed by the overall APIRH organization based upon a strategic plan, rather than as outcomes of organizing opportunities at the local level (such as the sexual harassment campaign).

The power asserted by the APIRH staff in Oakland magnified the dissonance already being felt by the Long Beach staff and HOPE girls, resulting in a growing lack of trust among all. From the HOPE girls' perspective, there were many contradictions between agency mission and action. Despite the fact that the Long Beach program focused on the needs of Southeast Asians, none of the APIRH Oakland staff were Cambodian or Southeast Asian. Although the HOPE girls were being trained on the topics of sexuality and empowerment, they felt kept in the dark about how the agency made decisions regarding local programming. Lastly, despite the fact that half of the Long Beach staff were Southeast Asian and queer, the girls never felt open to talking about the power struggles that may exist due to ethnicity, gender, and sexual orientation. Ultimately, the girls felt betrayed by the leadership of APIRH, who used words like "participation," "accountability," and "empowerment" but secretly held onto all the power to dictate local staffing and program decisions.

Distrust was also evident within APIRH's own organizational structure. For instance, APIRH Long Beach staff were asked to develop a six-month work plan for evaluating their long-term efforts, with a subsequent assessment by APIRH to be made as to the agency's capacity to sustain local community engagement efforts by June 2001. From the tone of conference calls between agency sites and staff, many HOPE girls quickly learned that APIRH had issues with local staff because the staff didn't fit into APIRH's vision of their work in Oakland. Unbeknownst to the Long Beach staff and girls, the APIRH board of directors were told by the agency leadership that there would be a "ramping down" of activities in Long Beach while APIRH decided what direction their strategic agenda would take them. While some key board members questioned whether the decrease in staff and programs represented a de facto decision to close down the Long Beach community-based activities, throughout this time they were told by staff that this was not the case. However, all cultural and support programs were slowly eliminated in Long Beach.

Despite the internal changes and conflicts, in public APIRH continued to voice support for their Long Beach HOPE activities, including at a public fundraising gathering in March 2001. At the Los Angeles house of one board member, approximately thirty local immigrant rights advocates, feminists, and other allies attended a "house party" fundraiser to create/enhance local support for APIRH's national agenda and local community organizing work. At that event, HOPE girls and local staff provided testimonies about their work and positive results in the community. In large part because of the evidence of these local programs, APIRH successfully raised several thousands of dollars. However, the irony of the fundraiser stories in light of the impending closure of many of the Long Beach programs further served to demoralize and anger the girls and Long Beach staff.

The tensions between the APIRH agency and the Long Beach Cambodian girls quickly came to a head. In the summer of 2001, approximately twenty of the current and past HOPE for Girls participants met with APIRH board members and directors at the Long Beach office to discuss their anger with the loss of their programs. At that meeting, board and staff were asked to account for why decisions had been made without local input from the girls, what was the status of funding that was earmarked for Long Beach activities, and the ultimate fate of their local efforts. The girls believed they owned the HOPE for Girls effort, and felt that they were giving the leadership of APIRH one last chance to account for their decisions and actions. However, APIRH staff (along with half of the board) believed that the girls' confrontational actions were inappropriate and unethical, and left the meeting unified in the decision to terminate the Long Beach program. At the next board meeting, half of the board members resigned in protest regarding the treatment of the girls and the impending closure of the program. Subsequently, the Long Beach APIRH office closed, with all physical and intellectual properties (such as the sexual harassment needs assessment data) transported back to northern California. Thus, despite clear working tenets of joint ownership in, and of, materials and information developed via participatory action research strategies, in the end none of the HOPE girls had access to any of the program and research materials that they had produced during the three years of HOPE's existence in Long Beach. Since that time, APIRH has changed its name to Asian Communities for Reproductive Justice. This change marked a departure of significant members of their board, and was an effort to reconstitute and redevelop a national focus to their advocacy work.

COMMUNITY POWER: THE BIRTH OF
A NEW GIRLS ORGANIZATION

In October 2001, thirty HOPE for Girls participants, former Long Beach staff, and resigned board members convened to discuss the development of a new Cambodian girls' organization. Throughout the day-long "retreat," the girls and adults discussed their vision for such an agency, including who else from the community needed to be involved, what the organization would promote, how the organization's governance would be structured, and who would form the interim steering group to move forward. This would be the birth of Khmer Girls in Action (KGA), a new nonprofit organization with the goal of promoting social, political, and economic justice for Cambodians in Long Beach. In addition to continuing the gender-based dialogical learning processes initiated during their time with APIRH, KGA would also promote community-based empowerment strategies that built upon the cultural and social strengths of Cambodian girls in order to support their development as future leaders, scholars, artists, and advocates.

Even at this early stage, retreat participants understood that part of their new agency's work would entail telling the history of their conflict-based organizational development. One important aspect of this involved dispelling a myth created by APIRH that the 1998 sexual harassment campaign was a participatory action research effort undertaken in true collaboration by APIRH staff with HOPE girls. Indeed, after the 2003 publication of a book chapter detailing the PAR experience (from the point of view of only APIRH Oakland staff),[16] KGA members appeared at a university forum to voice their ethical concerns regarding power to control short versus long-term collaboration and commitment to community-based work. As described by Chavez and her colleagues (2003), institutions exercise productive power by creating "the symbols and hierarchies of structural power that normalize and mask repressive relationships."[17] As illustrated by the case of KGA, such power structures can and do exist within the world of gender-based progressive institutions that must struggle with exemplifying the values and ideals that they espouse.

Thus, KGA was formally established in 2001 with the vision to promote social, economic, and political justice through the education and empowerment of Cambodian girls (ages fourteen through twenty-one years) in Long Beach, California. The word Khmer (pronounced "keh-my") represents both the people from Cambodia as well as their language, while the emphasis on girls reflects the continued need to address their unique struggles in their personal, family, social, and community lives. Although sexuality continues to be a starting point for KGA's empowerment work, since many young Khmer women do not know how to keep their bodies healthy and safe, the members themselves decide what root causes they want to address in their community. In only four short years, KGA has amassed an enviable list of youth-led and organized accomplishments, including the following:

- The Khmer Justice Program, which works with high school members to promote positive self-image and community justice. The program facilitates a sisterhood alliance, through which members analyze existing oppressive systems by discussing issues like race, gender, sexuality, sexual orientation, power, and class privilege.
- Individual support services, to ensure that members achieve their personal and academic goals. Services include regular, individual check-ins with members, as well as communication and coordination with adults (such as school administrators and counselors) to make sure members are getting the appropriate support they desire.
- Performance, literary works, and films, including "Her Turn to Talk," which documents and explores the history, experiences, and struggles of Khmer Americans in Long Beach.
- Social justice campaigns, such as protesting the deportation of Southeast Asians, and creation of a national, grassroots network, the Southeast Asian Freedom Network.
- Stable organizational leadership (which includes Cambodian girls and young women at every level), funding, and resources, including the identification of a fiscal sponsor, Community Partners (in Los Angeles), and the establishment of an office in Long Beach.

Throughout its work, KGA continues to build upon each new struggle to maintain shared visions and values about empowerment among members and agency representatives. Many of the HOPE for Girls members are now KGA staff and board members, and promote constant reflection about how to work with Khmer girls and adults, as well as community and mainstream organizations. They recognize the youth are often not in positions of power within their communities or agencies, but that if these youth can understand how to make decisions and anticipate consequences, they can be capable of addressing the many different dynamics that come with being empowered. Clarity in roles along with constant communication is important to building the infrastructure needed to sustain their new agency. Although young, they are taking ownership in organizational development.

KGA's goal is to increase the community's power and ability to challenge oppressive systems and institutions that are not accountable to immigrant and refugee needs. Members recognize that young women of color are often marginalized in social justice movements; therefore, KGA invests in building young women's leadership, strength, and voice to be leaders in this struggle. Thus, the many KGA members and staff embody a truly dialogic conscientization process of empowerment, so easily publicly described but not so easily realized by APIRH, for girls and women in Long Beach, California.

NOTES

1. J. Silliman, M. G. Fried, L. Ross, and E. R. Gutierrez, *Undivided Rights: Women of Color Organize for Reproductive Justice* (Cambridge, Mass.: South End Press, 2004), 1–4.

2. P. Freire, *Pegagogy of the Oppressed* (New York: Seabury Press, 1970); P. Freire *Education for Critical Consciousness* (New York: Seabury Press, 1973).

3. U.S. Bureau of the Census. *Census 2000 Summary File 2*, PCT 32.

4. Asian Pacific American Legal Center, *The Diverse Face of Asians and Pacific Islanders in California* (Los Angeles: APALC, Asian Law Caucus and the National Asian Pacific American Legal Consortium, 2005).

5. J. Gould, B. Herrchen, T. Pham, S. Bera, J. Goshi, and Richard Yoder, *California Potential Project Areas for Adolescent Pregnancy Prevention Programs* (UC Berkeley, School of Public Health, 1996).

6. A. Cheatham and E. Shen, "Community-based Participatory Research with Cambodian Girls in Long Beach, California," in *Community Based Participatory Research for Health*, ed. M. Minkler and N. Wallerstein (San Francisco: Jossey-Bass, 2003), 316–31; J. Silliman, M. G. Fried, L. Ross, and E. R. Gutierrez, "Asians and Pacific Islanders for Reproductive Health," in *Undivided Rights: Women of Color Organize for Reproductive Justice*, ed. J. Silliman, M. G. Fried, L. Ross, and E. R. Gutierrez (Cambridge, Mass: South End Press, 2004), 176–95.

7. Asian Pacific Islanders for Reproductive Health, *Asian/Pacific Islander Reproductive Health Study* (Oakland, Calif.: APIRH, 1992); Asian Pacific Islanders for Reproductive Health, *The Health and Well-being of Asian and Pacific Islander Women* (Oakland, Calif.: APIRH, 1995); Asian Pacific Islanders for Reproductive Health, *API Adolescent Youth Reproductive Health Needs Assessment* (Oakland, Calif.: APIRH, 1997).

8. P. Freire, *Pegagogy of the Oppressed*; N. Freudenberg, "Training Health Educators for Social Change," *International Quarterly of Community Health* 5 (1) (1984): 37–52.

9. J. Rappaport, "Terms of Empowerment/Exemplars of Prevention: Toward a Theory for Community Psychology," *American Journal of Psychology* 15 (1987): 211–44.

10. E. Shen and E. Luluquisen, *HOPE for Girls Curriculum, Summer 1997: Description and Evaluation Results* (Oakland, Calif.: APIRH, 1997).

11. Asians and Pacific Islanders California Action Network, *Letter to Principal Collins and Principal Ashley of the Polytechnic High School in Long Beach, California*. June 25, 1998.

12. A. Cheatham and E. Shen, "Community-Based Participatory Research With Cambodian Girls In Long Beach, California," in *Community Based Participatory Research for Health*, ed. M. Minkler and N. Wallerstein (San Francisco: Jossey-Bass, 2003), 316–31.

13. For a more complete description of APIRH's account of their sexual harassment community campaign, please refer to Cheatham and Shen, *Community Based Participatory Research for Health*.

14. F. Calpotura and G. Acebo, *Nothing Less Will Do: An Organizational Assessment of Asian and Pacific Islanders for Reproductive Health* (Oakland, Calif.: APIRH, May 1, 2000).

15. B. Israel, A. J. Schultz, E. A. Parker, and A. B. Becker, "Review Of Community-Based Research: Assessing Partnership Approaches To Improve Public Health," *Annual Review of Public Health* 19 (1998): 173–202.

16. A. Cheatham and E. Shen, "Community Based Participatory Research With Cambodian Girls in Long Beach, California."

17. V. Chavez, B. Duran, Q. E. Avila, M. M. Baker, and N. Wallerstein, "The Dance of Race and Privilege in Community Based Participatory Research," in *Community Based Participatory Research for Health*, ed. M. Minkler and N. Wallerstein (San Francisco: Jossey-Bass, 2003), 86 of 81–97.

10

Family, Citizenship, and Selfhood in Luong Ung's *First They Killed My Father*

Cathy Schlund-Vials

> Sometimes it's frightening for me to look back at my past experiences. Once in a while I wonder about my uncles and how they were killed. It is very hard for Cambodians to let their memories go.
>
> Sopheap K. Hang, "Memoir of a Child's Nightmare," in *Children of Cambodia's Killing Fields*, 33

> Those who are alive receive a mandate from those who are silent forever. They can fulfill their duties only by trying to reconstruct precisely things as they were.
>
> Czeslaw Milosz, Nobel Prize Speech, December 8, 1980

Within Asian/American studies, the Cambodian/American experience occupies a similar, yet by no means identical, discursive position as that of Holocaust survivors within the Jewish American literary canon. The small but growing canon of Cambodian/American literature is one marked and shaped by a period of time more widely known as the "Killing Fields,"[1] an era dominated by the horrific policies enacted by Pol Pot and the communist Khmer Rouge between 1975 and 1979.[2] It is estimated that, in this brief four-year period, over two million Cambodians perished as a result of execution, starvation, disease, and forced labor; this number represents about one seventh of the total population of Cambodia at the time of the genocide. The memory of this genocide, along with the documentation of this unspeakable moment in history, has served as the primary referent for the Cambodian/American experience in the United States to those inside and outside of these communities. Documented cinematically in the 1984

Academy Award–winning film, *The Killing Fields*, the memory and stories of
the genocide are the subjects of most, if not all, the literary narratives written by Cambodian/American authors and published in the United States.[3]

It is the place of Cambodia, and within the space of Cambodian/Ameri-
can memoirs about the genocide, that I situate my examination of an
emerging narrative genre that is characterized by dislocated and displaced
refugee subjectivities and memorialization. The question of the Cambodian
refugee's place, or citizenship, is integrally linked to the space of the Killing
Fields within literary narratives, and the connection between the process of
remembering and the construction of subjectivity will serve as the primary
foundation for this chapter. In order to build a context upon which to consider various aspects of narratives about the Killing Fields, I begin with a
brief synopsis of Holocaust literature. I will then return to the connection
between citizenship and the Killing Fields, which is inflected by gender and
familial relationships in the literary imaginary. Such a schema informs Luong Ung's *First They Killed My Father: A Daughter of Cambodia Remembers*
(2000), the text that serves as my entree into a larger discussion about contemporary Cambodian/American literature and its connection to gender
and sexuality.

The literary treatment of the Holocaust provides a productive frame for
examining Cambodian/American narratives about the Killing Fields because of similarities of form and content (testimonial literatures and histories of genocide). This event, as previously mentioned, holds a particular
discursive position in the cultural productions of those authors who survived the Holocaust and for Jewish American writers. The Holocaust becomes a space in which people can form ethnic and religious affiliations
that extend beyond nation-state borders to encompass a diasporic community located in multiple places. In his examination of the Holocaust mu-
seum in Washington, D.C., Harold Kaplan writes that "[t]he Holocaust, at
the edge of all moral boundaries, is where discourse stops as before the unspeakable, but also where it begins."[4] As a beginning and an end point,
trauma characterizes narratives about the Holocaust. The Holocaust has
served, in the dominant imagination, as *the* event defining Jewish experience in the twentieth century. Since World War II, texts written by Jewish
survivors about their respective experiences during the Holocaust have entered the U.S. literary marketplace, leading to at least a familiarity of a genre
marked by the representation of large-scale atrocities and trauma through
both eyewitness accounts and photographic representations. The unspeakable experiences of these survivors have been documented photographi-
cally; they have been memorialized in autobiographies, and such narratives
have also been spoken on the screen in recent films like *Schindler's List*
(Steven Spielberg, 1993) and *The Pianist* (Roman Polanski, 2002). In ac-
cessing the term "unspeakable," I want to stress that accounts of the Holo-

caust have been transmitted through various *public* cultural productions of private accounts of horror and tragedy that occur long after the event occurred. Moreover, the tension that occurs in the revelation of what is unspeakable (something that initially defies an understanding of what is considered humane) is precisely located in the act of telling, which breaks a traumatic silence. I also argue that this silence is individual and collective, given the millions who perished as a result of the Holocaust and other genocides—who can no longer speak—and the representation of these stories becomes an even bigger project connected to notions of selfhood and nationhood.

The larger contextualization of the Holocaust as a historical reality and a traumatic actuality provides a foundation for each cultural production about the Holocaust. And, the traumatic event becomes *the* space in which discussions of what really happened occur. Each representation of this genocide accretes further meaning because of the narratives that have come before. The prevalence of such narratives within the Jewish American literary canon supports Kaplan's assertion that this unspeakable historical event has become both the beginning and the end of discourses about both World War II and the Jewish European experience. Moreover, as James Young asserts: "For murdered people without graves, without even corpses to inter . . . memorial books often came to serve as symbolic tombstones."[5] Thus, the documentation of the Holocaust on the page and on the cinematic screen serves as a way to memorialize those who, in death, have not had a proper burial. Such documentation creates a space for those lost to be remembered and allows those who are living to provide them with a symbolic "laying to rest." These memorials also give the traumatized subject an opportunity to speak her/his story, and they provide that subject with a narrative of resistance located within the literary or cinematic imaginary. By remembering those who have been killed and by revealing the details of their deaths, survivors are able to recount crimes against humanity, testify against those who have committed such crimes, and provide a space in which the magnitude of loss is individualized and personalized for a readership. Additionally, the primary theoretical framework embedded in such literary productions is that of trauma, in which stories of atrocities committed against the individual body are metonymically extended to encompass the entirety of a community impacted by policies of genocide. To connect to a previous point, in retelling these narratives through the genre of memoir, Jewish authors are able to link up to a particular form of diaspora that is oriented around the Holocaust. Moreover, given the number of cultural productions about the Shoah, the reception of these narratives by audiences is informed by the public acknowledgement that the atrocity occurred (e.g., the Nuremburg trials) and the undeniable presence of a canon of literature. However, in the case of Cambodian/American narratives about the genocide, there is, in comparison to Holocaust literature, a relative erasure of the event within the United States. The comparative paucity of literary and cultural productions about the Killing Fields, coupled with the fact that U.S. foreign policy paved the way for this particular genocide, are important tensions to consider in the reading of such works.

Though a critique of U.S. foreign policy is rarely overtly rendered in Cambodian/American memoirs, the knowledge that the genocide is connected to U.S. efforts during the Vietnam War is a significant referent for considering the history of the Killing Fields.[6] What is more salient in Cambodian/American texts is the way in which trauma, as both a literary frame and as a theoretical foundation, is used to tell the national story of Cambodia through individual narratives of Cambodian citizens. And the telling of such a multifaceted story—linked to nationhood and selfhood—is undeniably connected to the erasure of this complicated story from the realm of U.S. history. For the Cambodian/American author, the question becomes a two-sided one of representation in that such stories are, in comparison to the Holocaust, largely unknown by American readers. On the individual level, the story revealed is imbued with the task of representing Cambodians directly impacted by the Killing Fields. With this in mind, the Cambodian/American author both "lays to rest" the Cambodian bodies affected by the Killing Fields *and* codifies the national history of Cambodia.

The issue of memorialization and resistance provides a transition into the primary focus of this chapter, which is centered on the reading of Cambodian/American narratives about the Killing Fields. It is the unspeakable, unimaginable moments of the Killing Fields that serve as the beginning and end point for Cambodian/American writers who, through their respective personal experiences, connect with the larger national narrative of Cambodia, a nation-state with a history haunted by the specter of Pol Pot and the Khmer Rouge. Of the narratives that have been published in the United States, the majority of stories are written by those who grew up and came of age during this period of time; most of the autobiographies are written from the perspective of those who survived the Killing Fields as children. The titles of three full-length autobiographies that have recently been published illustrate this characteristic: Molyda Szymusiak's (Buth Keo's) *The Stones Cry Out: A Cambodian Childhood, 1975–1980*; Chanrithy Him's *When Broken Glass Floats: Growing Up under the Khmer Rouge*; and Luong Ung's *First They Killed My Father: A Daughter of Cambodia Remembers*. Each memoir is written by a subject who, prior to the revolution, hailed from a professional, middle-to-upper-middle-class family. Such accounts emphasize coming of age under the Khmer Rouge regime. Though perhaps coincidental, the fact that all three authors are female reflects a reality of the survivor demographic in Cambodia after the dismantling of Pol Pot's government. So many men had been killed in Cambodia between 1975 and 1979 that, by the late 1980s, 64 percent of the adult population was female.[7] And the gender roles that were present before the revolution had shifted considerably as a result. For example, after the 1975 takeover, women were expected to perform the same duties as their male counterparts in the rural camps, whereas prior to the revolution they carried primarily domestic duties within the home. This shift is present in these autobiographies, which recount traditional gender roles prior to the revolution and the dissolution of these roles during the reign of the Khmer Rouge.

Moreover, the prevalence of childhood memoirs in the Cambodian/American literary canon can be attributed to the fact that the Khmer Rouge viewed children as the most "pure" in Cambodia and more malleable than their adult counterparts. As a result of this characterization, children were cast by the Khmer Rouge regime as ideal citizens because they were not "tainted" by Western or foreign influence, and children were envisioned as the bedrock for the new nation-state known as Democratic Kampuchea.[8] Thus, they were less likely to be executed than their adult counterparts, who were often considered "beyond" reeducation because of their past, prerevolutionary affiliations and professions. Yet it is also important to note that, under the Khmer Rouge, familial affiliations were used as the basis for execution, and children of those considered traitors to Angkar—the Khmer Rouge's ruling organization—were often killed with their parents. The crime of being one's daughter or son thus had severe consequences, and the canon of Cambodian/American literature reflects this actuality. For the aforementioned authors, there is a thematic focus of hiding and the need to keep familial affiliations secret. Such accounts emphasize that the Khmer Rouge policies of execution were partially predicated on a need to eliminate threats that were cultural and familial in scope. Thus, if one's father was deemed a threat to Democratic Kampuchea, his familial affiliations were, by proxy, considered equal threats. Thus, these authors often write about the need to hide one's past family affiliations in order to survive. Further, a model citizen under the Khmer Rouge was often defined by the lack of prerevolutionary selfhood, which carried with it the absence of a familial past. This model citizenship status was predicated on the notion that children represented a population that lacked memory.

This lack of memory embodied and desired in children on the personal, individual level was, during Pol Pot's reign, a governmental goal on the national level. Such a construction of citizenship occurred alongside other Khmer Rouge policies that were intended to bring about "year zero"—a time before any Western influence and perceived foreign corruption.[9] As Ben Kiernan maintains, part of the political strategy that undergirded the Khmer Rouge's rise to power was based on the destruction of two Cambodian institutions—Buddhism and the family. Temples were destroyed, monks were executed, and religious practice was outlawed during this time. According to Kiernan, the Khmer Rouge "mounted history's fiercest ever attack on family life,"[10] and children were no longer, according to the Khmer Rouge, affiliated with their parents but to Angkar. Loyalty to Angkar "was to replace all preexisting family bonds," and a new vocabulary was introduced and enforced that reflected this shift from familial to nation-state loyalty.[11] For example, previous words for "mother" and "father" were replaced with the more communist-centered "comrade."[12] This semantic shift, coupled with polices that separated children from their parents, illustrates the extent to which children under such a regime ceased to belong to pre-revolutionary familial constructions and instead became subjects of Angkar.

On another level, the changing nature of relationships between parent and child were replicated in sexual relationships between men and women. This change in partnerships—which, prior to the revolution (according to Ung's text), were built around abstract ideals of love—reflected a greater project of post-revolution nation-building. In the revolutionary space, women were viewed for both their capacity to work and their ability to reproduce new citizens for Democratic Kampuchea. Similarly, men were viewed for both their ability to contribute to the state through their respective acts of labor and in their ability to help rebuild the nation through their progeny. This is not to say that women's sexuality before the revolution was not partially predicated on the dominant-held gendered notion that women as wives served a reproductive role within the domestic sphere. It is important to note the ways in which one's gender role was circumscribed by class, and one's position within the home (as an economic contributor, a transmitter of culture, or a mother) varied according to this other modality. However, after the revolution, a woman's role became one that is both classless and state-sanctioned. And marriages were orchestrated according to the party line of reproduction, which did eliminate voluntary affiliations in favor of forced unions built solely around the state need for new citizens untainted by the past. Sentimental notions of love and companionship were dismissed in favor of a more concrete relationship of reproduction. And the absence of any discussion of other sexualities within this space in the memoir is also one reflective of a national identity circumscribed by state-sanctioned calls for production (whether such work takes place in the fields or in domestic spaces). The emergence of "Angkar" as parent and the familial terms connected to the leaders of the nation-state (in which Angkar was positioned as "father" and its leaders as "brothers") illustrates the ways in which one's selfhood (a citizenship affiliation) was mediated through the lens of kinship.

Thus, during the reign of the Khmer Rouge, the issue of citizenship—which, in this chapter, will refer to both political and social belonging—involved multiple shifts in the way subjects constructed and articulated familial affiliations. Cambodian/American narratives represent these shifts by emphasizing the loss of family members and childhood, as well as by nostalgically yearning for the time before the Khmer Rouge's rise to power. In this context, the act of affiliating with one's family over that of the dominant political body represents a substantive act of resistance against a totalitarian regime. As such narratives reveal, it is also the persistence of memory *and* the connection to family that continues in the face of such traumatic events. The act of remembering creates particular spaces for resistance in which "surviving victims hit back."[13]

This particular form of resistance, which is mediated through a familial frame and embodied in the act of remembering, emerges in Luong Ung's *First They Killed My Father: A Daughter of Cambodia Remembers. First They Killed My Father* will serve as the main text for my meditation on family, citizenship, and selfhood in Democratic Kampuchea, and the selection of this text over other autobiographies is purposeful in that it occupies a distinct position within the Cambodian/American literary canon. Ung's memoir is controversial in that it has been critiqued by those within the Cambodian/American community as inauthentic and inaccurate, and is, at this point, the only text that has received such criticism. The controversy illustrates the complicated and contested nature of representing the genocide for readers who were intimately connected to it and creates a dialogic space to consider other Cambodian/American narratives.

Before delving into Ung's autobiography, I want to develop a particular schema for considering the function of family frames within *First They Killed My Father*. Marianne Hirsch's deployment of family frames is an important foundation for this chapter. In looking at family photographs and the ways in which such visual narratives link up to issues of memory and history, Hirsch defines a family as "an affiliative group, and the affiliations that create it are constructed through various relational, cultural, and institutional processes."[14] Hirsch then connects such affiliations to dominant ideologies of what families should "look like" at particular moments in history. In her text, Hirsch examines the idea of family "in contemporary discourse and its power to negotiate and mediate some of the traumatic shifts that have shaped postmodern mentalities."[15] Thus, using Hirsch's model, family is an affiliation that is social and political, and the representation of such affiliations in the realm of photography is thus mediated by memories of trauma that often fall outside of what is depicted within the photograph frame.

Hirsch uses personal photographs to consider how her memories of the past shift the meaning of these visual texts. Though Hirsch uses a more personal narrative as an entrée into a discussion about the ways in which photographic memory represents a revisable form of remembrance that is fragmented, such a schema is useful in examining genocide narratives that attempt to construct memory on a personal, social, and historical level for readers who may or may not have experienced the events. Not only are such narratives reflective of a suturing of personal and political histories, but these texts are also reflective of various traumatic fissures that are located within a familial site. I would also extend this notion of "traumatic fissure" to the larger issue of citizenship and nationhood, which, in Cambodian/American literature, becomes a significant site upon which to further locate experiences living during the time of the genocide.

Ung's memoir begins with the assertion that what follows is "a story of survival: my own and my family's. Though these events constitute my experience, my story mirrors that of millions of Cambodians. If you had been living in Cambodia during this period, this would be your story too."[16] Within the autobiography, multiple texts are included—a map of Cambodia, family photographs, and genealogies—that become, as the narrative progresses, significant elements in the representation of a personal history that Ung connects to a larger national story of Cambodia before and after the Khmer Rouge takeover. Simultaneously, the family trees and family photographs that appear in the work, along with the narratival emphasis on family dynamics and memories, intersect with sociopolitical shifts in the nature of Cambodian citizenship after the Khmer Rouge. Ung's narrative can thus be read as a contemplation of both the dissolution of the family and the changing nature of citizenship under a totalitarian regime. The work's initial dedication—"In memory of the two million people who perished under the Khmer Rouge regime"—reinforces the sense that *First They Killed My Father* is a literary memorial to both her father (among other family members who are lost throughout the course of the narrative) and other Cambodian citizens. The loss of two million people serves as a constant referent for the rest of the narrative, and Ung, in her telling of the Cambodian genocide, conflates the space between familial and political story.

A particular gender position informs the construction of citizenship in the text. Ung presents, in her autobiography, a space in which she inhabits a multifaceted "daughter" role. As the title of memoir suggests and the narrative reinforces, Ung casts herself as a daughter in the familial sense and, as the subtitle for her memoir reveals, "a daughter of Cambodia." It is this layered sense of "daughterliness" and the behaviors and political affiliations connected with such a concept that become, as the narrative progresses, sites for resistance. In the beginning of the narrative, the reader is introduced to Ung as a "daughter who does not act like a girl" and who causes her mother minor grief because she chooses to "stomp around like a cow dying of thirst" in spite of the fact that her mother has "tried so many times to teach [her] the proper way for a young lady to walk."[17] This self-characterization contradicts other notions of feminine identity, which are embodied by Ung's mother, who wears fine jewelry and silk clothing, and by her sister Keav, whose only non-ladylike characteristic (according to the narrator) is that she "has the misfortune to like to gossip and argue too much."[18] Though seemingly superficial details, what emerges from these descriptions are constructions of femininity considered pre-revolutionary; moreover, these descriptions illustrate a particular class position. She describes her mother as both a socialite and one who goes, on a daily basis, to the market and prepares dinner, which reveals a traditional role within the domestic sphere and one not inflected by work outside of the home. Ung does not critique this gender position or gendered labor within the text. Rather, she idealizes her mother's actions. Additionally, this construction takes on a nostalgic sense of the social order in place before the revolution.

As the narrative progresses, it becomes apparent to the reader the extent to which a shift in gender roles has occurred when in the labor camp, for her mother is expected to work in the fields and become, after the murder of Ung's father, the primary provider for the family. This shift reflects the ideal position of a woman within the Khmer Rouge society; there is no delineation made between sites of labor. Prior to the revolution, a middle-class feminine identity, as illustrated by Ung's description of her mother's activities, was primarily located within and connected to the domestic space. After the revolution, such a class identity dissolves and women are expected to work in the same spaces as their male counterparts. No dominant-held delineation is made between what is traditionally "women's work" (which is domestically situated) and "men's work" (which occurs outside of the home). To reiterate a previous point, to be an ideal citizen to Angkar and the Khmer Rouge was thus linked to both a dissolution of previous class dynamics *and* gender roles. And Ung's narrative reflects this "Angkar"-driven construction of citizenship.

However, Ung complicates this notion of a seemingly "egalitarian" politics between men and women with the assertion that a woman's ultimate duty to the post-revolutionary nation-state body is to "marry soldiers" and "do what they were made for, to bear children for Angkar."[19] Ung further maintains that the Khmer Rouge views women as expendable and dispensable subjects who, if they do not fulfill this childbearing directive, "are never heard from again."[20] Ung, as narrator, privileges both a "traditional" familial frame and an understanding of sexuality that is entrenched in heterosexual relationships. Returning to a previously mentioned point and to Ung's narration of life under the Khmer Rouge, not only is the directive to bear children embedded in particular heteronormative gender constructions and roles but this ideology also dictates that women are producers of citizens for Angkar as a nation-state. This shift is mapped onto the female body in two specific ways; women are transformed, like their male counterparts, into classless entities, and the process of childbirth, previously connected to the

familial body, is instead linked to Angkar body politic.[21] However, as Ung's
narrative reveals, the treatment of men and women in terms of their ability
to reproduce was not completely egalitarian, and the disappearance of
women (and not men) who failed to produce children makes manifest the
gendered dynamics still in place during the reign of the Khmer Rouge.

Furthermore, Ung as a narrator reflects the changing gender and familial
dynamics in her self-characterization as a daughter throughout the course
of the narrative. At the beginning of *First They Killed My Father*, Ung presents
herself as a child who is inquisitive yet respects her father's commands; as
the memoir progresses, her role in the family shifts as a result of their experiences living under the Khmer Rouge regime. For example, in one scene,
Ung steals food from the family. Given the circumstances and the threat of
famine, this act of childish selfishness becomes a severe crime against the
family and the source of an intense amount of guilt for the protagonist.[22]
Yet, Ung arguably redeems her daughter position with her refusal both to
forget her family and to align herself completely with Angkar. Though she
performs an allegiance to Angkar in nightly meetings at the youth labor
camp, she undercuts her public performance with private reflections on her
family and with repeated assertions of her hatred of Pol Pot and the Khmer
Rouge. There is a disconnection between Ung's physical and emotional
selves in which the bodily action is contradictory to her thoughts of resistance. And such a fissure is necessitated by the political situation, which
forces Ung to perform publicly and react privately. Moreover, it is through
the persistence of memory, and Ung's repeated remembrances of her family, that she performs a daughter role that is subversive to the dominant impulse to forget put forth by the prevailing political structure. In remembering her family, Ung does not fulfill the ideal Angkar citizen role of
transferring her allegiances to the nation-state. Her resistance is connected
to being a "bad" daughter of the Khmer Rouge while simultaneously enact-
ing a "good" daughter position to her family.

Ung's personal memory is one that is inflected by familial history and national location. The first few pages of the autobiography include two forms
of maps—one is a family tree, the other is a map of Cambodia. These maps
appear in sequence, and such an order emphasizes further the sense that
Ung is first a "daughter" in the familial sense and then "a daughter of Cambodia." From the outset, Ung constructs her narrative according to a gendered notion of one's belonging within a familial frame, which she then extends to encompass the larger history of her homeland. The memoir is
organized chronologically, and each chapter heading is also dated. Thus,
Ung immediately historicizes the work, and the personal history of her family is linked with the larger history of Cambodia. For example, the trials and
tribulations faced by her family are linked, in the space of the narrative,
with political upheavals within Cambodia. Her narrative also begins with

the ascension of Pol Pot and the Khmer Rouge (the takeover of Phnom Penh). The supposed authenticity of the memoir is embedded in the assertion of witness, which is manifest in the use of a first-person narrative and by Ung's repeated assertions that she did indeed "witness" (that is, see firsthand) the atrocities she describes. She uses her familial experiences as the basis for knowledge of the political landscape of Cambodia in that she connects what has happened on the personal level to what was happening nationally to other Cambodian citizens. According to Ung: "I hate Pol Pot for murdering Pa, Ma, Keav, and Geak.[23] . . . I am too young to understand Pol Pot's strategies for creating a classless pure agrarian society."[24] What occurs in this brief passage is a collapsing of space between personal and political. Ung writes that she hates Pol Pot for what he, and by extension his regime, has done to her family, and then she immediately connects this personal assertion to the larger project of Democratic Kampuchea nationhood. Pol Pot's "strategies for creating a classless pure agrarian society"—a new national Cambodian identity—are tied to the dissolution of past familial bonds and the death of Cambodian citizens, including her own family members.

The motif of family that structures and informs the text is also reinforced by the inclusion of family photographs, which are taken from moments that occur before the Khmer Rouge's rise to power and after the dissolution, at least politically, of the regime in 1979. The photographs, like the family tree, accrete more meaning as the narrative progresses and details of living in the camps are revealed. The family album, which is placed in the middle of the text, serves as a referent for Ung's personal history and for Cambodia's political history. Ung's memories of childhood experiences are further mediated through the photographic narrative, which confirms for the reader the life she enjoyed prior to the Khmer Rouge's ascension and highlights the legacy of this history on her current family dynamic and the extent to which this dynamic is marked by loss. The photographs provide a space for both Ung and the reader to negotiate the traumatic narratives embedded in the text in that they constitute a visual referent that complements the literary descriptions of her family. In other words, as Ung describes her familial experience, the reader is given another text in which to visually locate her memories. And the photographs can also be read in terms of memory in that they capture the past in a way that is markedly different from writing due to the mechanical nature of the image. Though photographs are subjective in that they capture the shooter's perspective, they represent a mechanical reproduction that is unmediated by the remembrances that shape Ung's written text.

Concomitantly, Ung's *First They Killed My Father* represents an autobiographical and literary replaying of personal trauma in that it is firmly rooted in the telling of that personal history to the reader, yet it is also integrally linked to a more national, traumatic narrative of loss. The memoir, along with the photographs, comes together to form a literary memorial for both the living and the dead at the conclusion of the memoir. The written narrative, which is filled with details of life under the Khmer Rouge and enumerates the lives and deaths of family members, serves as a referent for the photographs that are placed in the middle of the text. The photographs are contextualized vis-à-vis the narrative. And they serve as another form of historical narrative and document that takes the reader through both pre-revolutionary and post-revolutionary moments. The inclusion of family photographs mirrors, quite literally, the familial representations that dominate the written text. The layering of multiple texts in the memoir serves an evidentiary role; the photographic record buttresses the descriptions that occur in the narrative by providing a visual representation of those bodies that have been impacted. Thus, Ung occupies a multisided position within the autobiographical rendering of her life under the reign of the Khmer Rouge; she is both the one who remembers and the primary subject of her memoir. To paraphrase Steven J. Rubin's work on the genre of autobiography, such a genre affirms personal identity and records social history.[25] Ung's work certainly fits within this rubric, yet the scope of her story—which intersects with a particular history of genocide—affirms her personal identity as Cambodian and records the sociopolitical history of Cambodia.

Yet it is also important to revisit what has been included and what has been omitted from *First They Killed My Father*, for such an analysis brings to light particular questions about intended audience and controversies that surround the text. The narrative, written in English and drawing from past narratives and knowledge about the Killing Fields, is intended for a U.S. audience, and this becomes apparent in what is included. For example, Ung makes mention of Pol Pot throughout the narrative, but for most of the time during the Killing Fields, Pol Pot's identity was not known by any but those in the highest levels of government. Though there is brief mention of U.S. foreign policy in the opening sections of the text, the primary narrative centers on the actions of the Khmer Rouge; there is little mention of U.S. bombings of the Cambodian countryside prior to 1975, which have been linked to a destabilization of the government and contributed to the rise of the Khmer Rouge. This particular omission provides an interesting space for further exploration. As a refugee, Ung's status as a U.S. subject could be complicated with a more in-depth indictment of her adoptive country's position within the Cambodian political sphere. Or perhaps such an omission speaks to a multifaceted, layered tension that is revealed at the conclusion of the narrative. The penultimate chapter of the memoir (prior to the epilogue) ends at the Bangkok International Airport, moments before Ung departs on a plane for the United States. What is apparent in this moment is a profound sense of hope—a desire that the traumatic events discussed in the previous chapters can somehow be transcended in the United States. Yet there is also an anxiety that is expressed about leaving her family behind, which includes both the living and the dead. Ung's sister, who is the first to perish, has died in a labor camp, her father is taken away by Khmer Rouge forces and executed, and her mother and younger sister are also taken by Khmer Rouge forces and killed. The rest of her family is separated, scattered in various labor camps and reeducation centers, and reunited at the conclusion of the narrative in a refugee camp.

Ung remembers her family both in real time and in the space of dreams, and her father figures keenly in these dream sequences. Returning to the anxiety of leaving, Ung, in a concluding dream sequence involving her father, tells him that she is going to a place that is "very far from Cambodia" and she fears that her father, among other family members, will be lost. In this scene, Ung's father reassures his daughter that, to paraphrase, wherever Ung goes, her father will find her.[26] The desire to forget the past is thus complicated by the simultaneous compulsion to remember her family and Cambodia. Ung writes: "When I came to America, I did everything I could to not think about them [my family]. . . . In my new country, I immersed myself in American culture during the day, but at night the war haunted me with nightmares."[27] The autobiography can be read as a literary outcome of these tensions—between a forgetfulness that is superficially possible in the United States and the lasting memory of the Cambodian homeland.

From this tension between forgetfulness and remembering, a gap is created in which to consider other contradictory moments within the text. In returning to the beginning of *First They Killed My Father*, Ung's position as one whose story "mirrors that of millions of Cambodians" is problematized by the fact that she is ethnically Chinese Cambodian and is thus a member of a minority group within Cambodia. This position is partially at the source of a controversy around the memoir, for Ung carefully enumerates, for the reader, the ways in which her Chineseness marks her as "other" within the larger Cambodian body politic. This distinction becomes racialized in Ung's memoir, and she consistently writes about her light skin and how this distinction is an integral aspect to her self-proclaimed position as an outsider. Although she situates herself as a "daughter of Cambodia," Ung is careful to qualify this status in the memoir by asserting within the first few pages of her narrative that she is the daughter of a Chinese mother and a Chinese Cambodian father. She describes her mother as having "Chinese" features—"perfectly arched eyebrows, almond-shaped eyes; tall straight Western nose; and oval face"—and juxtaposes these features with her father, who has "black curly hair, a wide nose, full lips, and a round face."[28] This status as other is revisited throughout the text, and Ung attributes the treatment of her family to the sense that, as a member of a racial group, she and her family are considered "racially corrupt."[29] She thus attempts simultaneously to occupy a position of insider and outsider. This negotiation occurs through the use of a family frame (as mentioned earlier in this particular chapter), and Ung casts herself as both a "daughter of Cambodia" and the product of an interethnic marriage. Though ethnically part of a minority group, Ung asserts that her experiences in reeducation and labor camps, coupled with the dissolution and decimation of her family, connect her to the larger narrative of Cambodia during the period of the Killing Fields. Her citizenship status, as she creates it, thus becomes Cambodian in scope because of her connection to this particular moment in history.

It is also this connection to Cambodian history generally and to the period between 1975 and 1979 specifically that has sparked controversy in regard to *First They Killed My Father*. The authenticity of her narrative has been questioned partially because of the details she includes in her autobiography, which, according to critics, represent exaggerations and fabrications of life under the Khmer Rouge. For example, her descriptions of Phnom Penh and her assertions of a middle-class status ("I know we are middle-class because of our apartment and the possessions we have"[30]) reveal a particular class bias and do not adequately, according to critics, address her own privilege within the text.[31] In other words, what is omitted, for the most part, are the countless Cambodians who inhabited a lower socioeconomic position than that of her family, and though mentioned intermittently throughout the narrative, Ung dismisses poorer Cambodians as "ignorant." Her casting of other Cambodians in this light distinguishes Ung's book from other previously mentioned narratives written by subjects from middle-class to upper-middle-class positions in that she creates within her memoir a distinction between those who lived in the city (who embody a more "Western sensibility") and those who lived in the villages.

Further, it is this peasant population that will be, according to Ung, more apt to commit crimes against her family because, in the words of her father, a former Lon Nol soldier, the villagers are intent to "make us the first scapegoats for their problems."[32] The enumeration of the treatment of her family, which involves several episodes of abuse and comments about her "foreignness," buttresses this claim of scapegoating within the text. Ung has also been critiqued for her racialized views that are manifest in *First They Killed My Father*, which are based largely on her characterization of the Khmer population as marked by "curly black hair, flat noses, full lips, and dark chocolate skin." This casting of "dark" attributes on Cambodian subjects occurs repeatedly in the memoir, and is one of the reasons why the Khmer Institute, a nonprofit organization committed to promoting the study of Khmer-related issues and the active production of knowledge by Cambodian/Americans, has questioned the authenticity of the autobiography and has asked the author to answer to accusations of exaggeration and racism in her text.[33] The importance of this controversy within the emerging and ever-growing space of Cambodian/American literature is that it brings to light the politics of representation as it connects to narratives about the Cambodian genocide. And what is at the heart of the controversy is Ung's position as a "daughter of Cambodia" and her assertion that her individual stories of loss connect to a more holistic rendering of Cambodian selfhood that is integrally linked to the genocide. In acknowledging both the familial frame Ung uses and the controversial nature of the text within the Cambodian/American literary realm, the problematic and contested notion of a national narrative embedded in trauma and the politics of representation are brought to light. Ung uses, through the course of her memoir, a family frame embedded in pre-revolutionary traditional gender roles and sexualities that mediate her rendering of the Killing Fields as both a daughter of those who perished and as a Cambodian female subject.

Moreover, Ung's status as a Chinese Cambodian takes on bodily dimension in that she claims to represent all of Cambodian experience while simultaneously inhabiting a minority body within the larger Cambodian population. And it is her description of other bodies that serves as both the source of debate and as a reflection of Ung's own sociopolitical subject position.

This debate over bodies and the representation of those bodies marks a significant dialogic moment upon which to consider other forms of Cambodian/American literary production and their overall relationship to Asian/American studies. The refugee subjectivity that is revealed through such narratives—the fact that such narratives are written by subjects who have been displaced and relocated—is one that has certainly been discussed within the field of Asian/American studies. And, as mentioned at the opening of this chapter, within Asian/American studies, scholars have acknowledged and explored the significance and specter of the Killing Fields within the lives of those Cambodian/American populations affected by such a history. However, what has yet to be done is an analysis of Cambodian/American literature as a particular genre that is intimately shaped by the traumatic and, as the debate over Ung's text attests, contested relationship between history, memory, and citizenship that is mediated through gender and sexuality. This chapter represents a beginning moment into that particular level of inquiry.

NOTES

1. According to Sucheng Chan, though the "Killing Fields" as a term is used to describe life under the Khmer Rouge, Cambodians more frequently refer to this period as *Samay Pol Pot* (the Pol Pot time). Sucheng Chan, *Survivors: Cambodian Refugees in the United States* (Urbana: Illinois University Press, 2004).

2. Pol Pot, whose name was not revealed until after the period of the Killing Fields concluded in 1979, is largely credited by historians and scholars as the leader and chief architect of what would become known as Democratic Kampuchea. Pol Pot was born on May 19, 1925, in Prek Sbauv in Kampong Thum province, north of Phnom Penh. The son of a prosperous farmer, Pol Pot's family was also connected to the Cambodian royal family. In 1949, Pol Pot won a government scholarship to study radio electronics in Paris. It was here that he was first introduced to and became fascinated by socialism, and connected with other Cambodians studying in the metropolis, including Ieng Sary, Khieu Samphan, Khieu Ponnary, and Song Sen, who would eventually become leaders of the Khmer Rouge. As part of the French Communist Party, Pol Pot used the Association of Khmer Students as a platform for leftist politics in Cambodia, and it is also in this place that open challenges to the Sihanouk government were initially formulated. As the Cambodian government became increasingly more unstable during the years of U.S. involvement in Southeast Asia, Pol Pot emerged as the leader of the Khmer Rouge, which would eventually gain power in 1975 after the April takeover of Phnom Pen. He became prime minister in 1977. Yet it is important to reiterate that his identity and the identities of other members of the "Angkar" group (the leadership of the Khmer Rouge) were kept for the most part secret. And to most inside and outside of Cambodia, Pol Pot continues to be referred to not by his name but by the label "Brother Number One."

3. Other narratives of the Cambodian genocide include: Chanrithy Him, *When Broken Glass Floats: Growing Up Under the Khmer Rouge* (New York: W. W. Norton, 2000); Bree Lafrenier and Daran Kravanh, *Music Through the Dark: A Tale of Survival in Cambodia* (Honolulu: University of Hawaii Press, 2000); Molyda Szymusiak (Buth Keo), *The Stones Cry Out: A Cambodian Childhood, 1975–1980* [1986] (Bloomington: Indiana University Press, 1999); Usha Welaratna, *Beyond the Killing Field: Voices of Nine Cambodian Survivors* (Stanford, Calif.: Stanford University Press, 1994); and Dith Pran, et al., *Children of Cambodia's Killing Fields: Memoirs by Survivors* (New Haven, Conn.: Yale University Press, 1999).

4. Harold Kaplan, *Conscience and Memory* (Chicago: University of Chicago Press, 1994), x.

5. James Young, *The Texture of Memory: Holocaust Memorials and Meaning* (New Haven, Conn.: Yale University Press, 1994), 7.

6. Beginning in March 1969, the United States began secret bombing raids on Vietnamese communist sanctuaries and supply routes inside Cambodia. Authorized by President Nixon and directed by national security advisor, Henry Kissinger, the raids were illegal because the United States had not officially declared war on Cambodia. In fourteen months, 110,000 tons of bombs were dropped. These raids continued into 1973, and it is estimated that 539,129 tons of bombs were dropped, about three and a half times more than the 153,000 tons dropped on Japan during World War II. Up to 600,000 Cambodians were killed in these raids.

The lack of overt criticism within Cambodian/American autobiographical productions of U.S. involvement in Cambodia is perhaps largely due to the fact that those writing about the events that occurred during the period of the Killing Fields are writing primarily from a refugee position within the United States. Thus, their political status as refugees who sought asylum in the United States circumscribes the extent to which criticism of the country of settlement is rendered.

7. James Garbarino, Kathleen Kostelny, and Nancy Dubrow, *No Place to Be a Child: Growing Up in a War Zone* (Lexington, Mass.: Lexington Books, 1991), 36.

8. According to Sucheng Chan, the Khmer Rouge "separated children above the age of 7 from their parents and placed them into youth work brigades under the supervision of young Khmer Rouge soldiers and political cadres. . . . [T]he Khmer Rouge used children, who were considered 'purer', less corrupt, and more malleable than adults, to spy on their parents and other older relatives." From *Survivors: Cambodian Refugees in the United States*, 19.

9. According to Sucheng Chan, "year zero" was taken from the French Revolution (*Survivors: Cambodian Refugees*, 18).

10. Ben Kiernan, "Introduction" in *Children of Cambodia's Killing Fields: Memoirs of Survivors*, compiled by Dith Pran, et al. (New Haven, Conn.: Yale University Press, 1999).

11. Sucheng Chan, *Survivors: Cambodian Refugees*, 25.

12. Sucheng Chan, *Survivors: Cambodian Refugees*, 25.

13. Ben Kiernan, "Introduction," xiv.

14. Marianne Hirsch, *Family Frames: Photography, Narrative, and Postmemory* (Cambridge, Mass.: Harvard University Press, 1997), 13.

15. Hirsch, *Family Frames*, 15.

16. Luong Ung, "Author's Note," in *First They Killed My Father* (New York: Harper Collins, 2000).

17. Ung, *First They Killed My Father*, 3.

18. Ung, *First They Killed My Father*, 9 and 13.

19. Ung, *First They Killed My Father*, 72.

20. Ung, *First They Killed My Father*, 71.

21. It should be noted that the issue of bearing children and Ung's characterization of this issue is contradicted by the Khmer Institute, which maintains that this represents an exaggeration by the author (see below).

22. Ung, *First They Killed My Father*, 90.

23. Keav and Geak are Ung's sisters.

24. Ung, *First They Killed My Father*, 169.

25. Steven J. Rubin, "Style and Meaning in Mary Antin's *The Promised Land*: A Reevaluation," in *Studies in American Jewish Literature*, ed. Daniel Walden, No. 5 (Albany: State University of New York Press, 1986), 29.

26. Ung, *First They Killed My Father*, 233.

27. Ung, *First They Killed My Father*, 235.

28. Ung, *First They Killed My Father*, 2–4.

29. Ung, *First They Killed My Father*, 62.

30. Ung, *First They Killed My Father*, 7–8.

31. For a detailed critique of *First They Killed My Father*, please refer to www.khmerinstitute.org/articles/art04.html. This particular site provides an in-depth analysis of Ung's text and raises issues of authenticity and veracity.

32. Ung, *First They Killed My Father*, 54.

33. The Khmer Institute put forth the following proclamation against Luong Ung:

We are not engaged in a crusade against the author; our crusade, if it can be described as such, is to expose the truth so that people may know what the Killing Fields really meant for Cambodians who lived through it. Although Ung's book is subtitled "A Daughter of Cambodia Remembers," it is apparent that she neither truly considers herself a "daughter of Cambodia" (except for the purpose of publicity) nor does she with any kind of accuracy "remember." Unlike the acclaim and support given to the movie *The Killing Fields*, many survivors of the Democratic Kampuchea regime find this book inaccurate, distasteful, and insulting. We believe in this case that misinformation is more dangerous than no information. It is sad that a person would distort and sensationalize such a tragic experience for personal gain. It dishonors the memory of the 1.7 million people who died and the legitimate stories of countless others who have [suffered] and still suffer because of the Khmer Rouge (www.khmerinstitute.org, accessed December 1, 2004).

11

Homosexuality and Korean Immigrant Protestant Churches

Eunai Shrake

"Homosexuality is unbiblical. The Bible does not endorse it."

"Doesn't it depend on how you interpret the Bible? Don't we have to take the historical context of the Bible into consideration?"

"You should not relativize [sic] the meaning of the Bible through contextual interpretation."

"If you truly believe the Bible word by word, why have you allowed me, a woman, to lead the youth group? The Bible does not approve women's leadership in the church, does it?"

"Whatever you say, I am not going to let those liberal Americans corrupt our young ones."

This excerpt from a discussion between myself and the senior pastor at an immigrant Korean/American church during a search committee meeting for a youth pastor, described in greater detail shortly, illustrates the type of confrontation on the issue of sexuality that is occurring in Korean/American churches today. Using this incident as an example, my intention in this chapter is to examine how Korean/American churches embody a synthesis of Confucian practice with fundamentalist theology when they address the issue of homosexuality. This chapter is not a theological debate on the issue of homosexuality but rather an opinion piece based on my personal observations of Korean/American churches over twenty years as an insider.

Like many Asian immigrant churches, Korean/American churches are often composed of two generations: the immigrant generation, who are mostly Korean-speaking adults, and the American-born and American-raised generation, whose primary language is English. Due to language and cultural differences, many Korean immigrant churches offer a separate English ministry for American-born youth and young adults. Holding master's degrees in theology and Christian education, I have worked as a part-time youth pastor in three different Korean immigrant churches for over ten years. When I began teaching full-time at a university, I turned my church work into voluntary services, mostly helping out English ministries in small Korean immigrant churches.

For the past five years, I have been serving as a volunteer youth pastor at a Korean/American Methodist church in the Los Angeles area. Because I was overburdened by the added responsibility in addition to my regular teaching job at the university, I asked the church to hire a paid youth minister to better serve the youth group. The church accepted my request and thus began the search for a youth pastor. I became involved in the search process as a search committee[1] member. After receiving numerous job applications, we narrowed the search down to three candidates. After the first two interviews, the search committee agreed that neither of these two candidates, despite being Korean/American, was a very good match for our youth group. The search committee was then presented with the third candidate, who seemed to be highly qualified in terms of seminary credentials, ministry experiences, and multicultural competence. The search committee members expressed their relief and gratitude that such a qualified candidate, who happened to be a Caucasian, was willing to serve this small Korean immigrant church. We agreed to interview this candidate with potential.

During the job interview, however, the benevolent atmosphere changed. In the midst of the questioning, the senior pastor suddenly asked the candidate about his opinion on homosexuality. As the pastor did not mention anything about the previous two Korean/American candidates' sexual orientations or thoughts on homosexuality, I was quite surprised by his line of questioning. The third candidate, though slightly perplexed, responded to the pastor's question in a calm manner. He stated that he supported gay/lesbian brothers/sisters and their civil as well as religious issues. The candidate's honest opinion regarding this issue prompted the pastor's opposition to hiring the candidate. When the search committee met to discuss the possible hire of the candidate for the position, the pastor strongly opposed the hire. When I asked the pastor why the issue of homosexuality was so important in selecting a youth pastor, he responded that the United Methodist church does not recognize homosexuality and the Bible clearly points out that homosexuality is a sin. He also added that to protect the integrity of the faith, Christians should not accommodate the worldly, especially American, liberal trends in this matter. The search committee members expressed their anxiety about not being able to find another capable youth pastor, but they failed to offer any theological rebuttal to the pastor's arguments against the issue of homosexuality. Moreover, when the pastor expressed his worries about the negative influence of American liberal lifestyles on the lives of the young children, the search committee members, most of whom were immigrant parents themselves, conceded to the pastor's position against the candidate. The candidate was dropped and the church missed a good opportunity to have a capable youth pastor.

This incident of homophobia is not uncommon in many Asian, especially Korean, immigrant churches. I have observed the same pattern in several Korean immigrant churches in which I have served, and there are Asian/American community leaders and scholars who also share the same observation.[2] The incident reminded me of the uproar in 2000, when certain Korean/American church members rallied against gay rights by voicing their support on the streets for Proposition 22, which barred recognition of same-sex marriage contracted outside of California. Why are most Korean immigrant churches so stubbornly conservative on issues of sexuality? Why is the argument against homosexuality so persuasive to the congregation?

In this chapter, I will analyze the prejudicial attitudes toward homosexuality in Korean/American churches by examining the dynamics of religion and sexuality in the evangelical Korean immigrant Protestant churches. I will argue that there are three major sources for the conservative standpoint against homosexuality in Korean immigrant churches:

1. A theological fundamentalist position taken by most Korean immigrant churches;
2. Confucian influence on Korean immigrant churches; and
3. The Korean immigrant churches' anxiety over American cultural liberalism.

In so doing, my analysis will focus on how these factors intertwine with each other in legitimizing the opposition by Korean immigrant churches to homosexuality. Although my work may be relevant to other Asian immigrant churches, I will focus on the Korean immigrant Protestant churches with which I am familiar.

FUNDAMENTALISM VS. EVANGELICALISM

First, the major source for the strong opposition to homosexuality comes from the theological conservatism of most Korean immigrant churches. Traditionally, Korean Protestant churches base their theological positions on the reformed tradition that stemmed from the teachings of such theologians as John Calvin, Martin Luther, John Wesley, and Karl Barth. Though these theologians took different views on many theological doctrines, they all agreed on their belief in the Bible as the central authority.

Since this tradition understood the Bible as the only definitive authority in Christian faith, discovering the original meaning of the Bible became a central concern for theologians and church clerics. As a result, there have been continuous controversies over how to deduce the "true" meaning of the Bible. Nevertheless, the reformed tradition set up the conservative trend in modern-day Christian theology.

Most Korean immigrant churches follow this conservative tradition. In practice, however, two different groups have emerged within conservative Protestant churches: evangelicals and fundamentalists.[3] Fundamentalists and evangelicals share many conservative doctrinal positions, including the inerrancy of the Bible, Trinity, virgin birth, and active evangelism, to name a few. However, they diverge in their ways of dealing with the changing needs of the society. The difference is mostly due to their differing degrees of rigidity in interpreting the Bible. For example, while both fundamentalists and evangelicals believe in the ultimate authority of the Bible, fundamentalists rigidly hold on to the literal interpretation of the Bible without consideration of sociohistorical context of the Biblical times, and thus are less flexible in responding to society's changes than evangelicals.[4] Consequently, they do not tolerate any disagreement and thus separate themselves from the so-called "secular" society. In so doing, fundamentalist Christians often rely on the opinions of certain clerics and theologians who command authority. In contrast, evangelicals acknowledge that there are a variety of interpretations of the Bible and its application to social diversity. While believing in the Bible as the revealed Word of God, evangelicals are more accommodating to different biblical interpretations and their applications than fundamentalists are. As a result, they are more tolerant to the challenges of new ideas and viewpoints than fundamentalists.

Whereas many Korean immigrant churches profess evangelicalism as their theological orientation, their actual practice tends to vacillate between fundamentalism and evangelicalism, depending on the issues in question. In other words, many Korean immigrant churches often switch from the evangelical position to the fundamentalist position on certain issues. For instance, most Korean immigrant churches tends to take a fundamentalist position on sexuality-related issues, including the issue of homosexuality. The strong opposition to homosexuality in the Korean immigrant churches is a clear example of the fundamentalist influence. Needless to say, to argue against homosexuality, Korean immigrant church leaders often employ the fundamentalist tactic of wielding the Bible as their primary weapon to justify their prejudice. What is more troublesome with the use of fundamentalist approach is the selective interpretation of a few passages from the Bible to defend a certain position while ignoring other religio-cultural customs practiced in the Bible of which they currently disapprove.

Typically, many conservative church leaders quote Leviticus 18 and 21 from the Old Testament and a couple of Pauline letters (Romans 1, I Timothy 1, and I Corinthians 6) to argue against same-sex relations.[5] However, they fail to point out that the very same Old Testament also sanctions polygamy, concubinage, and slavery, which are already rejected in modern society. Moreover, according to Boswell,[6] Levitical regulations as Jewish tradition have no hold on Christians; therefore, Leviticus 18 and 21 are irrelevant in explaining Christian hostility to homosexuality. As for the Pauline letters, Boswell claims that their purpose is not to stigmatize sexual behavior of any sort but to condemn the Gentiles for their general infidelity.[7] Also, the Pauline letters forbade women's leadership in the church. This position is currently irrelevant.

Furthermore, Jesus never mentioned homosexuality in the four Gospels. Selectively quoting Bible verses for their convenience, while ignoring the main message of God's love revealed in the Bible as a whole text, is self-serving at best, and hypocritical at worst.

This fundamentalist influence clearly manifested itself in the "search committee meeting turned into a debate over homosexuality" episode that I described earlier. As expected, the pastor referred to the above Bible passages in his argument against homosexuality. As a former theologian, I contested his argument by proposing alternative hermeneutical principles in Biblical exegesis such as form criticism,[8] which provides historical contexts for rediscovering the original meaning of the Bible.[9] However, my counterargument was quickly dismissed when the pastor accused liberal Christians of "relativizing" the meaning of the Bible. Chiding me for making a liberal argument, he revealed his unwillingness to hear any disagreement. Unwilling to disagree with the pastor, none of the committee members voiced their opinion on the issue. Instead, they appeared to be annoyed by my challenging the senior pastor, which they may have thought to be disrespectful behavior. This silent concession to the pastor's position points to another possible source for the opposition to homosexuality in Korean/American churches: Confucian influence.

CONFUCIANISM AND KOREAN IMMIGRANT CHURCHES

Since its establishment, Korean Christianity has adopted certain Confucian traditions, including its patriarchal family system, social hierarchy, legalism, and mannerism.[10] In other words, Korean Christianity exists in combination with Confucian social system. Thus, some people argue that Korean Christianity is basically a "Confucian-Christianity."[11] In this sense, most Korean Christians can be called "Confucian Christians," who identify themselves as Christians but have cultural values and social ethics that are based on Confucianism.

There is no doubt that this "Confucian Christianity" has been carried on in the Korean/American churches that have been founded by post-1965 immigrants,[12] a majority of whom have their cultural background in Korea. Indeed, Confucian moral values have great influence on Korean/American churches and congregation members. Many immigrant generation Korean/Americans arrived in the United States during the 1970s and 1980s when Korea was under stronger Confucian influence than current Korean society. Given the time period of their arrival, it should be noted that many Korean immigrants are even more Confucian in their cultural beliefs than their counterparts in Korea. This strong Confucian influence may play a role in the prejudicial attitudes toward homosexuality in the Korean immigrant churches.

Interestingly, however, there is no direct discussion of sexual orientation or homosexuality in Confucian writings. Nevertheless, Confucian society regards marriage and procreation as the individual's primary filial and social duties, thus obligating men and women to abide by traditional gender roles. Men are expected to have children to pass on their family name, while women are responsible for bearing male children to their husbands. Relations that result in the failure to fulfill one's filial and reproductive duties are seen as disruptive, and are thus condemned. Accordingly, homosexual relations can be considered as deviant behavior from Confucian norms.[13] This may be the reason why Confucians tend to disapprove of homosexuality.

However, in public discourses at many Korean immigrant churches that I have observed for the past two decades, church clerics and members rarely invoke Confucianism in making arguments against homosexuality. In my observations, the conservative attitude toward homosexuality is associated more with the Confucian authoritarian structure of Korean/American churches than with the Confucian ideology on sexuality. As a system of social ethics and moral codes, Confucianism places great emphasis on hierarchical social relationships in which each individual is expected to behave according to his place in the hierarchy. In the Confucian social hierarchy, individuals are expected to show unquestioning respect and obedience to people in authority positions based on age, gender, and social position. Integrating this Confucian hierarchy into its structure in most Korean/American churches, pastors command unquestioned authority over the congregation, especially in the areas of biblical interpretation and its application to issues of social life. In this regard, Confucian hierarchy provides an additional authority to clerics who already assume a position of authority that was created by theological fundamentalism. In other words, Confucian hierarchy is intertwined with the fundamentalist theological leaning of Korean/American churches in legitimizing clerical authority. Commanding this unmatched authority, clerics often legitimize their opinion on certain issues while silencing the congregation. Partly due to their lack of theological training and partly due to Confucian upbringing, Korean/American congregation members tend to follow their pastor's position on most religious and social issues.[14] This Confucian structural influence was quite evident in the committee members' unwillingness to disagree with the pastor in the search committee meeting I previously described. During the whole meeting, no one raised any questions about the pastor's argument against homosexuality. It seemed apparent that, due to their Confucian upbringing, which forbids disagreement with people in positions of authority, committee members were not willing to question the pastor's position on the issue.

The incident shows that Confucian hierarchical structure in the church, combined with fundamentalist theological orientation, can be held partially responsible for the persistently negative attitudes toward homosexuality in Korean immigrant churches.

RESISTANCE TO AMERICAN CULTURAL LIBERALISM

Another factor in the strong opposition to homosexuality in the Korean immigrant churches is related to Korean immigrants' perception of American culture. Many Korean immigrants tend to consider American culture as liberal and morally depraved; therefore they fear the liberal American cultural influence on their children. This anxiety over perceived American cultural liberalism arises from Korean/Americans' immigrant status.

New immigrants commonly resist certain aspects of American culture in order to preserve their cultural tradition. Hence, cultural resistance is a part of ethnic identity formation. In other words, new immigrants solidify their ethnic/cultural identity by adhering to their traditional culture while resisting the mainstream one.[15] Similarly, Korean/Americans tend to selectively adopt certain features of American culture, such as American materialism, while resisting others, especially American cultural liberalism.[16]

The strong opposition to homosexuality may be a part of this cultural resistance to American liberalism. Despite the general consensus of the medical and scientific world that one's sexual orientation is not a moral choice, many Korean/Americans consider homosexuality as a liberal lifestyle that goes against their moral values. Consequently, Korean/American parents, who want their children to follow their cherished Confucian moral tradition, are eager to protect their children from the corrupting influence of this perceived American liberal lifestyle. Out of concern for their children, Korean/American parents turn to the church for moral guidance, allowing the church and clerics to command cultural and moral authority in addition to religious authority. As a result, many Korean immigrants buy into the church's fundamentalist position on the issue of sexual orientation.

In assuming the roles of the guardian of culture and of the protector of children from moral corruption, Korean/American churches and clerics tend to shift social topics, including the issue of sexual orientation, into moral and cultural concerns. By equating Confucian morality with fundamentalist Christian moral values, churches use the Bible as a powerful tool to fundamentalize Korean traditional moral values, and thus to warn congregations against cultural liberalism. Accordingly, exploiting parental anxiety over American liberal moral values becomes a useful mechanism of the church to justify its fundamentalist moral standpoint. It also functions as an effective threat to force parents to conform to the church's position. In so doing, Korean/American churches use culture as a site for legitimizing church's conservatism. This is how the Korean/American churches' opposition to homosexuality became a statement of position rather than an issue of an open and sustained discussion.

I noticed that this method of cultural manipulation was quite effective in the search committee meeting in which I participated. It was somewhat obvious that the pastor linked the Caucasian candidate's race to American cultural liberalism, which in turn, triggered his fear of culture clash. When his fear was confirmed by the candidate's positive attitude toward homosexuality, he desperately tried to block the hire. When the pastor mentioned the need for protecting children from America's bad moral influence, his statement became an ultimatum ending the discussion.

I suspect that not all committee members agreed with the pastor's position against homosexuality. In other Korean/American churches where I previously worked, I occasionally met some members who expressed their opposition to the Korean/American church's conservative stance on many social issues, including homosexuality. However, the fact that no one questioned the pastor suggests that congregation members' extreme concern for their children's moral education superseded their ability to express honest opinions on the issue. Therefore, the committee members conceded to the fundamentalist argument against homosexuality. Uneasiness about the emerging American culture of Korean immigrant Christians, intermingled with their Confucian upbringing, played a consequential role in the silent concession to the pastor's conservative standpoint on homosexuality.

CONCLUSION

In this chapter, I discussed the reasons why Korean immigrant churches have persistently opposed homosexuality and why the church's position has been so persuasive to its congregation.[17] I argued that there are three factors intertwined with each other in strengthening and perpetuating the church's strong opposition to homosexuality: its theological conservatism, a Confucian hierarchy, and the community's biased view of American culture.

Given that these factors have operated inseparably in forming this prejudicial belief regarding sexual orientation, it may not be easy for Korean/American churches to break out of this tendency of being a community of prejudice. For the church to be consistent with its purported mission of openness and inclusiveness, it has to provide a non-prejudicial environment for the LGBT (lesbian, gay, bisexual, transsexual) community, including LGBT children and their parents. To alter this prejudicial mindset and prevent its perpetuation, I suggest changes on three fronts: clerical training, relationship structure in the church, and collaboration between church leaders and community activists.

First, church clerics and leaders should be (re)exposed to alternative sources for the understanding of the Bible. Theological schools and mainline Protestant churches in America should train their students to be open to a variety of biblical interpretations, especially in contextual interpretation of the Bible. In addition, theological schools and the church should also provide open forums on diverse social issues, including issues of sexuality, so that current as well as future clerics may learn to explore diverse ways in applying biblical messages to the modern day social context. In other words, theological schools and the churches, rather than sustaining a statement of position on certain social issues, should provide their students with more space to wrestle with both religious and social issues. This type of clerical training will enable church clerics and leaders to recontextualize the Bible and thus help them think out of the box of fundamentalist confinement. Once changes like this occur in the field of clerical training, then it would be possible for Korean/American churches to abandon over-literal misreadings of the Bible, and thus to replace their fundamentalism with evangelicalism.

Second, there should be a drastic change in the hierarchical structure in Korean/American churches. The best way to avoid human misjudgments would be reaching a consensus through sustained discussions and debates rather than allowing a handful of leaders to claim an absolute authority. Upon acknowledging this structure, church participants should work together on promoting a more democratic and egalitarian relationship. On the one hand, church clerics and leaders should learn to make open discussions available to their congregation instead of dominating the decisionmaking process on the issues surrounding congregation life. Clerics and leaders should work on changing the top-down structure in the church by participating in the discussion as equal partners with lay people. On the other hand, lay people should be encouraged to break out of the habitual silence by learning to express their opinions through active participation in discussion. In other words, both church clerics and lay people need to break free from the confinement of Confucian hierarchy so that they may freely exchange their ideas without worrying about disrespecting or being disrespected.

Once the church begins creating a more democratic environment, I believe that more socially open-minded lay people will come out expressing opinions that would be different from the church's claimed position, and this in turn would bring about a change in attitudes and beliefs on many social issues including homosexuality.

Lastly, to facilitate changes in Korean immigrant churches, there should be cooperation between church leaders and community activists. There has been a tendency for socially open-minded Korean/American community activists to leave the church due to their disappointment with its conservative stance in dealing with social issues. Instead of overlooking their departure, church clerics should invite these community activists back to the church and encourage them to share with the congregation their knowledge of, and expertise in, cultural diversity in the mainstream society. Community activists, in turn, should actively involve themselves in the church by helping clerics and lay people to overcome their ignorance about, and their ensuing anxiety over, mainstream cultural liberalism. Moreover, community leaders can assist clerics and lay people in differentiating social issues, such as the issue of sexual orientation, from moral issues by clarifying diverse social issues that may impact the congregation's life. Community leaders should also remind church clerics that unless they open themselves to diverse social issues and accommodate certain aspect of mainstream life, Korean/American churches will most likely fail to reach out to future generations who are more Americanized and thus more exposed to American cultural diversity. Once community activists start playing leadership roles in the church by collaborating with open-minded clerics, this will eventually bring about positive changes in the church's attitudes and beliefs on social issues, including the issue of sexual orientation.

The issue of sexual orientation and same-sex marriage will continue to be an important topic of our social and political debate that may have profound impact on the young generation of Korean/Americans. For this reason, if Korean/American churches wish to remain an important part of both immigrant and American-born generation Korean/Americans' lives, they should dispose of their disgraceful image as a community of prejudice by accommodating cultural diversity, including different sexual orientations.

NOTES

1. The search committee was composed of the senior pastor, two elders (one male and one female), two lay members (one male and one female), and myself as a youth pastor.

2. See, for example, Yun J. Cho, "Straight from the Church? Debate on Homosexuality in Korean American Churches" (paper presented at Asian and Pacific Americans Religion and Research Initiative [APARRI] Conference, 2002); and Jason Ma, "Straight from the Church: How Korean American Churches in California Rallied Against Gay Rights," *Asian Week* 21, 26 January 2000.

3. Fenggang Yang, "Gender and Generation in a Chinese Christian Church," in *Asian American Religions*, ed. Tony Carnes and Fenggang Yang (New York: New York University Press, 2004).

4. Yang, "Gender and Generation."

5. See, for example, Robert A. J. Gagnon, *The Bible and Homosexual Practice: Texts and Hermeneutics* (Nashville: Abingdon Press, 2002); and also Robert A. J. Gagnon and Dan O. Via, *Homosexuality and the Bible: Two Views* (Minneapolis: Fortress Press, 2003).

6. John Boswell, *Christianity, Social Tolerance, and Homosexuality* (Chicago: University of Chicago Press, 1980). In this groundbreaking work on the history of homosexuality, Boswell offers a revolutionary new interpretation of the attitudes and practices of the early Christian period vis-à-vis homosexuality. In this pioneering book, Boswell claims that the Christian church had not always been homophobic but had become so in the later thirteenth century as the church attempted to consolidate power. This sharply undermines the conservative beliefs that homophobia is an immutable feature in Christianity.

7. Boswell, *Christianity, Social Tolerance, and Homosexuality.*

8. Developed by preeminent German theologians Hermann Gunkel and Rudolf Bultmann, form criticism seeks to discover the original meaning of the Bible by analyzing each Bible text's literary genre and the historical as well as sociological setting. This process has been described as "demythologizing," and through this demythologizing process, the underlying, kernel message of God, called "kerygma," is to be uncovered.

9. Carl E. Armerding, *The Old Testament and Criticism* (Grand Rapids, Mich.: Eerdmans, 1983).

10. Andrew E. Kim, "Political Insecurity, Social Chaos, Religious Void and the Rise of Protestantism in Late Nineteenth-Century Korea," *Social History* 26 (2001): 267–82.

11. Many Korean theologians and Korean church historians argue that Christianity in Korea survived and prospered by accommodating to Korean Confucian culture. Some prefer to label it "Confucian-Christianity" or "Koreanized Christianity." See, for example, Young-Gwan Kim, "The Confucian-Christian Context in Korean Christianity," *B.C. Asian Review* 13 (2002): 70–91; and Jahyun Kim Haboush, "The Confucianization of Korean Society," in *The East Asian Religion: Confucian Heritage and Its Modern Adaptation*, ed. Gilbert Rozman (Princeton, N.J.: Princeton University Press, 1961).

12. Pyong Gap Min, "The Structure and Social Functions of Korean Immigrant Churches in the U.S.," *International Migration Review* 26 (1992): 1370–94.

13. Keith Pratt, *Korea: A Historical and Cultural Dictionary* (London: Routledge, 1999).

14. In the Korean/American churches I served, I rarely witnessed pastors who encouraged lay members to participate in theological seminars or conferences, or provided forums for theological debate. Rather, I witnessed some pastors promote conservative social/political agendas through their sermons, pressing lay members to

follow the pastor's position. This was particularly noticeable during the past two presidential elections when many pastors encouraged lay members to vote for the conservative candidate.

15. For further understanding of this "additive or adhesive" assimilation pattern, see Won Moo Hurh and Kwang Chung Kim, "Beyond Assimilation and Pluralism: Syncretic Sociocultural Adaptation of Korean Immigrants in the US," *Ethnic and Racial Studies* 16 (4) (1993): 496–513; and Pyong Gap Min, "Cultural and Economic Boundaries of Korean Ethnicity: A Comparative Analysis," *Ethnic and Racial Studies* 14 (1991): 225–41.

16. Liberalism in this context does not imply a liberal view of society or progressive political ideology. Rather, it refers to American diverse lifestyles that endorse individual freedom and choice, which may conflict with Asian moral and cultural values of family and group conformity. Despite the uncritical acceptance of Western culture since the early twentieth century, many Koreans consider homosexuality as an unwanted Western import of a liberal lifestyle, which they often equate with moral decadence.

17. The persistent anti-homosexual stance in Korean/American churches is puzzling to me considering the fact that Korean/American churches have been increasingly more tolerant to other issues of sexuality, such as women's active roles in the church (e.g., ordination), divorce, abortion, and contraceptives, on which they had traditionally taken a conservative stance.

12

Finding Fellatio

Friendship, History, and Yone Noguchi

Amy Sueyoshi

In March 1899 Kōsen Takahashi, an illustrator for the San Francisco Japanese-language newspaper *Shin Sekai*, fretted over the disappearance of his friend Yone Noguchi, who had quietly left the foggy city to travel. Takahashi was "nearly drowning" in his tears after having lost his dearest Yone. "Oh where is my sweetheart?" Kōsen declared. He was nearly "mad" searching for Yone, as he dreamed of their reunion when their "warm lips" would join in an "eternal" kiss.[1] At the turn of the century, Kōsen's longing for Yone might appear as an unusually passionate articulation of Japanese immigrant intimacy. However, the affectionate expression becomes doubly queer since it involved two men. What was the significance of Kōsen and Yone's relationship? Historians studying friendship among white women and men note that before the twentieth century, homosociability allowed for the acceptance of intense friendships between people of the same sex. Within this romantic friendship framework, the queer duo might appear mundane, deserving little historical notice. However, a closer look into Yone's intimate life, in particular his relationship with white western writer Charles Warren Stoddard, points to the lesser known existence of passionate and lasting same-sex relationships among first-generation or Issei men. Notably, these affections appeared to thrive relatively peaceably among immigrants who already felt alienated from the dictates of a larger mainstream moral code. Indeed, Yone's affairs would offer alternative realities of affectionate expression and alienation in the seemingly all-white world of American friendship as well as Japanese immigrant asexuality more than one hundred years ago.

For Yone, Kōsen, and perhaps other Japanese living in a largely homosocial immigrant community, the most significant relationships—those of deep discussions and even romantic if not sexual fulfillment—likely occurred between men. Yet Asian/Americanists more inclined to focus on the deprivation rather than delight of homosocial environments and historians' knowledge of acceptable intimate male friendships among white bohemians at the time have erased the unique significance these intimacies offer. For Asian/American history, these same-sex ties among Japanese point to how these men did not necessarily live devoid of romance in harsh bachelor communities. For the history of romantic friendship—read as a completely white, middle-class phenomena—Yone, Kōsen, and others reveal not just how men of color existed within this bastion of white male privilege, but also how race informed the desires of these white bohemians who considered themselves to be stewards of tolerance and internationalism. Passionate letters written by immigrant men such as Yone and Kōsen would not be just another browned version of American friendship. With their Japanese immigrant status, their intimacies would hold complicated interactions of exotification and alienation not just from whites but from themselves as well.

In 1975 Carroll Smith-Rosenberg first set the cornerstone for the study of same-sex friendships when she detailed how literate, middle-class, white women in the eighteenth and nineteenth century sustained intense emotional if not physical ties to one other. Using private letters, Smith-Rosenberg traced the socially acceptable "sensual and platonic" love these women friends and family members held for each other. Her article stirred decades of debate, particularly around the sexual orientation of these women.[2] While Smith-Rosenberg never mentioned the "L" word in her essay, she pointed to the dilemma in tracing intimacy among individuals of the same-sex in the past[3]: "[D]id the word 'love' connote to these women, as it does to us, the recognition of sexual desire . . . [o]r, alternatively, to feelings rooted not in sexual desire but in experiences of intimacy and affection that grew out of women's shared physical and psychological realities?"[4] Because of existing nineteenth-century norms for people to express themselves with effusive emotion, even graphic erotic words could not necessarily point to a sexual relationship.

As works on the normalcy of intense female networks proliferated, critics protested that "friendship" once again desexualized women. Blanche Wiesen Cook cautioned against the "historical denial of lesbianism," while Mary E. Wood noted that the use of "romantic friendship" avoided the more subversive label of lesbian and painted these relationships as pure and conflict-free.[5] By the late 1980s and early 1990s, scholars such as Lisa Moore and Emma Donoghue began writing about how some women saw their same-sex intimacies as different from acceptable female affection. Finally in 2004 Martha Vicinus synthesized and elaborated upon 150 years of friendship among educated, white women both in its acceptable and illicit forms.[6]

Unlike works on women, the study of male friendship from its begin-
nings has appeared more closely tied to sexuality, employing the word "homosexuality" rather than the ambiguous language of "friendship." Alan
Bray in 1982 titled his seminal book *Homosexuality in Renaissance England,*
a work often credited for founding friendship studies.[7] Two years later literary critic Eve Sedgwick named the male intimacies she examined as homosocial "desire" rather than "love" to emphasize its erotic nature. In 1994
Alan Sinfield's "same-sex passion" included physical as well as emotional
intimacy.[8]

While passionate exchanges between women appeared to form pacts of
emotional support, male relationships appeared to have sociopolitical results—namely, the preservation of class and patriarchal privilege. If these relationships did not reinforce social ordering among the men themselves,
they frequently replicated societal hierarchies by excluding women, the un-
lettered, or poor from their fraternal networks.[9] More recently, however,
works that favor the centrality of emotional "love" rather than sex have
been increasing, such as those by Jeffrey Merrick and George Haggerty. Others, such as Anya Jabour and Anthony Rotundo, have directly applied
Smith-Rosenberg's theories on romantic friendship to their own work. Bray
himself implemented a less singularly sexual framework in his most recent
work titled "The Friend."[10]

Moreover, source materials have dictated differences between female and
male friendship studies. While scholarship on women tends to rely heavily
on personal documents such as letters and diaries, publications on male
homosociality also extensively utilize literature, poetry, and plays, as well as
criminal records. Not only have men historically had more access to education and publishing than women, but legal and moral codes also more actively policed "sodomy" than genital contact between women. Those who
allegedly broke these codes left paper trails and fostered discourse on male-
male sexual intimacy.[11] Despite the differences, the two gendered fields
have a single similarity—both have yet to be significantly informed by critical considerations of race.

In the midst of a significantly diverse population in North America, the
current scholarship on U.S. friendship hardly considers people of color.[12]
Indeed, in a social world of middle-class whites mingling passionately as
equals with one another, those not white would likely not appear. Scholars
Walter Williams and Paula Gunn Allen noted the existence of American Indian women's communities of female intimacy as vastly distinct from and
unrelated to romantic friendships. The interracial homosocial interactions
within the diverse southern mines of the Gold Rush that historian Susan
Johnson traced more closely resembled networks of exploitation than any
passionate letter-writing endeavor between men. When Judy Wu documented Chinese/American physician Margaret Chung's intimate affairs

with women that began in the 1920s, lesbian identity rather than romantic friendships had already begun to overshadow female intimacies.[13]

Notably, in 1996 Karen Hansen, a sociologist well established in friendship studies, brought race to the field when she traced the correspondence of one African American woman to another.[14] During the 1860s in Connecticut, domestic worker Addie Brown wrote letters to Rebecca Primus, a teacher. Hansen articulated their significance in terms of race: "[I]t differs from the white women's correspondence in many ways, most importantly, in that it documents an explicitly erotic—as distinct from romantic— friendship."[15]

Evidence of what Hansen named as "bosom sex" proved their erotic relationship. In 1867 Addie, who worked at a school, wrote to Rebecca of one particular female student who wanted to sleep with her. After Addie finally consented, she wrote to Rebecca "[i]f you think that is my bosom that captivated the girl that made her want to sleep with me, she got sadly disappointed injoying it, for I had my back towards her all night and my night dress was butten up so she could not get to my bosom." She assured Rebecca: "I shall try to keep your f[lavored] one always for you." Hansen noted that comparable explicitness such as this remained absent among letters of nineteenth-century white women.[16]

However, the better-known English and white woman Anne Lister wrote explicitly of her sexual exploits with other women, albeit in her journal. When a widow in Paris climbed into her bed Lister wrote: "I was contented that my naked left thigh should rest upon her naked left thigh and thus she let me grubble her over her petticoats. All the while I was pressing her between my thighs. Now and then I held my hand still and felt her pulsation, let her rise towards my hand two or three times and gradually opened her thighs, and felt that she was excited."[17] In comparison to Anne's writings, Addie's might seem more girlish than erotic. Moreover, Hansen's argument that Addie's letters differed most significantly from white women's correspondence in its erotic content might ring uncomfortably familiar to black feminists who, since the late 1960s, have protested the hypersexualization of black women in scholarly studies and popular culture.[18]

Indeed, Addie's letters hold additional importance when their difference from white women's correspondence would not define their primary significance. Evaluated on their own, Addie's letters demonstrated a certain freedom within the free black community in her explicit expressions of same-sex affections. Addie's letters may also suggest how white women hoped to engage sexually with African American women in ways that white women did not articulate in their letters to one another, since the student that climbed into Addie's bed was in fact a "whit[ie]."[19] Notably, the intimate affairs of Japanese immigrant Yone, about whose departure Kōsen lamented tearfully in 1899, reveals similar parallels. Not only would Yone have intimate interactions with a white man, Charles Warren Stoddard, but Yone also expressed his same-sex affections more publicly than Charles. Their affair additionally appeared eroticized by racial difference, especially for Charles.

In 1893, at the age of nineteen, Yone traveled to the United States to facilitate his ambition to become an English-language poet. California writer Joaquin Miller introduced Yone to Charles as well as other literary figures.[20] Through the earliest years of the twentieth century, Yone wrote regularly to Charles, and Charles's letters in return brought "great pleasure," "certain sweet odor," and "sweetest thoughts" that Yone wished he could have every day.[21]

From the outset, Charles perceived Yone as his "sensual" "Orient[al]" friend, a poet filled with "fire" and "primitive eloquence."[22] In his personal notebook, Charles wrote his impressions of Yone: "Dearest Yone Noguchi! Eyes? His eyes are the windows of a temple, filled with the shadow of mystery. What a pernicious little body his is! As of ivory . . . as an idol that has wakened from a mystical dream. His soul—a, tis jewell in the lotus."[23] The use of words such as "Orient," "fire," "temple," "mystery," "ivory," and "jewel in the lotus" could only point to the most orientalist of fantasies that Charles painted upon Yone.[24] At their first meeting, Yone sensed Charles's disappointment. "It would have been more natural had I been barefooted and in a Japanese kimono," he recalled. Charles "condemned" Yone as "far too Americanized." Yone remained fully aware, if not annoyed, that Charles imagined him as a mystical persona from the Pacific: "Did he expect me to be another Kana Ana—a little sea god of his South Sea, shaking the spray from his forehead like a porpoise? I am positive he prayed that I would come to him in some Japanese robe at the least."[25]

Rather than recoil from Charles' racialization, Yone pursued Charles at his home in Washington, D.C., a gathering place known among friends as the "Bungalow." In 1900 they spent afternoons dozing comfortably together in a single armchair, chatted without end, and shared each other's most trivial secrets. In the evenings they slept in the same bed. Upon his return Yone wrote: "My Dear Charles, How rare your sweet magnetism! Your breath so soft and impressive like autumn rain! Your love—Thank God! So heavenly! Why shortest—how sad it was short!—, but loveliest visit to you was my dream realized, it cannot be forgotten. It was a great event in my life. . . . You are my ideal person."[26] During the Christmas holidays of 1901, Yone frequented the Bungalow almost every day.

Yet that same year after Yone relocated to New York, he hired writer Léonie Gilmour to edit his works and he reportedly fell in "love at first sight" with Ethel Armes, a reporter from the *Washington Post*.[27] While Léonie would become pregnant by Yone and give birth to his first child, Isamu, Yone proposed marriage to Ethel.[28] When Léonie moved to Los Angeles to live with her mother and raise the baby, Yone still hoped to marry Ethel and take her to Japan in July 1904. Charles disapproved of the union. He emphasized that Ethel and Yone lacked "a nature sufficiently practical to manage domestic affairs": "You should both be free, remain free of encumbrances so long as you live. This is my firm conviction."[29] As Charles expressed his unconditional "love" for Yone regardless of his decision to marry, the intimacy of their relationship exposed itself more fully: "How I long to see you; to hold you in my arms again and tell you how dearly I love you or how I shall miss you when you are gone far away. If I had my Bungalow and the money to run it I should implore you to come to me and dwell with me forever."[30] Interestingly, Charles's suggestion to live a life "free of encumbrances" included himself instead of Ethel by Yone's side.

Even as Yone planned to marry Ethel he wrote publicly of his love for Charles. In *National Magazine* with a circulation of nearly three hundred thousand, Yone detailed his deep "love" for Charles in 1904:

> Ho, ho, . . . in Charles's Bungalow! Til that day we had embraced each other only in letter. "Oh Yone, you would fit in there," Charles exclaimed. We both sat in one huge chair with a deep hollow where we could doze comfortably, its long arms appearing but a pair of oars carrying us into the isle of dream. We talked on many things far and near,—things without beginning and apparently without end. We agreed upon every point. We aroused ourselves to such a height of enthusiasm. . . . Is there any more delicious thing than to listen to his talk about nothing? How full of little stories he is![31]

Yone further recalled his elation when he first began writing to Charles, how he gathered flowers along a hillside, how he then offered his bouquet to an imaginary Charles, and how he blew kisses toward his bungalow in Washington, D.C.

Yone's open publication of his love for Charles in *National Magazine* and the later reprint of the same article in his autobiography, *The Story of Yone Noguchi Told by Himself*, differed dramatically from Charles's more measured public comments about Yone.[32] Yone likely believed that his public statements participated in a larger bohemian discourse of collegial gladhand and fraternal intimacy. What he perhaps did not realize was that he, perhaps more so than any other American of his time, publicly detailed the affections that passed in the privacy of cozy sitting rooms. As white bohemians and writers such as Charles appeared cautious in their sexuality to avoid the tragic fate of their British counterpart and alleged "sodomite" Oscar Wilde, Japanese men such as Yone and Kōsen may have engaged more innocently in intimate same-sex relationships in public ways.[33]

In 1899 Kōsen ardently and openly professed his love for Yone in successive letters to Blanche Partington, a virtual stranger. Yone had just recently hired Blanche to edit his English-language writings before publication and Kōsen had not yet met Yone's newest editorial assistant. In his letter to Blanche, Kōsen accused of Yone of being an "eloping lover" who had deserted him for the seductive calls of spring. Yone the "flying lover" had left Kōsen in a pool of sorrow and tears. Kōsen declared to Blanche that he stood on the brink of madness, "still wooing [Yone] ever and ever." He had "sacrificed" his "whole heart." Kōsen wrote: "I woo to him as a boy do so for a girl well! Yone is my lover forever." As if baring his own heart brimming with same-sex affection did not prove to be enough, Kōsen then exposed Yone's unusual proclivities as well. He explained: "Yone is most queer boy among all Nipponese, and very curiousnessness of his strange manner, his character is far different from average man." He added: "I have great deal to talk [to] you something [about] Yone." As Kōsen looked forward to meeting Blanche he concluded: "I am utmost queer fellow as much as Yone is. Perhaps you will [be] surprised as you see me." For Kōsen, discretion around his affection for Yone as well as his unusual character, whether it be sexual in nature or not, appeared to be the farthest thing from his mind.[34]

For these two and perhaps countless other unknown Japanese immigrants, their alien status in white America may have afforded them personal liberty to become more expressive. American whites seemed undaunted by Japanese expressions of same-sex affections, since they appeared to reflect merely what intellectuals and artists believed to be the asethetic and poetic "Japanese soul."[35] In 1905 Japanese internationalist Inazō Nitobe published his bestseller *Bushido*, dedicated to exposing the West to the "moral and ethical value[s] of Japanese men." With its passages on the beauty of male-male love, the book gained immense popularity in the United States with no moral censure.[36] In the absence of explicit advice against their open expressions of love between men, these Japanese may have written more freely in their unfamiliarity with unspoken American mores.

Meanwhile, the women who comprised Yone's messy matrimonial possibilities appeared aware of Yone's shortcomings as a husband. Though Ethel had planned on moving to Japan in 1905, their reunion never materialized.[37] While Léonie later moved to Japan in 1906 after much insistence from Yone, she also held little expectation. Before finally deciding to move to Japan, Léonie pushed Yone to seriously consider the implications of his invitation. She asked if he would be happy with the companionship of a wife he did not love—if he could continue to live with love "shut out" of his life: "[S]omeday I will come. And you can see Baby all you like. And we will have a proper separation when you get ready—and you will remarry according to your better and ripen judgment."[38] Léonie confided in others as well about her relationship. One friend noted: "She seems to accept that he doesn't love her, that he can't love her."[39] When Léonie informed Stoddard of her imminent departure to Japan, she remarked: "I quite agree with you that poets—at least some of them—were not made for domestic uses. So I shall open the door of the cage as soon as I get over there."[40] Yone also conceded to Léonie that there was something "awry" with himself. Shortly after the birth of Isamu, Yone asked for Gilmour's forgiveness; wished to God that he could love her, but could not; appreciated her kindness; and deplored his "temperament."[41] Though Léonie would eventually move to Japan, they lived in separate households until her own return to the United States. Ultimately, Yone would marry Matsu Takeda, a Japanese woman who he had employed to do his domestic work.

As a married man, Yone continued to write to Charles from Japan and confessed to thinking of him daily. He repeatedly invited Charles to visit and later move to Japan to live with him.[42] Yone's affectionate letters often pleaded for the comfort of Charles's company. He wrote: "[A]gain I am hungry (to) read your work, and touch on your feeling and fancy. Dear dad, I love you—you know that."[43] In an additional letter he conceded his neglect of Charles and pleaded with him to write back: "I must be wicked fellow to think I was perfectly honest and loyal to you. However, I was right in my heart and never forgot you. I feel lonesome for you today being alone at home as I said I felt loneliness for you today so I began to read *For the Pleasure of His Company*. That book makes me feel at one (with) your heart pulls and blood. I felt somehow happy afterward." Literary critics have tagged *For the Pleasure of His Company* as San Francisco's earliest gay novel.[44]

Charles occupied Yone's most intimate thoughts in an immeasurable way. His words revealed how Charles held his heart more tightly than even the women with whom he considered marriage. Their "love" remained significant and unique for the most personal reasons, a deeply emotional commitment that endured until Charles's death in 1909. Their intimacy additionally signaled how individuals of the same sex could hold remarkable friendships across racial lines with little consequence. Yone's explicit expressions of same-sex intimacy, paired with Addie's letters to Rebecca, suggest that non-whites may have engaged in the queerest of friendships with full knowledge of its personal significance and little turmoil over its social implication. Those already marginalized by race may have felt little compulsion to be regulated by Euro-American standards if it did not directly affect their livelihood.

Yone's intimacies further demonstrate how he stretched moral and racial boundaries of turn-of-the-century American sexual ideology. Not only did he articulate same-sex love, but also interracial marriage during times of increasing animosity toward both. While the prevalence and acceptability of passionate friendships between men likely facilitated his intimacy with Charles, his incomplete understanding of the tide of American morality may have left him free to openly express his sentiments. In early-1900s California, nativist groups began forming an anti-Japanese campaign. Nationwide, men too "dandy" and unusually intimate with other men had become increasingly suspect with the "outing" and incarceration of Wilde. America's romance with Japan as well as sensitive, well-groomed men who mixed well with other men seemed to be ending. In the very midst of changing American ideas about the Japanese and same-sex sexuality, Yone in his bohemian bubble may have fallen one lesson behind.

Furthermore, Yone revealed alternative narratives within well-researched early Asian/American histories that have assumed heterosexuality as the ideal norm. Immigration historians depicted these early years when men severely outnumbered women as a time of great deprivation.[45] While many likely suffered from the gender imbalance, Yone and others could have just as likely forged fulfilling intimacies within vibrant homosocial environments.[46] Yet Yone's unique relationship with Charles has largely gone unnoticed, perhaps because of the lack of evidence detailing explicit genital contact or maybe even due to the influence of presentist notions of Asian/American male asexuality that make it nearly impossible to imagine immigrants as love machines. Ironically, scholars in Japan have glossed over the significance of Kōsen's impassioned pleas for Yone as being typical of feverish bohemians of the time. Ultimately, the closeting of Yone's same-sex intimacies might lie in the ubiquity of heteronormativity.

No evidence of genital contact with Ethel exists, yet just four recovered letters proclaiming "love" and a possible marriage have produced at least some scholarship that recounts their relationship as more than just late-Victorian friendship.[47] Thus, while nuanced interpretations of same-sex friendships reflect thoughtful historical contextualization, they may just as likely point to the insidious nature of heteronormativity. Among differently sexed couples the mere articulation of "love" in letters immediately signals a romance of greater intimacy than friendship without rigorous inspection. Marriage or a birth of a child then confirms the assessment. There would be no investigation to see if the couple's union was one of genuine love, no requisite genetic testing to prove that the child was a product of both parents, no inquiry into the couple's relationship to examine if sexual intercourse was consensual. While legal documents appear all too ready to reveal heterosexual bonds, they seem more resistant to telling stories of same-sex couples and the intimacies they might have shared. Shots of semen into warm mouths, clitorises massaged to orgasm, personal pacts to care for one another, all appear largely undetectable in history outside of the handful of criminal records or sensationalized stories. Additionally, finding sex acts proves even more difficult among communities not necessarily socialized to be explicitly sexual. In the absence of finding fellatio, for example, the best conclusion for these affairs might very well be romantic friendship.

Sexual intercourse, however, might have little do to with the most intimate exchanges between people. An identical sex act might hold varied
meetings depending on geography, history, and culture. A gay male anally
penetrating his partner after an afternoon at Pride may likely have a different sexual identity and concept of his act than a man on the "down-low"
having the same anal sex with a man he just met under a freeway overpass.
Similarly, two men holding hands might signal a budding romance on Cas-
tro Street in San Francisco and merely weekend soccer mates on an un-
named street in Mindif, Cameroon. Ultimately, genital or any physical contact, even if available, might prove to be a faulty determiner of the "true"
nature of relationships.[48] It would appear that finding fellatio, or cunnilin-
gus for that matter, is far less important than mapping emotions when documenting the most important relationships of our past.

NOTES

1. Kōsen Takahashi, San Francisco to Blanche Partington, 24 March 1899. From
Ikuko Atsumi, *Yone Noguchi Collected English Letters* (Tokyo: The Yone Noguchi Society, 1975), 34–35.

2. Smith-Rosenberg's essay titled "Female World of Love and Ritual" appeared in
Signs: Journal of Women in Culture and Society I (1) (1975): 1–29. For the debates that
arose, see Ellen Dubois in "Politics and Culture in Women's History: A Sympo-
sium," *Feminist Studies* VI (Spring 1980): 28–36; Liz Stanley, "Romantic Friendship?
Some Issues in Researching Lesbian History," *Women's History Review* 1 (1992):
193–216; Sylvia Martin, "'These Walls of Flesh': The Problem of the Body in the Romantic Friendship/Lesbianism Debate," *Historical Reflections/Réflexions Historiques*
20 (1994): 243–66; Marylynne Diggs, "Romantic Friends or a 'Different Race of
Creatures?' The Representation of Lesbian Pathology in Nineteenth Century America," *Feminist Studies* 21 (1995): 317–40; Molly McGarry, Kanchana Natarjan, Dása
Franèiková, Tania Navarro Swain, and Karin Lützen, "Carroll Smith-Rosenberg's
'The Female World of Love and Ritual' after Twenty Five Years," *Journal of Women's
History* 12 (2000): 8–38; and Leila J. Rupp, "Romantic Friendships," *Modern American Queer History*, ed. Allida Black and John Howard (Philadelphia: Temple Univer-
sity Press, 2001).

3. The "L" in this case refers to the word "lesbian."

4. Smith-Rosenberg, *Disorderly Conduct*, 35–36.

5. Blanche Wiesen Cook, "The Historical Denial of Lesbianism," *Radical History
Review* 20 (Spring/Summer 1979): 60–65; Mary E. Wood, "'With Ready Eye': Mar-
garet Fuller and Lesbianism in Nineteenth Century American Literature," *American
Literature* 65 (1) (March 1993), 3.

6. The following works have more explicitly noted intimate relationship between
women as "lesbian," "lesbian-like," or "proto-lesbian": Lisa Moore, "Something More
Tender Still Than Friendship: Romantic Friendship in Early Nineteenth-Century Eng-

land," *Feminist Studies* 18 (3) (Fall 1992): 499–520; Emma Donoghue, *Passions Between Women: British Lesbian Culture, 1668–1801* (New York: Harper Collins, 1993); and Martha Vicinus, *Intimate Friends: Women who Loved Women, 1778–1928* (Chicago: University of Chicago Press, 2004). See also Ann Lister, *I Know My Own Heart: 1817–1824*, ed. Helena Whitbread (London: Virago, 1988); Ann Lister, *No Priest but Love: 1824–1826*, ed. Helena Whitbread (West Yorkshire: Smith Settle, 1992); Winfried Schleiner, "Le Feu Cache: Homosocial Bonds Between Women in Renaissance Romance," *Renaissance Quarterly* 45 (2) (Summer 1992): 293–311; Valerie Traub, *The Renaissance of Lesbianism in Early Modern England* (Cambridge: Cambridge University Press, 2002); Lillian Faderman, *Surpassing the Love of Men: Romantic Friendship and Love Between Women From the Renaissance to the Present* (New York: Perennial, 2001); and Lillian Faderman, *Odd Girls and Twilight Lovers: A History of Lesbian Life in Twentieth Century America* (New York: Columbia University Press, 1991).

7. I sardonically use the word "seminal" here to highlight the irony in crediting Bray's avowedly masculinist work published in 1982 as founding friendship studies seven years after Smith-Rosenberg's work appeared. In a special *GLQ* issue dedicated to Alan Bray in 2004, Jody Green called Bray the "founder of a new field, one we might call 'friendship studies.'" She went further to propose that "[w]ithout him, 'friendship studies' . . . might well not exist." Jody Green, "Introduction: The Work of Friendship," *Gay and Lesbian Quarterly* 10 (3) (2004): 320–21. According to Karin Lützen, Smith-Rosenberg's essay likely proved "queer before queer studies was invented."

8. For the publications that explicitly link male friendship to sexuality, see Alan Bray, *Homosexuality in Renaissance England* (London: Gay Men's, 1982); Eve Kosofsky Sedgwick, *Between Men: English Literature and Male Homosocial Desire* (New York: Columbia University Press, 1984), 1; Alan Sinfield, *The Wilde Century: Effeminacy, Oscar Wilde and the Queer Moment* (London: Cassell, 1994); and Karin Lützen, "The Female World Viewed from Denmark," *Journal of Women's History* 12 (3) (Autumn 2000): 37.

9. Jeffrey Merrick, "Male Friendship in Prerevolutionary France," *Gay and Lesbian Quarterly* 10 (2004): 405–32; Alan Bray, "Homosexuality and Signs of Male Friendship I Elizabethan England," *History Workshop Journal* 29 (1990): 1–19; Gregory W. Bredbeck, *Sodomy and Interpretation: Marlowe to Milton* (Ithaca: Cornell University Press, 1991); Bruce R. Smith, *Homosexual Desire in Shakespeare's England: A Cultural Poetics* (Chicago: University of Chicago Press, 1991); Goldberg, *Sodometries*; and Alan Stewart, *Close Readers: Humanism and Sodomy in Early Modern England* (Princeton, N.J.: Princeton University Press, 1997).

10. Merrick, "Male Friendship in Prerevolutionary France"; George E. Haggerty, *Men in Love: Masculinity and Sexuality in the Eighteenth Century* (New York: Columbia University Press, 1999); Anya Jabour, "Male Friendship and Masculinity in the Early National South: William Wirt and His Friends," *Journal of the Early Republic* 20 (1) (Spring 2000): 83–111; E. Anthony Rotundo, "Romantic Friendship: Male Intimacy and Middle Class Youth in the Northern United States, 1800–1900," *Journal of Social History* 23 (1989): 1–25; and Alan Bray, *The Friend* (Chicago: University of Chicago Press, 2003). See also Jeffrey Richards, "'Passing the Love of Women': Manly Love and Victorian Society," in *Manliness and Morality: Middle Class Masculinity in*

Britain and America, 1800–1940 (Manchester, UK: Palgrave Macmillan, 1987), 92–122; Peter Parker, *The Old Lie: The Great War and the Public School Ethos* (London: Constable, 1987); and Caleb Crain, *American Sympathy: Men Friendship, and Literature in the New Nation* (New Haven, Conn.: Yale University Press, 2001).

11. Michel Foucault, *History of Sexuality*, vol. 1, trans. Robert Hurley (New York: Vintage, 1980).

12. Faderman, *Surpassing the Love of Men*, 15.

13. Walter Williams, *The Spirit and the Flesh: Sexual Diversity in American Indian Culture* (Boston: Beacon, 1986); Paula Gunn Allen, *The Sacred Hoop: Recovering the Feminine in American Indian Traditions* (Boston: Beacon, 1986). The diverse southern mines included Miwoks, Chileans, Mexicans, French, Chinese, African Americans, and Anglo-Americans. Susan Johnson, *Roaring Camp: The Social World of the California Gold Rush* (New York: W. W. Norton and Company, Inc., 2001); Judy Tzu-Chun Wu, "Was Mom Chung a 'Sister Lesbian'?" *Journal of Women's History* 13 (1) (Spring 2001): 58–82; and Judy Tzu-Chun Wu, *Dr. Mom Chung of the Fair-Haired Bastards: The Life of a Wartime Celebrity* (Berkeley and Los Angeles: University of California Press, 2005). Lillian Faderman also cited Carole Ione, *Pride of Family: Four Generations of American Women of Color* (New York: Summit Books, 1991), 16–25. Faderman, *Surpassing the Love of Men*, 15.

14. For her previous works that address intimate, same-sex ties, see Karen V. Hansen, *A Very Social Time: Crafting Community in Antebellum New England* (Berkeley and Los Angeles: University of California Press, 1994); Karen V. Hansen, "'Our Eyes Behold Each Other': Masculinity and Intimate Friendships in Antebellum England," in *Men's Friendships*, ed. Peter M. Nardi (Newbury Park, Calif.: Sage Publications, 1992), 92–122; and Karen V. Hansen and Emily K. Abel, "Masculinity, Caregiving, and Men's Friendship in Antebellum New England," in *Families in the U.S.: Kinship and Domestic Politics*, ed. Karen V. Hansen and Anita Ilta Gary (Philadelphia: Temple University Press, 1998). I thank Deb Cohler for introducing me to Hansen's critical work on African American female friendship.

15. Karen V. Hansen, "'No Kisses Is Like Youres': An Erotic Friendship between two African American Women during the Mid-nineteenth Century," in *Lesbian Subjects: Feminist Studies Reader*, ed. Martha Vicinus (Bloomington: Indiana University Press, 1996), 184.

16. Hansen, "'No Kisses Is Like Youres,'" 186.

17. Lister, *No Priest but Love*, 65. See also Jill Liddington, "Anne Lister of Shibden Hall, Halifax (1791–1840): Her Diaries and the Historians," *History Workshop* 35 (1993): 45–77; and Anna Clark, "Anne Lister's Construction of Lesbian Identity," *Journal of History of Homosexuality* 7 (1996): 23–50.

18. Toni Cade Bambara, ed., *Black Woman: An Anthology* (New York: New American Library, 1970); Patricia Hill Collins, *Black Feminist Thought: Knowledge, Consciousness, and the Politics of Empowerment* (New York: Routledge, 1991). To Hansen's credit she immediately followed the sentence with a thorough footnote that clearly served as a disclaimer to her imaginably racist intent: "I do not mean to suggest that it represents correspondence typical of all African American women. I do not intend to generalize from the experiences of Rebecca Primus and Addie Brown. Nor do I mean that the explicit sexuality can be attributed to racial differences. Some white women's correspondence might be interpreted as erotic. This

correspondence documents only one case, a case which can be better understood by placing it in the context of both Black and white women's history." Hansen, "'No Kisses Is Like Youres,'" 205.

19. Hansen, "'No Kisses Is Like Youres,'" 186.

20. He first settled in San Francisco, where he quickly became disenchanted with life as a houseboy. Yone followed up on rumors that California writer Joaquin Miller offered his home to young Japanese men. From Joaquin's Oakland residence, the "Hights," where many artists sought refuge, Yone contacted Charles. Ikuko Atsumi, *Yone Noguchi Collected English Letters* (Tokyo: The Yone Noguchi Society, 1975); Edward Marx, "'A Different Mode of Speech': Yone Noguchi in Meiji America," *Recollecting Early Asian America: Essays in Cultural History*, ed. Josephine Lee, Imogene L. Lim, and Yuko Matsukawa (Philadelphia: Temple University Press, 2002), 288–306; and Yone Noguchi, *The Story of Yone Noguchi as Told by Himself* (Philadelphia: George W. Jacobs & Company, 1914).

21. Yone Noguchi, Oakland to Charles Warren Stoddard, 19 March 1900, Special Collections, Bancroft Library, University of California at Berkeley; Yone Noguchi, Oakland to Charles Warren Stoddard, 26 July 1901, Special Collections, Bancroft Library, University of California at Berkeley; and Yone Noguchi, Oakland to Charles Warren Stoddard, 26 November 1901, Special Collections, Bancroft Library, University of California at Berkeley.

22. Letter from Charles Warren Stoddard, Washington, D.C., to Yone Noguchi, April 1897; Noguchi, *Voice of the Valley*.

23. "Island Heights Notebook, 17 May 1904," Special Collections, Bancroft Library, University of California at Berkeley.

24. For more on Orientalism, see Edward Said, *Orientalism* (New York: Pantheon Books, 1978).

25. Yone Noguchi, "In the Bungalow with Charles Warren Stoddard: A Protest Against Modernism," *National Magazine* (December 1904), 306. My most recent research reveals that Yone also took part in orientalizing himself, perhaps wittingly, to appeal to bohemian and literary types who took pride in their worldliness. In many of Yone's letters he highlights his ethnic difference by including Japanese words or calling exceptional attention to his Japanese identity. Moreover, two books he published for the popular press, *The American Diary of a Japanese Girl* and *The American Letters of a Japanese Parlor-Maid* (published respectively in 1902 and 1905), distinctly take on exotic tones. In these works he interestingly adopts a female gender identity, perhaps signaling a quintessential orientalist move to embody the feminine.

26. Yone Noguchi, Oakland to Charles Warren Stoddard, 24 September 1900, Special Collections, Bancroft Library, University of California at Berkeley.

27. Atsumi, *Yone Noguchi Collected English Letters*, 12.

28. Yone's son, Isamu, born Isamu Gilmour, is in fact the acclaimed Asian/American artist and sculptor Isamu Noguchi.

29. "Island Heights Notebook, 1 August 1904," Special Collections, Bancroft Library, University of California at Berkeley; Yone Noguchi to Charles Warren Stoddard, Cambridge, Mass., 1 August 1904, in Atsumi, *Yone Noguchi Collected English Letters*, 185–86.

30. Charles Warren Stoddard, Cambridge, Mass., to Yone Noguchi, 1 August 1904; in Atsumi, *Yone Noguchi Collected English Letters*, 185–86.

31. Noguchi, "In the Bungalow with Charles Warren Stoddard: A Protest Against Modernism."

32. For the reprinted article, see the last chapter in Yone Noguchi, *The Story of Yone Noguchi Told by Himself* (London: Chatto & Windus, 1914). Roger Austen noted how Stoddard, knowing public sentiment toward homosexuality, felt compelled to censor his most private life. Austen described Charles as living a "double life"—a gay life in the Pacific Islands and one of seeming heterosexuality in the continental United States. As the medical community published statements stigmatizing same-sex relationships as sexual perversion, Charles increasingly lived to hide his secret world. Roger Austen, *Genteel Pagan: The Double Life of Charles Warren Stoddard*, ed. John W. Crowley (Amherst: University of Massachusetts Press, 1991), 57.

33. Oscar Wilde was well known among American bohemian circles of the time. An acclaimed playwright, poet, novelist, and aesthete, he gained infamy when British courts found him to be a "sodomite." After two years of hard labor, authorities released Wilde in 1897. Stoddard frequently copied Wilde's pithy quotations in his journals and made notes about Wilde's publication such as *De Profundis* and *Picture of Dorian Gray*, two texts in which Bosie, Wilde's male lover, is said to have been an inspiration. Even after Wilde's scandal he continued to support him in his notebook. Charles Warren Stoddard, "III. Extracts—Bank Stock Notebook, V. Extracts—Bank Stock Notebook, VI. Extracts—Bank Stock Notebook, 190?" Special Collections, Bancroft Library, University of California at Berkeley. For more on Wilde's life, see Michael S. Foldy, *The Trials of Oscar Wilde: Deviance, Morality, and Late-Victorian Society* (New Haven, Conn.: Yale University Press, 1997).

34. Kōsen Takahashi, San Francisco, to Blanche Partington, 24 March 1899; Kōsen Takahashi, San Francisco, to Blanche Partington, 29 March 1899, in Ikuko Atsumi, *Yone Noguchi Collected English Letters* (Tokyo: The Yone Noguchi Society, 1975), 34–35.

35. The late nineteenth century marked the height of "Japonisme," Western exaltation of Japan as a place of "ascetic superiority" and "sensual sensitivity." Jean-Pierre Lehmann, "Old and New Japonisme: The Tokugawa Legacy and Modern European Images of Japan," *Modern Asian Studies* 18 (4) (1984), 758. See also Earl Miner, *The Japanese Tradition in British and American Literature* (Princeton, N.J.: Princeton University Press, 1966).

36. Theodore Roosevelt reportedly bought sixty copies to give to friends and family. F. G. Notehelfer, "Nitobe Inazō: Japan's Bridge Across the Pacific," *Journal of Japanese Studies* 22 (2) (Summer 1996): 451. For more on Nitobe, see John F. Howes, ed., *Nitobe Inazō: Japan's Bridge Across the Pacific* (Boulder, Colo.: Westview Press, 1995).

37. The undoing of their affair did not appear to be initiated by Yone. In April 1905, Yone rather mysteriously asked Charles if Ethel had discovered his relationship with Gilmour. He wrote in a postscript: "Did Ethel ask you about Los Angel's woman?" Yone Noguchi, Tokyo, to Charles Warren Stoddard, 25 April 1905, in Atsumi, *Yone Noguchi Collected English Letters*, 192.

38. Léonie Gilmour, Pasadena, to Yone Noguchi, Tokyo, 24 February 1906, in Atsumi, *Yone Noguchi Collected English Letters*, 196–97. With the birth of Isamu, Léonie appears to have believed that she was married to Yone, when in fact Yone may have simply misled her to believe so.

39. This in fact appeared to be a letter from "Elizabeth" reporting to Ethel about Léonie's closeness to Yone. Elizabeth to Ethel Armes, 23 March 1905, Special Collections, Bancroft Library, University of California at Berkeley.

40. Gilmour planned to make a "Japanese boy" out of her son Isamu and teach at Tsuda College. Léonie Gilmour Noguchi to Charles Warren Stoddard, 6 December 1906, Special Collections, Bancroft Library, University of California at Berkeley.

41. Elizabeth to Ethel Armes, n.d., Special Collections, Bancroft Library, University of California at Berkeley.

42. Yone Noguchi, Tokyo, to Charles Warren Stoddard, 27 January 1905, in Atsumi, *Yone Noguchi Collected English Letters*, 190; Yone Noguchi, Tokyo, to Charles Warren Stoddard, 25 April 1905, in Atsumi, *Yone Noguchi Collected English Letters*, 192; Yone Noguchi, Tokyo, to Charles Warren Stoddard, 20 October 1905, in Atsumi, *Yone Noguchi Collected English Letters*, 193; Yone Noguchi, Japan to Charles Warren Stoddard, 27 January 1905, Special Collections, Bancroft Library, University of California at Berkeley.

43. Noguchi scholars have cited the use of "dad" as evidence a relationship more akin to father and son between Yone and Charles. Stoddard scholar Roger Austen, however, recounted how Charles in fact had sexual relationships with his "kids." Austen, *Genteel Pagan*.

44. Yone Noguchi, Japan, to Charles Warren Stoddard, San Francisco, 26 July 1906, Special Collections, Bancroft Library, University of California at Berkeley. For more on Stoddard's novel, see Roger Austen, *Playing the Game: The Homosexual Novel in America* (Indianapolis: Bobbs-Merrill, 1977); Austen, *Genteel Pagan*.

45. Yuji Ichioka, *The Issei: The World of First Generation Japanese Immigrants, 1885–1924* (New York: The Free Press, 1988); Sucheng Chan, *Asian Americans: An Interpretive History* (New York: Twayne Publishers, 1991); and Ronald Takaki, *Strangers From a Different Shore: A History of Asian Americans* (New York: Penguin Books, 1989).

46. Jennifer Ting and Madeline Hsu also suggested that Chinese immigrant men might have found fulfillment rather than deprivation in these early homosocial communities. Jennifer Ting, "Bachelor Society: Deviant Heterosexuality and Asian American Historiography," in *Privileging Positions: The Sites of Asian American Studies*, ed. Gary Y. Okihiro, et al. (Pullman: Washington State University Press, 1995), 271–80; Madeline Y. Hsu, "Unwrapping Orientalism, Unwrapping Orientalist Constraints: Restoring Homosocial Normativity to Chinese American History," *Amerasia Journal* 29 (2) (2003): 230–53.

47. Note that these letters are not even exchanges that occurred directly between Ethel and Yone but rather letters between Yone and a third party. Biographer Ikuko Atsumi recounted Yone's engagement to Ethel in the introduction to her collected English letters of Yone Noguchi. Atsumi, *Yone Noguchi Collected English Letters*, 12. For the four letters, see Charles Warren Stoddard, Cambridge, Mass., to Yone Noguchi, New York, 28 July 1904, in Atsumi, *Yone Noguchi Collected English Letters*, 183; Yone Noguchi, New York, to Charles Warren Stoddard, 29 (1904?), in Atsumi, *Yone Noguchi Collected English Letters*, 184; Charles Warren Stoddard, Cambridge, Mass., to Yone Noguchi, 1 August 1904, in Atsumi, *Yone Noguchi Collected English Letters*, 185–86; Yone Noguchi to Charles Warren Stoddard, 4 (1904?), in Atsumi, *Yone Noguchi Collected English Letters*, 187.

48. Friendship scholars have long been proclaiming that the question of genital contact remains irrelevant to their argument. Smith-Rosenberg, *Disorderly Conduct*, 58; Faderman, *Surpassing the Love of Men*, 19; and Martha Vicinus, ed., *Lesbian Subjects: A Feminist Studies Reader* (Bloomington: Indiana University Press, 1996), 2.

13

Ghosts

Julie Thị Underhill

Several uncles in Việt Nam went by way of tigers, a family curse of sorts. And once, for wearing untraditional attire to the burial grounds, my mother was nearly attacked beside the uncles' graves by three incarnated tigers whose missing limbs echoed the uncles' fatal wounds. Since the spirit world avenges displays of ancestral and family disrespect, years later my great-grandmother visited us at night as a huge-clawed tiger intent on drowning her granddaughter for evacuating Việt Nam. And so my mother's restless dead meshed with other brutal mythologies of my Texas childhood, as ghosts followed three people from war.

The least relevant here, my father, lived with my mother for a year in Can Tho before their escape six hours prior to the fall of Saigon. As an American contracted to repair military aircraft in Việt Nam, his fits of rage and startled responses coincided with manic depression, paranoid-schizophrenic tendencies, alcoholism, and heroin addiction. His ghosts emerged in tandem. Once arriving in the United States, his marriage to my mother lasted four tumultuous years. By contrast, my stepfather seemed gentle and jovial. A U.S. Army captain who'd flown combat helicopters in Việt Nam for six tours, upon returning home he drugged himself to forget and trivialize war, life, and death. Yet in those six years in combat lurked phantoms, unraveled covertly. On the other hand, after thirty years of coercion and crossfire in a culture riddled with ancestry and apology, my mother's spirits were too numerous to count on two hands, although I learned names, anatomies, and whereabouts of the more prominent. A Vietnamese military widow and refugee who'd left behind five children, her apparitions were for continual reckoning.

As a child I read in *Amityville Horror* the old folk wisdom that after botched exorcisms you can evacuate from phantasms by moving away, across water. Yet by my own observation, no inconceivable stretch of South China Sea, Pacific Ocean, imagination, time, incense, drinking, gardening, incantations, diverting, TV watching, sleeping, forgetting, cooking, pleading, working, smoking, childbearing, misdirected sorrow and rage—*nothing* prevented trespasses by my family's disgruntled dead.

In Việt Nam, the dead are intimately woven into the world of the living, and inadequate funerals make for malevolent ghosts. So you fear the angered and roaming retributions of the improperly honored or those never buried. Even when an apparition never or rarely came, my mother would suspect that the deceased was not properly appeased, despite funerary rites to ease the soul into the other world. Her first husband, Kip, had been a South Vietnamese Army (ARVN) captain killed in action in Quảng Ngãi, after thirteen years of marriage. In 1973, she exhumed and identified his three-month decomposed body to carry it three days' distance to give him a final grave and to offer his four children somewhere to mourn. A committal to his family's cemetery had ushered him from the "army of wandering souls," Việt Nam's unfound dead whose loved ones still search for their remains. Yet as husband and wife they'd had their problems, too late to address. Then came his death, then her evacuation.

In my childhood my mother had no photos of her late husband. She sketched Kip's likeness from memory, in smeary shaded pencil commensurate with my own idea of a spirit. Perhaps because of my stepfather's jealousy she kept the drawing in the attic and so I came to believe Kip mostly stayed there. Often she cried or sat with that thousand-mile stare, missing their daughters and son, then orphaned to extended family.

The children of Việt Nam, my stepfather would say, might slip a grenade into your fuel tank, its pin held by a rubber band that would slowly disintegrate. Eventually you'd explode, mid-flight, with your crew. But he didn't speak of retribution against the ubiquitous enemy, nor did he lament striping those rice paddies, jungles, and villages with fire. Instead he amused us. The Cobra, his preferred combat helicopter, he praised as "*the* way to fight a war . . . in air-conditioned comfort." He told charmed stories about the haunted monastery hidden by mountain fog, where he watched *Gone With The Wind* on projected 16mm film while smoking Việt Cộng–supplied pot as the guerrillas watched from the fence's other side, a ceasefire of mythic quietude, whites of eyes gleaming in the dark.

Yet often he fielded my mother's questions, her rhetorical tirade against the stupidity of U.S. military efforts. "Do you know how easy it was to get you people to blow up a village in South Việt Nam, your *friendly* territory?!" she'd inquire at the dinner table. "VC shoot from the edge of the village and run! You return fire and blow up the whole fucking village killing everybody! Everyone in surrounding villages knows the GIs did it and they'd get scared of you! Easy for the VC to win them over and they use your firepower to do it!"

I only slowly grasped the subtleties of guerrilla psychological civil imperialist counterinsurgency warfare in the intersection of my parents' terrors. I mostly spent my waking hours catching tadpoles, minnows, and crawdads in the woods—alone or with friends, dog, or brother. I then spent my unwaking hours fending off my stepfather's clandestine attempts to pour some disused part of him into a vessel far too small. After four years, I told a school counselor. I was removed at age nine by child protective services, put into foster care, and later placed with my biological father. My stepfather was tried and convicted of a felony. After a year in prison, he returned home to my mother and three siblings. Then, ten years after I testified against him, in a rare moment alone during my annual family visit, my stepfather let me in on something.

While piloting a mission in Cambodia (before *we* were even *in* Cambodia) he was radioed by his commanding officer. No one on the ground could stomach—at the moment—an execution-style shooting. On a rural road they'd allegedly caught two bicycling girls carrying arms, wearing white. Then his commanding officer issued him the coordinates. "Your mom says I could have been lied to, that the girls might not have had any weapons, only sticks in their baskets. Hell, I didn't want to do it either, but from the air it's not as difficult—more removed—and they'd given orders." So as the Cobra leaned in upon them and as he pulled trigger and as the pair of rockets bore down on the pair of girls—each no older than twelve years—one of the girls turned and looked over her shoulder straight at him. In her only opportunity for insurrection she withstood him, as he killed her, a gaze unflinching until he disintegrated her and her sister-friend into fire.

Our adjacent motherlands were ruptured by his war, a war he later married into while still engaged in heart and mind. Perhaps his early years with me had been some sort of renunciation—a less brutal destruction this time, within attempts at tenderness, in distorted apology to the Cambodian girl he destroyed. It's worth saying that by comparison to my siblings, after a sweltering summer outside, I resemble dark-stained wood. My browned skin and black hair must've contributed—it certainly hadn't been my eye contact—*so that every time you've worn white*, he admitted after knowing me for fifteen years, *you've reminded me of that girl*. As his stepdaughter, with a mother from Việt Nam, I'd long embodied war remorse he needed to vindicate. With me he tried to lessen and loosen his embodied shame, irrelevant to new dishonor. In time, he could even call it love.

With or without love, ghosts often manifest proportionate to guilt. The last time we spoke, six years ago, my stepfather hadn't remembered telling me about my resemblance to the Cambodian girl. He even insisted that the worst thing about war is that he's been "bored ever since," bereft of the adrenaline euphoria of risking and beating death every day for seventy-two months. And like a postwar amnesty of war crimes to keep the empowered in command and despite my court testimony that landed him with a felony, my mother still refuses to learn any details of my stepfather's "so-called" abuse, conceals the word from my siblings, says I can't reveal anything until she and her husband are dead, insists that whatever I've gone through "could not be worse than war." Probably because at age five she was fondled by a friend of her father's and then at age twelve raped by a "friendly" soldier, who later became her first husband's commanding officer. She's suffered and inflicted such pain that she probably can't handle more guilt. In any case, hers is the only measurable pain, and only her nocturnal ghosts come bearing claws.

During my childhood, to make reparations with the spirits, my mother would pray and offer feasts of fruit in bowls while I would stand aside coveting their gleaming skins. "Aren't they done yet?" At my impropriety she would scowl *no*. Yet how can you tell when an apparently ravenous entourage of ghosts has finished their last courses? How could I ask them, if I couldn't speak their language? How to satiate an invisible immortal? I'd obliged my life—my family and body—quite noticeably. Otherwise I was too new to the world, the inheritances of war too frequent and consuming, to gracefully navigate cultural dislocation and postwar trauma.

Even if I had never worn white, the looking back persists, pillars of salt withstanding. Even if I wouldn't "be here" if not for my mother's choice of a second husband and their hasty escape from the city as it fell to the northern army. Even if she didn't see those abandoned children for sixteen agonizing years, no sooner than the death of the youngest. Even if her oldest child—whom she left a twelve-year-old—had not attempted escape to the United States—and to her mother—for which she was detained, tortured, and raped for two years in a Cambodian prison. Even if he hadn't been exorcising through me his extermination of a Cambodian peasant girl. Even if she hadn't tried to drown herself in the Mississippi River while pregnant with me, stopped by my ill-tempered kicks but mostly by the Cape Girardeau police. Even if he hadn't married someone whose scathing words indict him in an unthinkable madness and whose children smell to him of genocide. Even as war—unconfined by chronology, ideology, or geography—continues to flaunt empire's arrogance by infusing each defenseless life with death's continual unraveling.

Index

About the Contributors

Noël Alumit is the award-winning writer of *Letters to Montgomery Clift* (Alyson). His second novel, *Talking to the Moon*, was published in 2007 by Carroll and Graff. He is also a performance artist with work produced on both coasts.

Anjali Arondekar is an associate professor in the feminist studies department at the University of California, Santa Cruz. She works in the fields of South Asian studies, colonial historiography, feminist theories, queer theory, critical race studies, and nineteenth-century interdisciplinary studies. Her book *For the Record: On Sexuality and the Colonial Archive in India* is forthcoming from Duke University Press.

Dan Bacalzo received his Ph.D. in performance studies from New York University. He is an adjunct lecturer in the drama department at NYU and works as the managing editor of TheaterMania.com.

Eugenie Chan is a playwright based in San Francisco, California. Over the past fifteen years, Chan's award-winning plays have been seen at The Public Theatre, Magic Theatre, Cutting Ball Theatre, Thick Description, Perishable, Northwest Asian American Theatre, Brava! For Women in the Arts, Opera Piccola/StageBridge, PlayLabs, and the Bay Area Playwrights Festival, among other venues.

Sylvia Chong is an assistant professor in the English department at the University of Virginia. She is the recipient of the Society for Cinema and Media

Studies dissertation award. Her book *The Oriental Obscene: Violence and the Asian Male Body in American Moving Images in the Vietnam Era* is in progress.

Richard Fung is an internationally renowned essayist and filmmaker whose work has been published and shown in numerous venues. He is co-author (with Monika Kin Gagnon) of *13: Conversations on Art and Cultural Race Politics* (Artexte) and is an associate professor in the faculty of art at the Ontario College of Art & Design.

Cathy Irwin received her Ph.D. in English from the University of Southern California. She is an assistant professor of writing and creative writing at the University of La Verne. She lives in Los Angeles, California.

Stacy Lavin did her graduate work in the Duke University Department of English and is a Marion L. Brittain Fellow in the School of Literature, Communication, and Culture at the Georgia Institute of Technology. She specializes in nineteenth- and twentieth-century British and American literature with an emphasis on modernism, media studies, and the cultural study of science. Her current project, "In the Loop: Experimental Writing and the Information Age," synchronizes the work of Gertrude Stein, Samuel Beckett, and William S. Burroughs with an emerging emphasis on data processing, information, noise, and computation in the scientific and humanistic disciplines.

Ruthann Lee is a Ph.D. candidate in the graduate program in sociology at York University, and she completed her M.A. in the Department of Sociology and Equity Studies in Education at OISE-UT in 2003. She collectively edited the anthology *Han Kut: Critical Art and Writing by Korean Canadian Women* (Inanna Publications). Her work integrates anti-racist, feminist, and queer cultural theory.

Gina Masequesmay is an associate professor in the Asian American studies department at California State University–Northridge. She is a sociologist with research interests on the intersections of race, class, gender, ability, and sexuality.

Sean Metzger is assistant professor of English and theater studies at Duke University, where he is also affiliated with the programs in sexualities studies and women's studies, as well as the Asian/Pacific Studies Institute. His book *Looks Chinese: Fashioning Asian/American Spectatorship* is in progress.

Fiona I. B. Ngô is an assistant professor in Asian American studies and gender and women's studies at the University of Illinois, Urbana-Champaign.

Ngô is an interdisciplinary scholar interested in comparative ethnic studies, music cultures, transnational sexualities, mixed-race identities, and the Southeast Asian diaspora.

Pauline Park chairs the New York Association for Gender Rights Advocacy (NYAGRA), the first statewide transgender advocacy organization in New York (www.nyagra.com), which she co-founded in June 1998. Park led the campaign for passage of Int. No. 24, the transgender rights law enacted by the New York City Council as Local Law 3 of 2002. She earned her master's degree from the London School of Economics and her Ph.D. in political science from the University of Illinois at Urbana-Champaign, and she has written widely on LGBT rights and queer API issues as well as intercountry adoption.

Cathy Schlund-Vials is an assistant professor of Asian American studies and English at the University of Connecticut.

Eunai Shrake is an associate professor in the department of Asian American Studies at California State University–Northridge, where she teaches courses on multicultural education with a special emphasis on Asian American students and their culture. She has a master's degree in theology from Austin Presbyterian Theological Seminary in Austin, Texas, and a Ph.D. in education with a concentration in social sciences and comparative education from University of California at Los Angeles. Her research focuses on cross-cultural studies in the areas of parenting styles, ethnic identity development, and adolescent problem behaviors.

Amy Sueyoshi is an associate professor jointly appointed in ethnic studies and sexuality studies at San Francisco State University. She has published on topics ranging from cross-dressing, same-sex marriage, and Asian American pornography in journals such as *Frontiers* and *Amerasia*. Currently, she is finishing a book manuscript on the intimate life of Japanese immigrant poet Yone Noguchi. Previous to academia she worked as a grassroots organizer for Asian Americans for Equality and the U.S. Peace Corps. Additionally, she is actively involved in the Asian queer women's community in both the United States and Japan. She volunteers as APIQWTC's fundraiser, a consortium of over twenty different queer Asian women's and transgender organizations in the San Francisco Bay Area. Moreover, she has lectured on sexuality and social justice in Osaka and continues to serve as a liaison for women scholars and activists in Japan seeking intellectual exchange with the United States around issues of social justice for ethnic and sexual minorities.

Sora Park Tanjasiri, Ph.D., MPH, is associate professor in the Department of Health Science at California State University–Fullerton. Her research focuses on the community health needs of diverse populations, particularly Asian/Americans and Pacific Islanders (AAPIs). In addition to her professional work, Dr. Tanjasiri also serves as an advisor to numerous non-profit organizations and coalitions, including serving on the board of directors of the Orange County Asian Pacific Islander Community Alliance. Her collaborators on this chapter include past and current members and board of Khmer Girls for Action (KGA): Cynthia Choi, Sophya Chum, Phiravy Chung, Que Dang, Mary Anne Foo, Ra Pok, and Diep Tran.

Julie Thị Underhill's poetry appears in Maxine Hong Kingston's *Veterans of War, Veterans of Peace* (2006). Her photography includes portraits and landscapes from El Salvador, Malawi, Mexico, Spain, the United Kingdom, the United States, and Việt Nam. Her interviews are featured in the Peabody Award–winning "Crossing East" series on Asian/American history, in the Secret Asian Woman radio documentary, and also in *ColorLines* magazine. While a fellow of the William Joiner Center for the Study of War and Social Consequences at the University of Massachusetts in Boston, in 2006 she filmed *Second Burial*, a portrayal of her Cham grandmother's final ceremonies in Thôn Phuróc Lập, Việt Nam. As a chancellor's fellow at the University of California in Berkeley, she is currently a doctoral student in the Department of Ethnic Studies.

Breinigsville, PA USA
30 June 2010
240907BV00001B/7/P